Praise for *Modern Mainframe Development*

This book is a comprehensive treatment of modern mainframe software development. It is masterfully written and thoroughly researched.

—*Cameron Seay, mainframe evangelist*

Every chapter speaks in practical terms on how to leverage the strengths of the mainframe platform.

—*Russ Teubner, cofounder and CEO of HostBridge Technology*

Tom's clearly done his homework on the current and future state of the mainframe. His conviction that hybrid cloud architectures will rule the future lays the foundation for an important and insightful breakdown of the exciting opportunities mainframe modernization presents for enterprise organizations.

—*Gil Peleg, CEO and founder of Model9*

This book is evidence that as the mainframe is modernizing, it will be critical for the next (and some of the current) generation of "mainframers" to level up faster and cover more ground. This book fast-tracks some of that ground that used to take years.

—*Paul Gamble, z/OS Systems Programmer—Automation, Shared Services Canada*

The term *mainframe* has had negative connotations for years. But Tom has done a great job in explaining the technology and how it is a solid option for businesses.

—*Lionel Dyck, z/OS enthusiast and cofounder of the Zigi open source project*

Modern Mainframe Development

COBOL, Databases, and Next-Generation Approaches

Tom Taulli
Foreword by John McKenny

Beijing · Boston · Farnham · Sebastopol · Tokyo

Modern Mainframe Development

by Tom Taulli

Published by O'Reilly Media, Inc., 1005 Gravenstein Highway North, Sebastopol, CA 95472.

O'Reilly books may be purchased for educational, business, or sales promotional use. Online editions are also available for most titles (*https://oreilly.com*). For more information, contact our corporate/institutional sales department: 800-998-9938 or *corporate@oreilly.com*.

Acquisitions Editor: Suzanne McQuade
Development Editor: Michele Cronin
Production Editor: Gregory Hyman
Copyeditor: Sharon Wilkey
Proofreader: Piper Editorial Consulting, LLC

Indexer: Ellen Troutman-Zaig
Interior Designer: David Futato
Cover Designer: Karen Montgomery
Illustrator: Kate Dullea

March 2022:   First Edition

Revision History for the First Edition
2022-03-16:   First Release

See *https://oreilly.com/catalog/errata.csp?isbn=9781098107024* for release details.

This work is part of a collaboration between O'Reilly and BMC. See our statement of editorial independence (*https://oreil.ly/editorial-independence*).

978-1-098-10702-4

[LSI]

Table of Contents

Part II.   Modern Topics

Foreword

For over 60 years, the mainframe has been the system of record for leading businesses, governmental agencies, and institutions of learning. Today, the vast majority of the world's largest banks, insurance companies, airlines, and retailers continue to rely on the mainframe. If you've shopped, planned a vacation, or done banking online or through a mobile app, your transaction was almost certainly processed by a mainframe.

The mainframe's reliability, consistency, security, and performance have cemented its role as the workhorse of the digital economy, and reliance on the platform shows no signs of letting up. In fact, 92% of respondents to the 2021 BMC Mainframe Survey see it as a platform for long-term growth. As new technologies arise and demand for better, faster services and applications intensifies, the mainframe continues to evolve to meet changing market needs and power innovation.

The programming environment has advanced from punched cards to ISPF green screens to modern integrated development environments in which developers can edit, debug, and deploy source code from one interface. Meanwhile, modern development solutions have enabled the use of automation throughout the software delivery life cycle and opened the mainframe to integration with cross-platform development tools, monitoring and security software, and modern frontend applications.

These advanced automation capabilities and an "open-borders" approach go hand in hand with increased adoption of DevOps and Agile development on the platform. Modern processes, and the tools that support them, help increase the quality of applications and the speed and efficiency with which they are developed. In short, it is an exciting time for the mainframe, as it continues to build upon its reputation of reliability, security, and scalability and expand its integration with other platforms in support of continuous innovation.

This bright future also presents wonderful career opportunities on the mainframe. DevOps and Agile development open the door to greater collaboration with developers on other platforms, spurring the creation of applications and services that have the potential to change the digital landscape. Modern tools and an ever-expanding list of cross-platform integrations enable developers to do meaningful work on the platform that drives the world economy. Across a wide range of industries and organizations, from financial services to medical, insurance, retail, and the public sector, the need for skilled mainframe developers is boundless.

In this book, Tom Taulli introduces the mainframe and the systems behind it, covering the history of the platform, its unique role in the modern digital economy, and the architecture, processes, and people that make it such a powerhouse. In exploring its most commonly used programming language (COBOL) and examining database and transaction management on the platform, Tom provides the foundation upon which readers can build a working knowledge of mainframe development.

Modern Mainframe Development serves as a valuable overview of the platform's history and future while also thoroughly explaining its systems and processes. As experienced mainframe developers retire, taking with them decades of accrued knowledge, and the industry shifts toward a new generation of mainframe professionals, the importance of this resource cannot be overstated.

I hope that you, the reader, will use this book to lay the groundwork for further exploration of the platform and the opportunities it presents. Once you've experienced its power and capability for innovation, I'm confident you'll develop the same passion for the mainframe that has inspired my career.

— John McKenny
Senior vice president and general manager
Intelligent Z Optimization and Transformation at
BMC

Preface

Digital transformation is the main driver for global enterprises. According to software company ServiceNow, businesses will spend a staggering $7.4 trillion (*https://oreil.ly/tO72U*) on digital transformation during the next three years. A key reason is that larger enterprises need to remain competitive and relevant. Otherwise, relentless disruption will occur.

Yet true digital transformation does not mean ripping out mainframes and other legacy systems. This would be extremely expensive and risky. Besides, mainframes have major advantages. They can process huge amounts of information and allow for highly secure processing, which are essential for large enterprises. Many of these transactions are mission-critical, such as those for banking, insurance, and energy.

In the years ahead, the main strategy for digital transformation will be to pursue a hybrid approach. Traditional mainframes and applications will integrate with modern systems. Developers will need to have a solid understanding of mainframe architectures and ecosystems. This will allow for creating systems that get results and make an impact on the organization.

What's Covered

The topic of mainframe development is expansive. To help readers better understand this, I divided the book into two parts:

Part I
> This part covers traditional aspects of mainframe development. We'll delve into details of the COBOL language as well as how to run programs with Job Control Language (JCL). We'll also look at the main databases for the mainframe—Db2 and IMS—as well as CICS transaction systems. The book then covers traditional tools for development, such as ISPF and TSO.

Part II

Since mainframes run many critical operations for businesses, these machines have become increasingly important for next-generation technologies. So this book looks at categories including artificial intelligence, DevOps, and robotic process automation. We'll also cover various strategies for migrating mainframe environments to cloud platforms. These approaches are still in the early phases but represent great opportunities for developers.

Who Is This Book For?

The book is focused at the beginner level. The good news is that mainframe development concepts are not necessarily complicated—although they can be somewhat tedious. In light of this, the book's intended audience includes the following:

Newbie

Someone who does not have much technical experience but is looking at a new career as a mainframe developer. This book provides the fundamentals.

Experienced developer

Someone who has a background in Java, Python, or another language. This book highlights the major differences between these modern languages and those for the mainframe (like COBOL).

Systems programmer

Someone who works on configuration but may not understand how mainframe development works. This book is a helpful guide for someone who wants to make a transition to being a coder.

Mainframe developer

Since the book covers many areas, even experienced developers can glean insights from it.

Business manager

Some chapters provide nontechnical content about mainframes (Chapter 2), languages (Chapter 4), and emerging trends like DevOps (Chapter 9), artificial intelligence (Chapter 10), robotic process automation (Chapter 11), and mainframe modernization strategies (Chapter 12).

The Approach to This Book

Mainframe topics can be dry. The coding can easily become wordy, and lots of configuration is required. However, I have tried to spice up the material by using real-life use cases, fun facts, and humor. I have also interviewed numerous executives, founders, and experts at companies like BMC, Broadcom, IBM, Rocket Software, Model9, Heirloom Computing, and Advanced, just to name a few.

Conventions Used in This Book

The following typographical conventions are used in this book:

Italic

Indicates new terms, URLs, email addresses, filenames, and file extensions.

`Constant width`

Used for program listings, as well as within paragraphs to refer to program elements such as variable or function names, databases, data types, environment variables, statements, and keywords.

`Constant width bold`

Shows commands or other text that should be typed literally by the user.

`Constant width italic`

Shows text that should be replaced with user-supplied values or by values determined by context.

 This element signifies a general note.

Using Code Examples

Supplemental material (code examples, exercises, etc.) is available for download at *https://oreil.ly/modern-mainframe-development-code*.

If you have a technical question or a problem using the code examples, please send email to *bookquestions@oreilly.com*.

This book is here to help you get your job done. In general, if example code is offered with this book, you may use it in your programs and documentation. You do not need to contact us for permission unless you're reproducing a significant portion of the code. For example, writing a program that uses several chunks of code from this book does not require permission. Selling or distributing examples from O'Reilly books does require permission. Answering a question by citing this book and quoting example code does not require permission. Incorporating a significant amount of example code from this book into your product's documentation does require permission.

We appreciate, but generally do not require, attribution. An attribution usually includes the title, author, publisher, and ISBN. For example: "*Modern Mainframe Development* by Tom Taulli (O'Reilly). Copyright 2022 Tom Taulli, 978-1-098-10702-4."

If you feel your use of code examples falls outside fair use or the permission given above, feel free to contact us at *permissions@oreilly.com*.

O'Reilly Online Learning

 For more than 40 years, *O'Reilly Media* has provided technology and business training, knowledge, and insight to help companies succeed.

Our unique network of experts and innovators share their knowledge and expertise through books, articles, and our online learning platform. O'Reilly's online learning platform gives you on-demand access to live training courses, in-depth learning paths, interactive coding environments, and a vast collection of text and video from O'Reilly and 200+ other publishers. For more information, visit *https://oreilly.com*.

How to Contact Us

Please address comments and questions concerning this book to the publisher:

> O'Reilly Media, Inc.
> 1005 Gravenstein Highway North
> Sebastopol, CA 95472
> 800-998-9938 (in the United States or Canada)
> 707-829-0515 (international or local)
> 707-829-0104 (fax)

We have a web page for this book, where we list errata, examples, and any additional information. You can access this page at *https://oreil.ly/modern-mainframe-development*.

Email *bookquestions@oreilly.com* to comment or ask technical questions about this book.

For news and information about our books and courses, visit *https://oreilly.com*.

Find us on Facebook: *https://facebook.com/oreilly*

Follow us on Twitter: *https://twitter.com/oreillymedia*

Watch us on YouTube: *https://www.youtube.com/oreillymedia*

Acknowledgments

My journey for writing this book has certainly been interesting. It started in July 2020 when I wrote a blog post (*https://oreil.ly/x2UJG*) for Forbes called "COBOL Language: Call It A Comeback?" I did this primarily because of the COVID-19 pandemic, which led to the overloading of state unemployment systems. The COBOL code had not been maintained to handle the enormous volume.

The post gained instant traction and wound up being my second most popular, with more than 31,000 views. It sparked debate and was picked up by other blogs. I even got some criticism for using a graphic of a punch card; some people thought that this was yet another case of the media treating mainframes as obsolete—even though this was not the point of my blog post.

I wondered: could this post be just a one-off? Or maybe true interest in mainframe development endured? To see, I wrote other posts, and they too were popular. I even put together a two-hour online course about COBOL. It did quite well.

I then wondered again: maybe there could be a book on the topic? I checked out Amazon and saw few titles available, and most were outdated. So I reached out to an editor at O'Reilly, Suzanne McQuade, and pitched the idea. She loved it, and so I began work on the project.

The process was great, and I learned a lot along the way. My editor, Michele Cronin, was extremely helpful. I also had the support of super-smart technical reviewers. They included Dr. Cameron Seay, co-chair of the Open Mainframe Project COBOL Working Group and an adjunct instructor at East Carolina University.

For this book, I have also interviewed various executives and experts. The interviewees include Rajesh Raheja, senior vice president and head of Engineering at Boomi; Ross Mauri, general manager of IBM Z; Gil Peleg, CEO and founder of Model9; Gary Crook, CEO at Heirloom Computing; Elpida Tzortzatos, an IBM Fellow and CTO of z/OS; Russ Teubner, CEO and cofounder of HostBridge Technology; Ben Chance, vice president of Intelligent Automation at Genpact; Dr. Alex Heublein, president of Adaptigent; Jeff Cherrington, vice president of Product Management for System Z at Rocket Software; David McNierney, product marketing leader at Broadcom; Justin Stone, senior director of DevOps Platforms at Liberty Mutual Insurance; Margaret Lee, senior vice president and general manager of Digital Service Operations Management at BMC; Scott Silk, Astadia's chairman and CEO; and Lionel Dyck, cofounder of the zigi open source project.

Finally, I want to thank BMC, which sponsored the book and provided great insights. Thanks especially to John McKenny, senior vice president and general manager, Intelligent Z Optimization and Transformation, and Sheila Watson, director of public relations.

PART I

Fundamentals of the Mainframe

CHAPTER 1

Why Be a Mainframe Developer?

The long-term prospects for tech employment are particularly bright. Just look at the results of research from the US Bureau of Labor Statistics (*https://oreil.ly/ImnJH*). The forecasted employment growth for technology occupations is expected to be about 13% from 2020 to 2030, which is significantly faster than the average for all occupations. The number of jobs projected to be added during this time is roughly 667,600.

But for those looking at career opportunities—or exploring a change—mainframe development is likely one of the last areas in tech considered. In fact, the odds are pretty good that many people will not even think about this category.

This should be no surprise. The media usually does not cover mainframe topics or trends. What's more, these systems often handle applications that power infrastructure, which makes it difficult to get a sense of what they can do. Besides, it's not like any one can go to a Best Buy and purchase a mainframe. These machines are expensive and complex. They also require a team of talented IT professionals.

The mainframe is a mystery for many people. And the common perception is that the industry is a backwater, with little growth.

But sometimes perceptions can be wrong, and this is certainly the case with the mainframe industry. Since the technology is generally for large companies, opportunities exist for developers to work on systems that impact many customers and users. Often the technologies support mission-critical applications, such as those that process ATM transactions or insurance claims.

Mainframe systems are also undergoing much transformation. This means they allow for the use of modern tools for DevOps, AI, integrations with mobile applications, and APIs.

So in this chapter, we will look at some of the driving forces of the mainframe industry and why it is a great option for any developer.

Fear of Disruption

In the mid-1990s, Harvard professor and entrepreneur Clayton Christensen coauthored a pathbreaking paper titled "Disruptive Technologies: Catching the Wave" (*https://oreil.ly/JaJ5E*). He set forth the core reasons for how technology can disrupt an industry. One of his key insights was that even strong companies could easily be vulnerable.

Christensen calls this the *innovator's dilemma*. An incumbent company will generally invest in sustainable innovations for existing products to maintain revenue and profit growth. But a startup does not have to worry about an existing product. It can take big risks and try revolutionary innovations, and if these get traction with customers, the results can be devastating for incumbents.

Nowadays the innovator's dilemma has become a palpable fear for many large companies, and many of them have mainframe systems. The belief is that if these companies don't adopt more innovative technologies, upstarts will ultimately prevail. This fear is perhaps the biggest catalyst for change in the mainframe industry and will mean long-term need for experienced developers.

To get a better sense of this fear, just look at Jamie Dimon, CEO of JPMorgan Chase. His firm is heavily dependent on mainframes.

In a 2020 shareholder letter, Dimon pointed out that disruptive technologies represent one of the biggest threats to his company. This is the case even though JPMorgan Chase has continued to grow strongly, despite the impact of the COVID-19 pandemic. In 2020, company revenues increased from $118.5 billion to $122.9 billion, and profits jumped from $29.1 billion to $36.4 billion, which was a record for the company. The company remains focused on gaining market share, investing in new technologies, and looking at ways to bolster its risk systems.

But in his shareholder letter (*https://oreil.ly/Es43y*), Dimon noted, "Banks have other weaknesses, born somewhat out of their success—for example, inflexible 'legacy systems.'" He then pointed out the threat of fintech companies that have been revolutionizing financial services, such as with mobile apps: "From loans to payment systems to investing, they have done a great job in developing easy-to-use, intuitive, fast and smart products. We have spoken about this for years, but this competition now is everywhere. Fintech's ability to merge social media, use data smartly and integrate with other platforms rapidly (often without the disadvantages of being an actual bank) will help these companies win significant market share."

But fintechs are not the only problems for traditional companies like JPMorgan Chase. Dimon also highlighted the impact of the mega tech operators like Amazon, Apple, Facebook, and Google. He wrote, "Their strengths are extraordinary, with ubiquitous platforms and endless data. At a minimum, they will all embed payments systems within their ecosystems and create a marketplace of bank products and services. Some may create exclusive white label banking relationships, and it is possible some will use various banking licenses to do it directly."

This stark honesty is definitely refreshing. It also is a positive sign, as Dimon is aware of the competitive environment and the need for investing in technologies. It's table stakes.

His example will encourage many other CEOs to take action. And this will ultimately mean even more urgency for modernization of legacy systems—leading to increasing demand for those developers who work on these technologies.

Software Is Eating the World

Marc Andreessen has a knack for anticipating the next big trend. In the early 1990s, he created the Mosaic browser, which became the basis for the iconic internet startup Netscape. Later in the decade, he went on to create Opsware, which was one of the pioneers of the cloud business.

But it was in 2011 that Andreessen set out to write his vision of the technology world. The article, published in the Wall Street Journal, was entitled "Why Software Is Eating the World" (*https://oreil.ly/su0SW*).

Writing 60 years after the invention of the microprocessor, Andreessen claimed that technology infrastructure had finally reached a point where industries could be transformed on a global scale. One reason for this was cloud platforms, especially Amazon Web Services (AWS). These platforms made it possible for any company to easily and inexpensively spin up an app. There was no need to buy servers, pay huge fees for data center access, or hire network specialists.

Another key factor was the ubiquity of broadband internet. In 2011, more than 2 billion people had access, compared to only 50 million in 2000.

According to Andreessen, "My own theory is that we are in the middle of a dramatic and broad technological and economic shift in which software companies are poised to take over large swathes of the economy."

This was definitely prophetic. Since then, we've seen Uber disrupt the traditional taxi industry, Netflix upend entertainment, and social media transform the broadcast industry, just to name a few examples.

But this is not to imply that traditional industries—which often rely on mainframes—are doomed. They are not. They actually have major advantages, like access to huge amounts of data, substantial financial resources, trusted brands, and talented employees.

Their mainframe systems are also a benefit. They are highly secure and reliable, and can handle massive workloads. As traditional companies continue to develop apps and websites, they are finding ways to leverage the mainframes, not get rid of them.

Interestingly enough, Andreessen highlighted various examples of traditional businesses successfully leveraging technologies. For example, he mentioned that the oil and gas industry has been a pioneer of data visualization, analytics, and supercomputers. These technologies have been used to improve the discovery of new sources of energy.

In the agricultural industry, companies like Deere & Company and Caterpillar have embedded sophisticated data-gathering systems in their tractors and equipment. This has then been melded with satellite data. With all this, AI has been used to make better decisions and even improve the development of newer systems.

Here are some other examples from Andreessen:

Walmart

From its early days, CEO and founder Sam Walton invested heavily in technologies. During the 1960s, he focused on using IBM mainframes to improve his company's supply chain. No doubt, this reliance on technology was a key for Walmart becoming the world's largest retailer.

FedEx

The company is one of the largest buyers of technology, which has been critical for logistics. Andreessen writes that FedEx "is best thought of as a software network that happens to have trucks, planes and distribution hubs attached."

Airlines

The industry innovated reservation systems, one of the first examples of mainframe use during the 1960s. Airlines also use data to price tickets and optimize routes.

In other words, those who want to work in the tech industry often end up working with traditional businesses and their mainframe systems. This will provide exciting opportunities for developers who want to take on tough challenges, such as fending off startups and retooling legacy systems.

COVID-19

The COVID-19 pandemic has shown the vulnerability of the global population. A new virus can easily spread at lightning speed and lead to massive closures. But the pandemic has also showed our amazing abilities in innovation and creativity. In record time, companies like Moderna, Pfizer, and BioNTech were able to develop revolutionary vaccines that have proven to be extremely effective.

It's true that the long-term consequences of the COVID-19 pandemic are far from clear. But it seems likely that it will factor significantly into the decision making of businesses. Major changes have already occurred in approaches to global supply chains. Digital transformation has also accelerated.

In April 2020, Microsoft CEO Satya Nadella had this (*https://oreil.ly/uc1a4*) to say about it: "We've seen two years' worth of digital transformation in two months. From remote teamwork and learning, to sales and customer service, to critical cloud infrastructure and security—we are working alongside customers every day to help them adapt and stay open for business in a world of remote everything."

Perhaps one of the biggest changes has been a move to hybrid work approaches, blending in-office and home work. Millions of people have become accustomed to using tools like Zoom, DoorDash, Airbnb, and Slack.

A McKinsey global survey (*https://oreil.ly/xXLFa*) of executives bolsters Nadella's argument of much quicker adoption of new technologies. The respondents indicated that the digitization of customer and supply-chain operations accelerated by a factor of three to four years. They also indicated that the changes would not be temporary. For the most part, digital transformation has become an extremely powerful trend.

According to McKinsey, "For most, the need to work and interact with customers remotely required investments in data security and an accelerated migration to the cloud. Now that the investments have been made, these companies have permanently removed some of the precrisis bottlenecks to virtual interactions. Majorities of respondents expect that such technology-related changes, along with remote work and customer interactions, will continue in the future."

Here are some of the other takeaways of the survey:

- The respondents are three times likelier to have 80% of their customer interactions be digital.
- There has been a seven-year increase of the rate at which companies have developed products and services. This has been driven primarily by industries like healthcare, financial services, and professional services.

- For various corporate measures, the one that has increased the most has been the budget for digital transformation.
- About one-quarter of respondents reported a decrease in their physical footprints.

The impact on mainframes has been notable. Historically, many business leaders have been resistant toward investing in modernization. After all, these systems were rigid and carried risks for changing mission-critical functions. But COVID-19 drove an urgency to change the status quo—and this came from senior executives and managers.

Government Modernization

The opportunity for mainframe development is not just about modernizing IT for businesses. It is also about governments across the world. As you'll see in the next chapter, one of the biggest catalysts for the standardization of mainframes during the 1960s was the US Defense Department.

As a result, mainframes remain pervasive within government agencies and institutions. However, meeting the needs of the 21st century will require significant retooling of these systems.

The COVID-19 pandemic has highlighted this. When the pandemic emerged in April 2020, many unemployment insurance systems crashed. The legacy IT systems were simply not built to handle such spikes in applications.

The situation was so dire that New Jersey governor Phil Murphy gave a speech (*https://oreil.ly/xKyAn*) in which he said, "Given the legacy systems, we should add a page [to their online call for health professionals] for COBOL computer skills because that's what we're dealing with. We have systems that are 40-plus years old. There will be lot of post-mortems, and one of them on our list will be how the heck did we get here when we literally needed COBOL programmers."

Many states had to scramble to find solutions, which spurred innovation. Just look at Texas: when the pandemic hit, its unemployment insurance system was instantly swamped as the number of claims rose from 13,000 per week to more than 400,000. To deal with the surge in volume, government authorities looked at ways to enhance existing mainframe systems. One move was to migrate the website to a cloud service provider. But mainframe capacity was also increased by 200%. Next, the Texas government implemented a modern voice response system that used chatbots. Interestingly enough, this helped with basic issues, such as retrieving user IDs and passwords for applications. After all, many of these people had not used unemployment insurance in many years and had forgotten their credentials.

According to Clay Cole (*https://oreil.ly/tFdlw*), director of the Texas Unemployment Insurance Division, "Even though we had legacy systems, our information technology teams were very nimble and were able to modify our software programming in order to allow us to deliver these new programs, and we did so."

Texas is certainly not alone in striving for modernization. This is a top-of-mind goal for all state governments. The federal government is ramping up efforts as well.

For example, the Technology Modernization Fund (TMF) was launched in 2017 (*https://oreil.ly/4W9lx*). The goal of this federal government program is to streamline the process for agencies to obtain funding for IT modernization programs.

Some of the areas that the TMF focuses on include high-priority systems, cybersecurity protection, public-facing digital services, and cross-government collaboration services.

> The US federal government is the world's largest buyer of technology. Its spending is more than $100 billion per year (*https://oreil.ly/YZAHF*).

Future of Mainframe Development

Common Business Oriented Language (COBOL) is the main computer language for mainframe development. Chapter 4 provides some background on this, and later chapters show how to use the code.

While COBOL has its issues, it is still a robust language. Just look at a survey from Micro Focus (*https://oreil.ly/a0w8h*). About 70% of respondents indicated that they were not interested in replacing and retiring COBOL applications. Instead, their focus was on using the language to modernize existing systems.

This is what Chris Livesey, senior vice president of Application Modernization and Connectivity at Micro Focus, had to say: "As we see the attitudes around COBOL modernization with changes to where and how it needs to be delivered and how its usage continues to grow, COBOL's credentials as a strong digital technology appear to be set for another decade. With 60 years of experience supporting mission-critical applications and business systems, COBOL continues to evolve as a flexible and resilient computer language that will remain relevant and important for businesses around the world."

Here are some of the other findings of the Micro Focus survey:

- 92% of respondents said they believed that their organization's COBOL applications were strategic, up from 84% in 2017.
- From 2017 to 2020, the average COBOL application code base has gone from 8.4 million to 9.9 million lines.
- 63% of respondents said that their modernization efforts will focus on new functionality and improving existing processes.

Career Opportunities

As companies look to modernize their systems, they are running into a major problem: a talent shortage. It is increasingly difficult to find prospects who have the right skills, such as the ability to code in COBOL. According to PwC's 23rd Annual Global CEO Survey (*https://oreil.ly/PBtw1*), about 74% of respondents indicated that this was a major concern and could limit growth. Of course, the COVID-19 pandemic has had a notable impact, as 40% of employees have been considering a job change, according to Microsoft's 2021 Work Trends Index (*https://oreil.ly/d3Ome*).

Such issues have definitely been aggravated in the mainframe industry. One reason is that only a few dozen colleges teach COBOL. Moreover, many Baby Boomers will retire in the next decade, and this will mean even fewer COBOL programmers.

Of course, these trends bode extremely well for developers who are looking at a career in the mainframe industry. With demand increasing and the supply of qualified developers falling, compensation rates will rise. According to Leon Kappelman (*https://oreil.ly/9xJcf*), a professor of information systems at the University of North Texas, "Undergrads who take the school's two classes in mainframe COBOL 'tend to earn about $10,000 per year more starting out than those that don't.'"

Employers will also increasingly look at ways to train and mentor new prospects. In fact, it is common for larger enterprises to have their own educational programs or bootcamps.

Employment arrangements will also likely be more flexible. With remote work and hybrid approaches becoming more common, opportunities will be available for people across the globe. It's also becoming more common to hire qualified mainframe developers as freelancers.

The technology talent shortage will likely have adverse impacts on the US economy. Based on research from Korn Ferry (*https://oreil.ly/v68IQ*), it could mean losing out on over $160 billion in annual revenues from 2020 to 2030.

Interestingly, some employers are even forgoing the need for a traditional four-year degree. Rather, apprenticeship programs will bolster the necessary skills.

Even the federal government is looking at taking a role. In 2021, the House of Representatives passed the National Apprenticeship Act (*https://oreil.ly/4AhxY*), which would earmark $3 billion for new programs.

The proposed Grace Hopper Code for Us Act (*https://oreil.ly/pzcI9*) also was introduced into Congress in 2021. It would provide $100 million in grants to colleges to provide education for legacy systems and languages. But assistance would also be available for students from age 6 through 12. Some of the supporters of the bill include IBM, University of Alabama at Birmingham, and North Carolina Agricultural and Technical State University.

One of the sponsors of the bill, Pennsylvania representative Matt Cartwright, noted (*https://oreil.ly/lnO1h*), "The importance of IT professionals cannot be understated, especially given the weaknesses the COVID-19 pandemic showed in government IT systems. Lack of IT infrastructure can ultimately impact the government's ability to respond in the time of a crisis, and skilled IT professionals can help ensure our preparedness."

One argument against mainframe development is that it is not particularly exciting. Further, some people fear learning languages that may ultimately become obsolete. But for the most part, the work of mainframe development can be very fulfilling. Again, there is an opportunity to have a major impact on a large company whose systems impact potentially millions of people.

For example, about 20% of the 15,000 developers and HR managers who responded to a survey from CodinGame (*https://oreil.ly/EfW1L*) said that solving interesting technical challenges was the most important part of taking a job. This came after flexible hours and healthy work-life balance (18.5%), salary (13%), and company culture (10.9%).

 A study from iCIMS (*https://oreil.ly/umHzS*) shows that it takes about 66 days to fill a technology role, which is 50% longer than other roles.

Conclusion

In this chapter, we took a look at key drivers for growth of the mainframe industry. One of the most important is fear in the executive suite, as fast-growing startups pose an existential threat to larger companies. They do not have to deal with legacy systems and have the benefit of a thriving venture-capital market. Another threat comes from the mega tech operators like Amazon, Apple, Facebook, and Google.

As a result, larger companies have had more urgency to invest more in digital transformation. They certainly understand that "software is eating the world," as Andreessen said in 2011.

The COVID-19 pandemic has been another big factor. Some of its impacts are likely to be long-lasting, including remote-working arrangements and higher levels of IT investment.

Given all this, modernizing legacy mainframe systems carries more urgency, which should be a long-term catalyst for growth for developers. Larger companies certainly have advantages, including their financial resources, strong brands, and significant customer bases. Thus, developers have an opportunity to be a part of these exciting transformation efforts.

We also have seen that governments will be a source of growth. They have expansive mainframe systems that need to be modernized. To this end, Congress is already looking at ways to develop relevant programs.

The bottom line: mainframe development represents a solid career path. In the next chapter, we'll continue this discussion by walking through some background information on mainframes.

CHAPTER 2

World of the Mainframe

In 1985, Stewart Alsop started the *P.C. Letter*, which quickly became a must-read for the rapidly growing tech industry. He would go on to create several conferences and to become an editor of *InfoWorld*.

For the most part, Alsop had a knack for anticipating the next big trends. But he was not perfect. In 1991, he wrote the following (*https://oreil.ly/RQZTO*): "I predict that the last mainframe will be unplugged on 15 March 1996."

At the time, this prediction was not necessarily controversial. The king of the mainframe—IBM—was struggling against the onslaught of fast-growing companies like Dell, Compaq, and Sun Microsystems. There was even buzz that the company could go bust.

But to paraphrase Mark Twain, the death of the mainframe was greatly exaggerated. This technology proved quite durable. In 2002 Alsop admitted his mistake and wrote, "It's clear that corporate customers still like to have centrally controlled, very predictable, reliable computing systems—exactly the kind of systems that IBM specializes in."

And this is the case today. Keep in mind that the mainframe is a growth business for IBM and is likely to be important for key trends like the hybrid cloud, ecommerce, and even fintech. Since 2010, more than 250 companies have migrated their workloads to IBM Z systems.

The mainframe is also pervasive across the world. Consider that this technology (*https://oreil.ly/8ipeZ*) is used by the following:

- 92 of the world's top 100 banks
- All 10 of the world's top insurers

- 18 of the top 25 retailers
- 70% of Fortune 500 companies

In this chapter, we'll take a look at the mainframe, detailing its history, pros and cons, capabilities, and future.

What Does "Mainframe" Mean Anyway?

The first use of the word *mainframe* was in 1964. But it is not clear who coined the term. A glossary from Honeywell mentioned it, as did a paper for a company journal (authored by IBM engineer Gene Amdahl).

The concept of the mainframe came from the telecommunications industry. It was used to describe the central system of a telephone exchange, where lines were interconnected.

The term *mainframe computer* was used to describe the CPU, which connected to peripherals. But it would also become synonymous for a large computer system that could handle huge amounts of data processing.

OK, then, how is a mainframe different from a supercomputer? Well, a *supercomputer* is focused on scientific applications. These machines are also the most expensive in the world and process huge amounts of data. For example, the Fugaku supercomputer has over 7.6 million cores and can operate at 442 petaflops (a *petaflop* is one quadrillion floating-point operations per second).

Mainframes, on the other hand, are usually designed for business purposes and are ideal for managing transactions at scale. A supercomputer has only a fraction of the mainframe's I/O capabilities.

A Brief History

The earliest computers were mainframes. These machines were housed in large rooms—which could be over 10,000 square feet—and had many electric tubes and cables. Because of the size, the mainframe would often be referred to as *Big Iron*.

A major catalyst for the development of mainframes was World War II. The US government saw this technology as a superior way to calculate ballistics of weapons, plan logistics, and crack enemy codes.

The first mainframe is considered to be the Harvard Mark I. Its inventor, Harvard mathematics professor Howard Aiken, wanted to build a system that could go beyond using paper and pencil. He proposed his idea to IBM, which agreed to back the effort.

Development of the Harvard Mark I began in 1939, but it would not be launched until February 1944. One of the first uses of the Mark I was to do calculations for the Manhattan Project (*https://oreil.ly/pKjjw*), the US effort in World War II to build a nuclear bomb.

This electromechanical computer was 51 feet long and 8 feet high. The weight? About 5 tons. It contained 500 miles of wire and 3 million connections, along with 2,225 counters and 1,464 switches. The system could calculate three additions per second, one multiplication per six seconds, and a logarithm within a minute. To input instructions, there was a paper tape drive as well as stored memory. The output was provided through an electric typewriter. The machine would prove quite durable: it operated for roughly 15 years.

What Are Punch Cards?

A *punch card*, or *punched card*, is a piece of stiff paper marked with perforations to represent information. These were not used just by early computers, though. Punch cards were employed as early as the 1700s. They helped to provide the patterns for textile mills.

By the 1830s, Charles Babbage was using punch cards for his Analytical Engine, a mechanical general-purpose computer. In the 1890 US Census, Herman Hollerith used them for counting the population. Completing the massive project took only two and a half years, instead of the typical seven years.

Hollerith's business would eventually morph into IBM, and punch cards would remain a lucrative business for decades. They would also become essential for programming mainframe computers.

Here's how it worked: a person entered code in an electric typewriter that would make holes in the punch cards. This could easily result in a large stack. The programmer would then hand these off to a computer operator, who would place them in a card reader. This system began the processing at the top left and then read down the first column. It would go to the top of the next column until all the code was read on the card. Through this process, the information was converted into machine language that the computer could understand. Interestingly enough, it could take hours or even days to get the output back!

Growth of the Mainframe

No doubt, mainframe technology grew more powerful, and the systems would find more usage within the business world. Consider that the main automation systems for the office included typewriters, file cabinets, and tabulation machines.

A critical breakthrough in mainframes for business came in 1959 with IBM's launch of the 1401 system. It used only transistors and could be mass produced. It became a huge seller for IBM.

As a result, the mainframe started to transform the business world. Yet problems were also emerging. A mainframe was often a custom device for a particular use case, such as for inventory or payroll. Each also had a unique operating system. Therefore, software would have to be rewritten when a new mainframe system was deployed, which was expensive and time-consuming.

But IBM CEO Thomas J. Watson Sr. realized that this could not last. The complexity of managing a myriad of systems was just too much. The company had to deal with six disparate divisions, each with its own departments for R&D, sales, and support. This is why Watson set out to rethink his computer business.

At the heart of this was the development of the System/360 (the name referred to the 360 degrees of a compass, symbolizing that the mainframe was a complete solution). The original budget of roughly $2 million quickly proved to be far off the mark. IBM would ultimately invest a staggering $5 billion for the System/360 (in today's dollars, this would be about $300 billion!). This represented the largest investment during the 1960s, behind only the US space program.

The investment was not just a huge financial risk. IBM was going to essentially make its existing machines obsolete. The company also would need to come up with innovations to allow for a new type of computing architecture.

It was Amdahl who led this ambitious effort. A critical goal was to ensure that a customer could upgrade from a smaller machine to a larger one without having to rewrite the software and buy new peripherals. In other words, there would be backward compatibility.

And yes, this would ultimately be one of the most important advantages for the System/360. For example, if you wrote a program for the computer in the 1960s, it would still be able to run on today's IBM mainframe.

But allowing this kind of continuity required a way to standardize the instruction code. At the time, the main approach was to embed the instructions within the hardware, which often proved to be inflexible.

IBM's innovation was to develop a software layer, called *microcode*, that used 8-bit bytes to interact with the hardware (before this, the memory was addressed with varying bit sizes). This made it possible to allow for changes in the instruction set without replacing the whole computer system.

Another key goal for the System/360 was simultaneous access by a large number of users. This would lead to the business of time-sharing, in which companies could rent a mainframe. This innovation would also be leveraged in the creation of the internet during the end of the 1960s.

In the end, Watson's bet would pay off in a big way. When the System/360 was launched on April 7, 1964, the demand was staggering. Within a month, IBM received more than one thousand orders (*https://oreil.ly/onPfI*).

Initially, the company built 5 computers and 44 peripherals. Here are some of the machines:

Model 20

> This was the most basic system. It could handle binary numbers but not floating-point numbers, and had up to 32 KB of memory. The Model 20 would become the most popular in terms of units sold.

Model 65

> The maximum memory was 1 MB, and the machine could handle floating-point numbers and decimals. Time-sharing was available from IBM's Time Sharing Option (TSO).

Model 75

> Built specifically for NASA (five units were built), this machine was instrumental in helping with the Apollo space program. For example, the Model 75 helped with the calculations for the space vehicles and even was critical in helping to make the go/no-go decisions for flights. According to Gene Kranz, flight director for the Apollo missions (*https://oreil.ly/GkhJ2*), "Without IBM and the systems they provided, we would not have landed on the Moon."

The mainframes were certainly not cheap. Each could easily cost over $2 million. But many companies saw this technology as a must-have for being competitive. They would even showcase their mainframes by placing them in glass rooms at headquarters.

They would also become part of the entertainment culture. The System/360 would have cameo appearances in various films like *The Doll Squad* and *The Girl Most Likely To*....

Competition from other mainframe companies certainly existed. The main rivals included Sperry Rand, Burroughs, NCR, RCA, Honeywell, General Electric, and Control Data Corporation. But they were often referred to as the "seven dwarfs" because of the dominance of IBM. The company has uninterruptedly remained the number one player in the market, and this has been due primarily to the impact of the System/360.

Mainframe Innovation

IBM did not rest on its laurels. The company continued to invest heavily in its mainframe business.

One breakthrough innovation was *virtualization*. IBM launched this in 1972 with its System/370 mainframe. With virtualization, it was possible to get more resources from existing machines. This was accomplished by using sophisticated software called a *hypervisor*, which made it possible to turn a mainframe into multiple machines. Each was treated as a separate system—called a virtual machine (VM)—with its own operating system and applications.

Virtualization would be a game changer, with advantages like the following:

Cost savings
> A company could greatly reduce its physical footprint since there was not much need to buy new computers. Lower energy expenses were also a benefit.

Agility
> It was fairly easy to spin up and manage a VM.

Lower downtime
> If a machine went down, you could move a VM to another physical machine quickly.

Another innovation, commercialized in the mid-1970s, was the *Universal Product Code* (UPC). IBM researcher George Laurer led a program to use a mainframe to connect with a supermarket scanner for labels. He would use bar codes to make unique identifiers. The result was a significant improvement in automation for retailers.

The Terminal

From the 1960s through the 1990s, the *terminal* was a common way for nontechnical users to access a mainframe. For example, a terminal might be used by a travel agent to book a flight or an insurance agent to process a claim.

The terminal was often called a *green screen* because the characters were green (there were also no graphics). They were based on cathode ray tube (CRT) technology, and the size of the screen was 80 x 24 characters.

But these machines were also known as *dumb terminals*. Why? Because they were not computers; they just transmitted data.

But as personal computers (PCs) grew in popularity, they would become the norm for accessing mainframes. During the 1980s, IBM's Disk Operating System (DOS) was able to connect to mainframes (this was done through DOS/360). Then, in the

1990s, the Microsoft Windows platform became a common way to gain access to these machines.

Mainframe Challenges

By the 1980s, IBM's mainframe business was starting to come under pressure. One of the reasons was the growth in minicomputers, which were much cheaper but still quite powerful. Digital Equipment Corporation was the pioneer of this category and would become a juggernaut.

Then came the PC revolution. With applications like spreadsheets, databases, and word processors, this technology became pervasive in businesses. However, IBM was still able to navigate the changes. Mainframes continued to serve important needs, especially for large-scale data processing.

Fast-forward to today: IBM's mainframe business remains a key source of cash flow for the company and is even seeing a resurgence in growth. The latest version is the z15 (Figure 2-1), which has memory of up to 40 terabytes, over 100 processors, and compute power of up to 9,215 million instructions per second (MIPS).

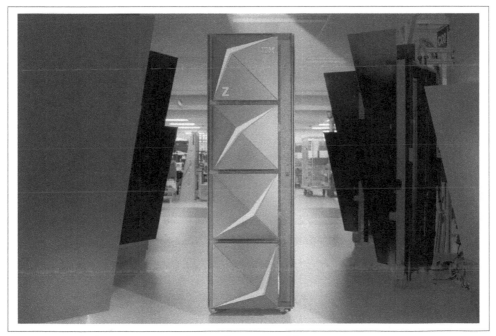

Figure 2-1. The latest IBM mainframe, the z15 model

Why Have a Mainframe?

A big reason the mainframe has lasted so long is that getting rid of it would be incredibly expensive. It would also be risky. What if the migration did not work? This could be a huge problem, because mainframes often handle mission-critical operations.

Jeff Cherrington, vice president of Product Management for System Z at Rocket Software, described the situation this way: "While there are reasons to complain about mainframe processing—large, single-line-item costs compared to more dispersed spending on distributed or cloud, the increasing attrition of seasoned mainframe staff, and the 'uncool' factor of the mainframe—for many specific use cases and many industries, it still represents the best value for IT spend."

Let's take a closer look at the advantages of using a mainframe:

Performance
> Mainframes have hundreds of processors that can process terabytes of data through input storage systems and efficiently generate output. This is certainly critical for handling such things as customer records, invoices, inventory, and other business applications. Mainframes also have *vertical scale*: resources can be upgraded or downgraded depending on the volumes.

Flexible compute
> It's a mistake to think that mainframes are only for large companies. IBM has programs to allow startups to access the technology, such as through the cloud.

Reliability
> Mainframes are built to run continuously (the uptime is at 99.999%). The *z* in z15 is short for "zero downtime." To this end, a mainframe has systems that monitor for errors, which are built into both the hardware and operating system (OS). Mainframes also can quickly recover from mishaps. To enable this, there is redundancy in the mainframe. Continuous reliability is definitely essential for many business applications, such as with ATMs, credit card systems at retailers, and processing of insurance claims. In fact, a z15 mainframe is a capable of withstanding an 8.0 magnitude earthquake.

Serviceability
> Mainframes are built to make it easy to change the systems, such as by swapping out processors. Consider that mainframes are built with a modular design based on *books*. They can be easily configured to customize for processors, memory, and I/O.

Security and encryption
> The z14 and z15 have encryption built into the hardware. Moreover, they're the only servers that have achieved Common Criteria Evaluation Assurance Level 5

(EAL5), which is the highest degree of security. This is certainly a key selling point for companies in highly regulated industries, such as banking, healthcare, insurance, and utilities.

Cost-effectiveness

It's true that mainframes are not cheap. But they may ultimately be more cost-effective than alternatives. The cost per transaction may be much lower than, say, having to manage many smaller servers. Mainframes also have the advantage of lower energy costs because the processing is centralized and conservation systems are built in (this includes an energy meter). The average watt per MIPS is about 0.91, and this is declining every year. Note that energy costs can, over time, be the biggest expense for an IT system.

Modernization

IBM has continued to invest heavily in innovating its mainframe system. A big part of this has been the adoption of open source software, such as Linux, Git, and Python. In addition, IBM bought the biggest player in the market, Red Hat, for $34 billion. Innovations have been made in cutting-edge areas like AI, the native cloud, and DevOps. Interestingly enough, breakthroughs have occurred in the design of the IBM mainframe door. The IBM z15 is made of aluminum and acoustic form shapes, which allows for a low level of noise while helping to cool the system. There is even a patent on the design. As Watson Jr. once said (*https://oreil.ly/saGEd*), "Good design is good business."

The OS

As a developer, you will usually not spend much time with the mainframe's OS. This will instead be the focus for systems programmers. Regardless, it is still important to understand some of the basic concepts.

So what is the OS for the IBM mainframe? No doubt, considerable changes have occurred over the years. The OS has seen a myriad of names, including OS/360, MVT, OS/VS2, and OS/390.

The most current version is the z/OS. This 64-bit platform got its start in 2000 and has seen major upgrades. But again, it has maintained backward compatibility, as its core still has much of the same functionality as the original System/360.

64-bit means that a system can address up to 16 exabytes of data. This is the equivalent of 1 million terabytes. To put this into human terms, it would be enough to store the entire Library of Congress 3,000 times over.

While z/OS is similar to typical operating systems, there are still some notable differences. For example, the memory management does not use the heap or stack. Instead, z/OS allocates memory to programs based on using large chunks or several of them.

Here are some of the other capabilities of the OS:

Concurrency
> This allows for more than one program to be executed at the same time. This is possible because a CPU's resources are usually idle or not heavily used.

Spooling
> Certain functions, like printing, can cause problems in terms of handling the process. Spooling manages the queue for files, which are stored on disk.

Languages
> z/OS supports a myriad of languages like COBOL, assembler, PL/I, Java, C, C++, Python, and Swift.

POSIX compatibility
> This provides Unix file access.

Yet z/OS is not the only OS supported on the IBM Z. There are five others: z/VSE, z/TPF, z/VM, Linux, and KVM. Let's look at each.

z/VSE

z/Virtual Storage Extended (z/VSE) was part of the original System/360 architecture. But the focus for this OS has been for smaller companies.

The original name for z/VSE was Disk Operating System (DOS). But this is not to be confused with the OS that Microsoft developed in the 1980s. IBM's DOS was used to describe how the system would use the disk drive to handle processing.

Even though z/VSE was a slimmed-down version of z/OS, the OS was still powerful. It allows for secure transactions and batch workloads and integrates with IBM's Customer Information Control System (CICS) and Db2. z/VSE has also proven effective with hybrid IT environments.

It's also common that, as a company grows, it will eventually migrate to z/OS. The process for doing so is relatively smooth.

z/TPF

z/Transaction Processing Facility (z/TPF) was developed to handle IBM's Semi-automatic Business Research Environment (Sabre) airline reservation system, which was launched in the early 1960s. The project was one of the first examples of using transactional operations with a mainframe.

The language for the system was based on assembler to allow for high speed and efficiency. But this proved complicated and unwieldy. This is why developers would move over to using the C language.

z/TPF is an expensive system that can be leveraged across various mainframes. But it can be cost-effective for customers that have enormous transactional workloads.

z/VM

z/Virtual Machine (z/VM) was introduced in 1972 when IBM developed virtualization. The z/VM allowed for the use of a *type 1 hypervisor* (also known as a *bare-metal hypervisor*). In this system, the software layer is installed directly on top of the physical machine or server. Generally, higher performance and stability result, since there is no need to run inside an OS (z/VM can host thousands of instances of operating systems). Essentially, a type 1 hypervisor is a form of an OS.

A *type 2 hypervisor*, on the other hand, runs within an OS. This is usually used with environments with a small number of machines.

Linux

Linus Torvalds created the Linux OS in 1991 while he was a student at the University of Helsinki. He did this primarily because he did not want to pay for the licensing fees for existing operating systems. So Torvalds made Linux open source, which led to significant adoption. Another factor for its success was the emergence of the internet as a means of software distribution.

Linux has proven to be robust and adaptable. It has also become pervasive within enterprise environments.

Regarding IBM, it adopted Linux for its mainframes in 2000, and this was key in the company's modernization efforts. Then in 2015, IBM launched LinuxONE, which was a Linux-only mainframe system.

When using Linux on an IBM mainframe, there are some factors to note:

Access
>You do not use a 3270 display terminal. Instead, Linux uses X Window terminators or emulators on PCs. This is the standard interface.

ASCII
>This is the character set. But a traditional mainframe system will use an IBM alternative, called Extended Binary Coded Decimal Interchange Code (EBCDIC12).

Virtualization
>You can use Linux with z/VM to clone different Linux images.

KVM

Kernel-based Virtual Machine (KVM) is an open source virtualization module for the Linux kernel. It essentially makes it function as a type 1 hypervisor.

IBM has adopted KVM for its mainframes to allow for better deployment of Linux workloads and consolidation of x86 server environments. The software has an easy installation process and uses the typical Linux administration console (it's possible to operate 8,000 Linux VMs at the same time). By using KVM, a mainframe can leverage technologies like Docker and Kubernetes.

Processor Architecture

The processor architecture for the modern IBM Z mainframe looks similar to the original developed in 1964. The architecture has three main components: the CPU, main storage, and channels. The CPU processes the instructions that are stored in the main memory. To speed this up, a cache system is built into the processor. The virtualization capabilities for the main memory also rely on caching, which means offloading data to the disk.

The channels are the input/output devices like terminals and printers. These are connected to high-speed fiber optic lines, which boost the performance.

A typical IBM Z system has a multiprocessor as well. This is another way to help enhance the speed of the machine. But a multiprocessor can help with reliability. If one of the processors fails, another one can take over the tasks.

LPAR

A logical partition (LPAR) is a form of virtualization that divides a machine into separate mainframes (it's based on a type 1 hypervisor). The current z15 system allows for up to 40 LPARs.

Each LPAR has its own OS and software. Except for the z/OS, an OS will not know that another one is running on the machine. Each partition has complete independence. To allow for seamless operation across the machine, the z/OS uses cross-memory services to handle the tasks for the various LPARs.

Allocation of resources is flexible. For example, it is possible to use one or more processors per LPAR or to spread them across multiple LPARs. It's even possible to assign weightings for the resources; for example, LPAR1 could have two times as much processor time as the LPAR2.

Part of the advantage of the LPAR architecture is reliability. If one partition goes down, another one can take over.

But when a developer uses an LPAR, they will notice nothing different. It will be acting just like any other mainframe system.

Consider that the LPAR technology relies on Processor Resource/Systems Manager (PR/SM, pronounced *priz-em*). This is based on *firmware*, which is software that is embedded into the hardware. With PR/SM, a mainframe has built-in virtualization that allows for the efficient use of CPU resources and storage for the LPARs.

Another technology to note is the systems complex (sysplex), which allows for the communications and clustering of LPARs. With this, you get district instances of the z/OS (this is often referred to as an *image*). This can allow for better sharing of workloads, handling resources, and dealing with recovery. There are two types of sysplexes: base (or mono) and parallel. The *base* essentially allows for standalone systems to make connections with high-speed fiber cables. Examples include working with applications that use Db2, Information Management System (IMS), or CICS.

A *parallel* sysplex is managed with the coupling facility (CF) LPAR. This can be either a separate LPAR or a dedicated hardware device.

Disks

Disk storage is extremely important for mainframe computers, as they are used to manage enormous amounts of data. This is why it is critical to have a general idea how this technology works.

A *disk drive* is made up of a stack of circular disks that consist of magnetic material to store data. In the middle is a hole, enabling the stack to be placed on a spindle. This allows the disk to be spun at a high rate.

The surface of a disk is divided into *tracks*, and each has various *sectors*. This is the case whether for a PC or a mainframe.

To access the data, a disk drive will use an actuator that moves ahead to a location of a particular sector (all of them are moved in unison). This can be done because there is a memory address for each sector.

IBM uses different terminology to describe its mainframe disk drive. The drive is called a *direct access storage device* (DASD, pronounced *dazz-dee*), which still has the original IBM System/360 architecture. What's more, a sector is instead called a *cylinder*.

Mainframe disk drivers are definitely fast. But of course, since they are mechanical, the speed is much slower than working with memory or the CPU. As a result, mainframe developers look for ways to minimize the accessing of the disk drive.

Note that a DASD is connected to the mainframe via arrays. Caching is used to help speed things up, and controllers manage the processing and provide for sharing of the system.

Batch and Online Transaction Processing

In the early days of mainframes, the primary approach for handling data was batch processing. An example of this is inputting data during business hours and then processing everything at night, when there is less activity. Another use case is processing payroll: information is collected for a couple weeks and then processed at the end of the period.

Batch processing may seem unusual to developers who have experience with modern languages like Java or Python, because usually no user input (or minimal user input) happens with the mainframe. Rather, a program is run by using Job Control Language (JCL), and a job is scheduled to process the data.

It's important to keep in mind that batch processing can be a cost-efficient way to manage large amounts of data, and it remains a common use case for mainframes. But batch processing has notable limitations. Let's face it, certain types of activities need to be processed in real time. For a mainframe, this is known as *online transaction processing* (OLTP).

A classic case of this technology is the Sabre platform for handling airline reservations. It was able to handle millions of transactions across the United States. Then OLTP would be used for other real-time processing areas like credit cards and banking.

Nowadays, a mainframe typically uses a system like CICS for real-time transactions. It can process up to 100 million transactions and port to databases like Db2.

Mainframe Trends

For 15 consecutive years, BMC Software has published an annual survey of the mainframe industry. The latest one (*https://oreil.ly/CBKty*) included more than one thousand respondents.

The good news is that the prospects for the industry look bright. About 54% of respondents indicated that their organizations had higher transaction volumes, and 47% reported higher data volumes.

Here are some of the other interesting findings from the survey:

- 90% of respondents believe that the mainframe will be a key platform for new growth and long-term applications.
- Roughly two-thirds of extra-large organizations had over half of their data in mainframe environments—indicating the critical importance of the technology.
- While cost has usually been the highest priority, this changed in 2020. The respondents now look at compliance and security as the most important. Data recovery was another area that saw a rise in priority.
- About 56% of respondents were using some form of DevOps on the mainframe. But this was seen as part of a journey, with cultural change still in progress for many.
- The survey showed that some of the reasons for the adoption of modern DevOps were for benefits like stability, better application quality and performance, security, and improved deployment. The efforts have also led to the use of AI, such as with AI operations (AIOps) to help automate processes.

The Mainframe "Shop"

An IT organization that manages mainframe systems is known as a *shop*. Each has its own approaches, strategies, standards, and requirements. However, certain types of roles are common across many shops.

Here's a look at the main ones:

Systems programmer
> This person provides engineering and administration for the mainframe and z/OS. Some of the duties include installation, configuration, training, and maintenance. But a systems programmer also helps provide analysis and documentation for hardware and software.

Systems administrator
> Depending on the organization, this person may serve essentially the same role as a systems programmer. But for larger companies, there will be clear differences,

with the roles more specialized. A systems administrator usually spends more time helping with data and applications, whereas a systems programmer is more focused on the maintenance of the system.

This separation in duties may also be due to the importance of security and auditing. For the most part, you do not want a person to have too much access to certain parts of the mainframe.

The systems administrator may have specialties as well. Examples include the database administrator and the security administrator.

Application programmer or designer
This person develops, tests, deploys, and maintains applications. This may involve using a language like COBOL, PL/I, Java, C, or C++.

The specifications for the program will often come from a business analyst or manager.

Systems operator
This person monitors the operation of the mainframe. If there is a problem, they can take action (say, to stop and restart a system) or notify the right person.

Production control analyst
This person manages batch workloads, helping to ensure there are no errors.

Vendor support
Usually, this means calling someone at IBM for assistance! The company has a long history of world-class support.

Granted, it seems like maintaining a mainframe installation requires many people. But given that a system has significant scale, the headcount is actually fairly small. This should mean a lower total cost of ownership of the mainframe compared to the equivalent blade servers. It also helps that a mainframe will have a variety of automation systems.

Conclusion

As we've seen in this chapter, the mainframe is alive and well. This type of machine can handle certain workloads at scale that would not be practical or economical for other systems. Growth prospects for the industry continue to look bright.

CHAPTER 3

The Development Environment

Nowadays it is easy for anyone to learn a modern programming language. Often this knowledge is free since most of the software is open source. For Python, for example, plenty of tutorials are available on YouTube.

But when it comes to mainframe development, the situation is much different. Not as many online resources are available. What's more, few people have access to an actual mainframe. It simply costs too much.

So what to do? Luckily, free software is available to emulate a mainframe environment as well as several integrated development environments (IDEs), and even web-based platforms.

In this chapter, we will look at these offerings. The chapter also shows the types of tools you are likely to have access to from your employer.

Accessing a Mainframe

Thousands of people can interact with a mainframe that is managed by z/OS. But before you can get access, your employer will provide you with the necessary login credentials. A background check may even be required before you can use the system. It's common to have a high level of security for mainframes because these machines usually contain critical data.

A common approach to provide mainframe access is through the use of emulator software, Eclipse or Visual Studio code. With this, you will have different types of software systems to make a connection:

TN3270 emulator

> This is the most common way to access a mainframe. This software will make a direct connection.

File Transfer Protocol (FTP)

> This is a way to manage files on a mainframe.

Secure Shell (SSH) client

> A common open source tool for this is PuTTY. This software makes it possible to create a Unix system session on the mainframe.

Let's go through the process of accessing and using a mainframe system. You first enter your user ID and press the Return or Enter key. However, if you are on a PC, this will be the Ctrl key on the right side of the keyboard. This can take some time to get used to.

Next, you enter the password, which has a default of one to eight characters. You then need to type this in again to verify it. Figure 3-1 shows what the screen looks like.

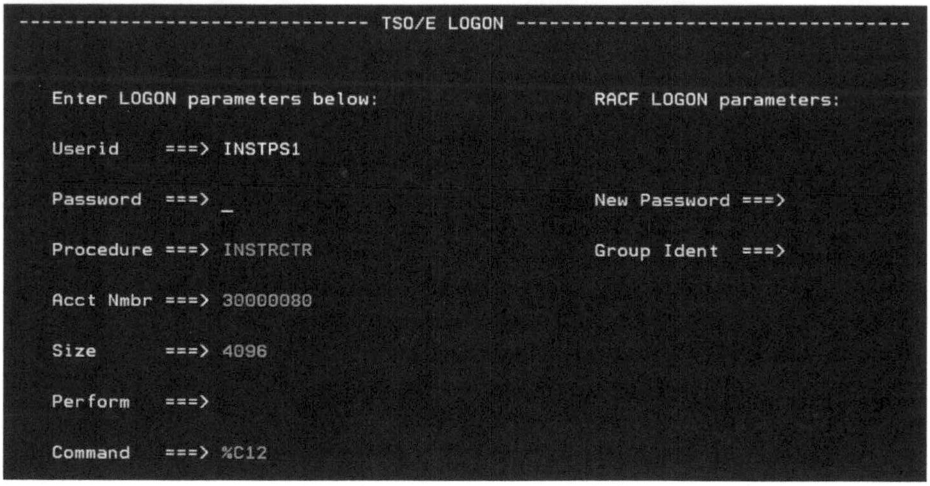

```
------------------------------ TSO/E LOGON ------------------------------


    Enter LOGON parameters below:            RACF LOGON parameters:

    Userid    ===> INSTPS1

    Password  ===> _                          New Password ===>

    Procedure ===> INSTRCTR                   Group Ident  ===>

    Acct Nmbr ===> 30000080

    Size      ===> 4096

    Perform   ===>

    Command   ===> %C12
```

Figure 3-1. A login screen for a mainframe computer

After you log in to the system, z/OS will issue numerous messages. If they cannot fit on the screen, you will see three asterisks (*) at the bottom, as you can see in Figure 3-2. You then press Enter to go to the next page of messages.

```
ICH70001I INSTPS1  LAST ACCESS AT 14:17:28 ON MONDAY, FEBRUARY 14, 2022
INSTPS1 LOGON IN PROGRESS AT 14:27:49 ON FEBRUARY 15, 2022
    ***********************************************
    ***       THIS SYSTEM IS TO BE USED FOR       ***
    *** IBM MANAGEMENT APPROVED PURPOSES ONLY ***
    ***   USE IS SUBJECT TO AUDIT AT ANY TIME   ***
    ***              BY IBM MANAGEMENT            ***
    ***********************************************
Allocating ISPF/PDF environment...
Test for Netmail
You have no messages or data sets to receive.

If you are unable to access ispf, please ensure that the
command line of your TSO logon panel has %xx where
xx is the curriculum code of the class you are supporting.
In most cases the curriculum code is the last two characters of
the default group for your ID.

You may also enter the %xx call here if it was not in
your command field.

%C12
***
```

Figure 3-2. Initial messages when you log into a mainframe computer

You may then go to the Interactive System Productivity Facility (ISPF) primary
option screen, which is where you will spend most of your time with your mainframe
development (Figure 3-3). It's important to keep in mind that you can gain access to
this through TSO by entering **ISPF**. You'll learn about this in the next section.

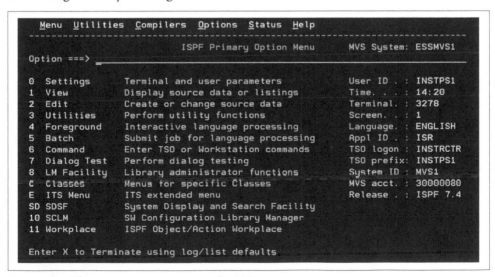

```
   Menu  Utilities  Compilers  Options  Status  Help
-----------------------------------------------------------------------
                       ISPF Primary Option Menu        MVS System: ESSMVS1
  Option ===>

   0  Settings     Terminal and user parameters        User ID . : INSTPS1
   1  View         Display source data or listings      Time. . . : 14:20
   2  Edit         Create or change source data         Terminal. : 3278
   3  Utilities    Perform utility functions            Screen. . : 1
   4  Foreground   Interactive language processing      Language. : ENGLISH
   5  Batch        Submit job for language processing   Appl ID . : ISR
   6  Command      Enter TSO or Workstation commands    TSO logon : INSTRCTR
   7  Dialog Test  Perform dialog testing               TSO prefix: INSTPS1
   8  LM Facility  Library administrator functions      System ID : MVS1
   C  Classes      Menus for specific Classes           MVS acct. : 30000080
   E  ITS Menu     ITS extended menu                    Release . : ISPF 7.4
   SD SDSF         System Display and Search Facility
   10 SCLM         SW Configuration Library Manager
   11 Workplace    ISPF Object/Action Workplace

   Enter X to Terminate using log/list defaults
```

Figure 3-3. The primary option menu for ISPF

TSO

Time Sharing Option (TSO) has dozens of commands, depending on the products installed. The system also is based on the command line; you'll see no graphics, just text on the screen. In fact, for many mainframe developers, TSO is not used much.

So then why is TSO important? One reason is that the technology provides the foundation for other technologies like ISPF. TSO also provides for native access to z/OS. As a result, it's a good idea to have a general understanding of it.

You can access TSO by pressing the X key in ISPF to exit the program. You will then get the READY prompt, which you can see in Figure 3-4.

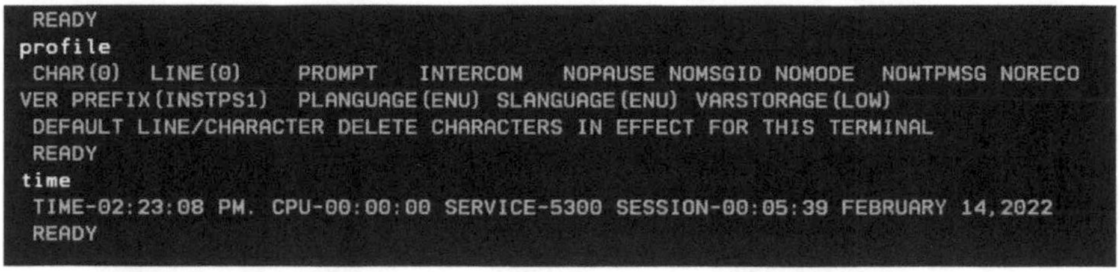

```
READY
profile
 CHAR(0)  LINE(0)    PROMPT   INTERCOM   NOPAUSE NOMSGID NOMODE   NOWTPMSG NORECO
VER PREFIX(INSTPS1)  PLANGUAGE(ENU) SLANGUAGE(ENU) VARSTORAGE(LOW)
 DEFAULT LINE/CHARACTER DELETE CHARACTERS IN EFFECT FOR THIS TERMINAL
 READY
time
 TIME-02:23:08 PM. CPU-00:00:00 SERVICE-5300 SESSION-00:05:39 FEBRUARY 14,2022
 READY
```

Figure 3-4. TSO screen

As you can see, we have entered the `profile` command to get some basic information on the user account as well as the `time` command. You can also send messages to other users on the system by using `send`:

```
send 'test message' user (tt25)
```

This means that user tt25 will receive the message after logging in.

Another useful command is `listc` (short for *list catalog*). This shows a list of the datasets currently available on your TSO session. You can then handle tasks like renaming a dataset:

```
rename 'tt103.invoices.data' 'tt104.invoices.data'
```

Or you can edit a dataset, such as by using the following:

```
edit 'myfile.jcl.new' cobol
```

You can enter COBOL commands in the dataset. Then once you are finished, you type **save**.

ISPF

Interactive System Productivity Facility (ISPF) is a menu-based system. It is essentially made up of different panels, which you can think of as web pages. It's true that ISPF may seem archaic and old. But it is actually quite fast and efficient.

Before we look at the various parts of ISPF, let's first review the basic navigation. You can move to the different input fields on the screen by using the mouse, arrow keys, or Tab keys. To move to the different panels, you enter the menu number at the Option ===> prompt. If you want to move to the prior panel, press the End key.

The ISPF screens can be customized. So the illustrations in this book may not necessarily look like the ones you will see on your system. But for the most part, many mainframe development shops will have many of the same features.

For example, if you want to go to the Settings panel, type **0** and press Enter. This takes you to the screen shown in Figure 3-5. You can customize the ISPF environment—for example, changing the location of the command prompt or providing for longer descriptions in pop-ups.

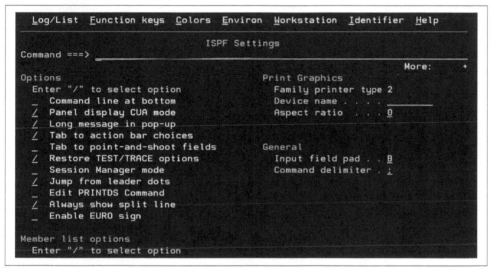

Figure 3-5. The Settings screen for ISPF

There are some other options to consider. On the primary option screen of ISPF, you can disable the copyright message by pressing Enter. You can then type **pfshow off** in the command prompt to turn off the message that shows how to use the function keys. These two actions can free up lots of space on the screen.

Even if a menu option is visible on ISPF, this does not mean you can use it. A mainframe shop will often restrict certain functions of the system.

Note that ISPF has a set of program function (PF) keys, which you can customize. Table 3-1 shows some examples.

Table 3-1. The PF keys for ISPF

PF key	What it does
Ctrl (on the lower-right side of the keyboard)	Enter
F1	Help
F2	Split screen
F3	Exit or return
F7	Page up
F8	Page down
F10	Navigate through data to the right
F11	Navigate through data to the left
PA1 or Program Action key (Alt-Insert or Esc)	Stop a process or task (this is often if the system is in an infinite loop)
Ctrl (lower-right side of the keyboard)	Unlock the keyboard

In an ISPF panel, some content may not fit on the screen. But you can use the arrow keys to navigate across horizontally or vertically.

Datasets

On a typical PC system, a file is a long string of bytes. But often delimiters indicate to the OS the beginning and ending of certain types of data (a delimiter is often in the form of a carriage return).

But a mainframe generally has a different approach. The data is often in the form of records. Because of this, the length of each will be established beforehand.

What's more, a file is not called a file. It is known as a *dataset*. You need to provide a variety of parameters, such as the following, to configure and manage a dataset:

Volume serial
    The name of the DASD, which is up to six characters.

Device type
    The disk device used.

Organization
    Shows how data is processed, which could be sequential, random, virtual storage access method (VSAM), basic direct access method (BDAM), linear, or partitioned.

Record format
    Records can be fixed-length (the most common approach) or variable.

Record length
> The number of characters for each record.

Space
> The amount reserved for the dataset. This can be expressed in units such as tracks of cylinders on the disk.

The dataset often includes data for input and output operations. Depending on the format, you can read it on your screen.

Keep in mind that a dataset can be put into a *catalog*. This grouping structure enables you to access a dataset without indicating where it is stored. A catalog is a helpful way to manage and navigate a system as the number of datasets can be large.

Datasets are not just for data files. They can also be used for storing applications, the operating system, libraries, and variables.

Main Types of Datasets

On the mainframe, various datasets are available. But in this section, we'll take a look at the following:

- Sequential file
- Partitioned dataset
- Virtual storage access

Sequential File

The easiest type of dataset to work with is *sequential*, which has records that are stored consecutively on the disk. There are other names for this, such as queued sequential access method (QSAM).

In a sequential dataset, added records are appended to the end of the file. This type of dataset is also defined by using JCL.

In some cases, sequential datasets can be stored on tapes. But this is much less common nowadays. Rather, the most common approach is for storage on disks.

Partitioned Dataset

A *partitioned dataset* (PDS) is similar to the concept of files within a directory or folder. But on the mainframe, each member inside has an address, which makes it possible to get direct access to the records. Each member also has records that are stored sequentially, and the names of the files are listed alphabetically. Moreover, to define a PDS, you use JCL or ISPF, and the process is fairly straightforward.

A key advantage of using a PDS is the grouping of organization functions. They make it much easier to navigate a complex web of files on a system.

A PDS is also efficient. Consider that it can store multiple members on a single track on a disk. But it is also possible to aggregate PDSs into large libraries, which can make processing easier for complex files.

What about the drawbacks? Several notable ones exist. One is that when a PDS is replaced, the pointer to the file is deleted. This makes it so the space cannot be effectively reused. Because of this, periodic cleaning of the disk must occur, such as with the IEBCOPY utility.

Next, the directories are limited in size. When you set up an allocation, it remains fixed. So if you want additional space, you need to create a new PDS.

Finally, as a PDS gets larger, more disk drive activity may occur, which slows the processing. What's more, the searching of the directory is done alphabetically. And this can make things even slower.

But an alternative is available: the *partitioned dataset extended* (PDSE). It has a directory and members and can also be created with JCL or ISPF. However, there are some differences. For example, a PDSE is available on one volume.

Yet a PDSE has some important benefits as well. You can have a directory of 522,236 members and 15,728,639 records per member. Searching is fast because the system relies on indexing. Finally, there is no need for a utility to clean up the drive.

Now all this is not to imply that you no longer need a PDS. Far from it. Both are necessary in mainframe development. It's really about understanding the use cases and the limits.

Virtual Storage Access Method

The *virtual storage access method* (VSAM) is a combination of a dataset and an access method. No doubt, these features make the technology powerful.

The developer of VSAM is IBM, which launched this technology back in the 1970s. As a result, it has been well-established and has evolved over the years.

Essentially, VSAM was developed to make file processing easier. It has also been made available for COBOL and CICS development (you'll learn more about this later in the book).

The VSAM system uses catalogs for organization of the datasets, and this is done with high performance and efficiency. Security, such as password protection, is built-in.

In a VSAM dataset, you can read records either sequentially or randomly. VSAM datasets come in four types:

Key-sequenced dataset (KSDS)
> This is the one you will see the most. It provides major advantages. You can access records randomly and use variable-length records. Moreover, KSDS is sorted on a key field, which makes processing more efficient.

Entry-sequenced dataset (ESDS)
> This is similar to a sequential file organization. Records are identified by a physical address, and storage is based on the order in which records are inserted into the dataset. But deletion is not allowed. And since there is no index, it is possible to have duplicate records. ESDS is common in databases like IMS and Db2.

Relative record dataset (RRDS)
> This shares many of the functions of ESDS. But an important difference is that records are accessed using the relative record number (RRN), which is based on the location of the first record. Also, the records are fixed length, and deletion is allowed.

Linear dataset (LDS)
> This dataset is based on byte streams, which are found in operating system files. However, the LDS structure is not used much when it comes to application development.

Yet VSAM has drawbacks. For instance, you can use it only on a DASD drive, not tape drives. But then again, tape drives are not used much anymore.

Another limitation is that a VSAM can have higher levels of storage requirements. This is because its functions require more overhead.

In addition, VSAM is mostly for mainframe development. You cannot use it for such things as modules, JCL, and source programs.

Finally, the VSAM dataset is proprietary. This means that it is not readable by other access methods. In fact, you cannot view it using ISPF, unless you use special software.

Catalogs

Of course, large numbers of datasets are usually spread across many disk drives. To manage all this, z/OS uses a catalog system and volume table of contents (VTOC) that track the locations. When you want to access a file, you do not have to know the volume serial number; the z/OS will find this in the catalog. This is part of the Integrated Catalog Facility (ICF).

There are two types of catalogs. One is the *master catalog*, of which there is only one. The other is the *user catalog*, and you can have as many as you want.

All VSAM files are automatically cataloged. This makes them easier to use with JCL.

ISPF and Datasets

One of the most common ISPF panels is used to locate datasets that are available on your system. To navigate to this panel, select 3 on the primary option screen and then choose 4 for DSLIST. Figure 3-6 shows what you will see.

```
   Menu   Options   View   Utilities   Compilers   Help

 DSLIST - Data Sets Matching INSTPS1                        Row 1 of 26
 Command ===>                                        Scroll ===> CSR

 Command - Enter "/" to select action           Message        Volume
 ---------------------------------------------------------------------
          INSTPS1                                               *ALIAS
          INSTPS1.CBL.CALC1000                                  SMS036
          INSTPS1.CBL.CALC2000                                  SMS036
          INSTPS1.CBL.COBOL                                     SMS132
          INSTPS1.CBL.IND1000                                   SMS039
          INSTPS1.CBL.IND2000                                   SMS032
          INSTPS1.CBL.RPT1000                                   SMS032
          INSTPS1.CBL.SEQ1000                                   SMS031
          INSTPS1.CBL.SEQ2000                                   SMS133
          INSTPS1.CBL.SRT1000                                   SMS132
          INSTPS1.COBOL                                         SMS032
          INSTPS1.COBOL.LOADLIB                                 SMS231
          INSTPS1.COBOL.SEQ                                     SMS031
          INSTPS1.DAT.CUSTMAST                                  SMS134
          INSTPS1.DAT.ERRTRAN                                   SMS132
          INSTPS1.DAT.INVMASTS                                  SMS132
```

Figure 3-6. Showing the list of datasets

Again, z/OS has a sophisticated system for searching datasets, which is based on a master catalog. The same goes for storage. A particular DASD volume can have many datasets. They are then located based on the volume serial number, dataset name, and the type of device. Unlike a PC filesystem, there are no pathnames.

Besides a DASD, a mainframe disk drive can be referred to as a disk pack, head disk assembly (HDA), or disk volume.

On the DLIST screen, you can move the cursor to the left side of one of the datasets and enter a command. For example, typing **e** opens the edit screen.

A myriad of rules and conventions constrain the naming of datasets. Of course, each name must be unique. Dataset names often have several parts, which are separated by periods (but there is no period at the end).

In Figure 3-6, one of the dataset names is INSTPS1.TSO.JCL. The first name is known as the *high-level qualifier* (HLQ), which may be the username or a name that is based on the security system. The last one is the *lowest-level qualifier* (LLQ). You can have 22 of these, for a total of 44 characters. But for the most part, it is a good idea to not make them too long.

For a name, the first character must be an uppercase letter from A to Z or a special character, which includes #, @, and $. You can then have up to seven more characters, which can be uppercase letters, numbers, the special characters, or a hyphen.

Here are some conventions for dataset names to consider:

- For source code, you will usually see the name of the language, like COBOL, PL/I, C, JAVA, and so on.
- An executable will have a name like LOAD, LOADLIB, or LINKLIB.
- A partitioned dataset to store an executable will typically have LOAD or LINK in the name, for example, USERNAME.LOADLIB/USERNAME.LINKLIB/USERNAME.LOAD.
- If it is a JCL file, it will likely have JCL in the name. But it could also have CNTL or JOB. PRC, PROC, or PROCLIB indicates that the dataset has JCL procedures. Later in this chapter, we will cover JCL.
- A library will have LIB in the name.
- The dataset name could have a description of the function of the dataset. Some examples include INV (for inventory) and CUSTMAST (for customer master).

To create a dataset, there are several approaches. You can use the ALLOCATE command at the TSO terminal. But a more common way is to use ISPF (you navigate to 3.2) or JCL.

 After a while, a mainframe developer will memorize the panel number sequences, which can speed up navigation. One of the most widely used is 3.4, which will get you to the DLIST panel. This is known as *ISPF concatenation*. You separate the screen numbers with a period, which provides a convenient shortcut.

Creating a File with ISPF

Now that you have a general understanding about datasets, their structure, and use cases, let's take a look at how to create one. We could use TSO or ISPF, but we'll focus on ISPF, which is more common.

On the main screen, select 3 for Utilities to access the Utility Selection Panel shown in Figure 3-7.

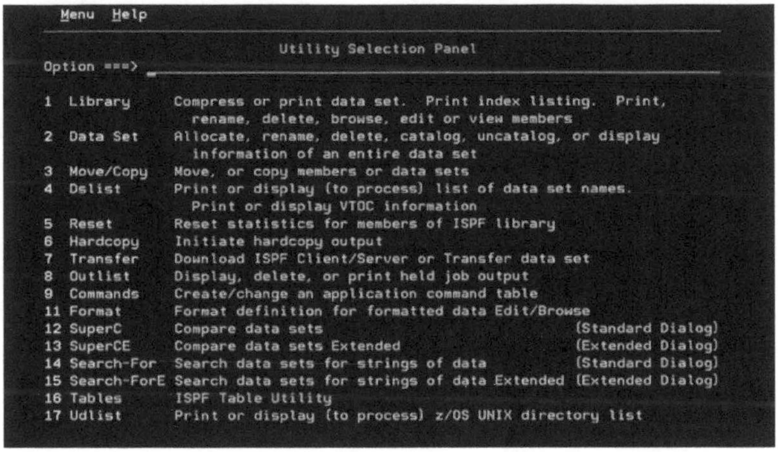

Figure 3-7. The Utility Selection Panel, where you can start creating a dataset

Next, select option 2 for Data Set. This begins the process of the allocation. You'll see the Data Set Utility screen (Figure 3-8).

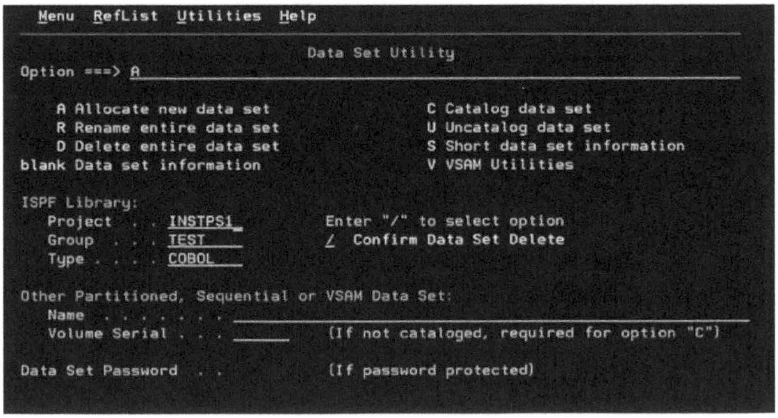

Figure 3-8. The Data Set Utility, where you specify the name of the dataset

At this panel, you will create the name for the dataset. The Project is for your user ID, and the Group is in reference to essentially the directory for the members. For Type, you indicate the type of file, which is COBOL. This is important. It ensures that you'll have the correct editor when you work with the file.

Now press Enter to access the Allocate New Data Set screen in Figure 3-9.

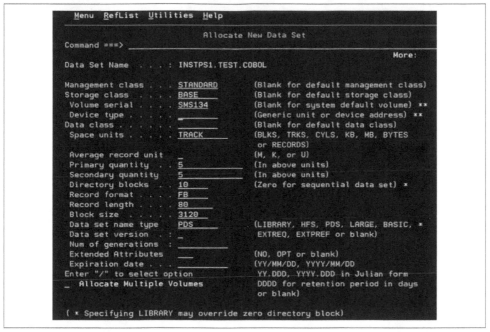

Figure 3-9. The Allocate New Data Set screen for setting the parameters for the dataset

This screen has a lot of details. But the important ones are in the second half, where you set the size for the file, record length, and record format. Then you need to make sure that the "Data set name type" is set to **PDS**. If you leave this blank, it will be assumed that you want a sequential file.

Press Enter to be taken to the Data Set Utility screen. If it reads "dataset allocated" at the top right, you have a new dataset.

But there is no member inside it. So you need to create one. Go back to the main screen for ISPF and select 2. This brings up the Edit Entry panel (Figure 3-10).

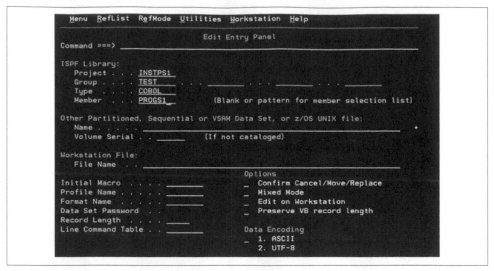

Figure 3-10. The Edit Entry panel screen for creating a member

At the Member option, enter the name. I put in PROGS. But you can put what you want so long as it is unique and does not exceed eight characters.

After you press Enter, you will get the editor for the file (Figure 3-11).

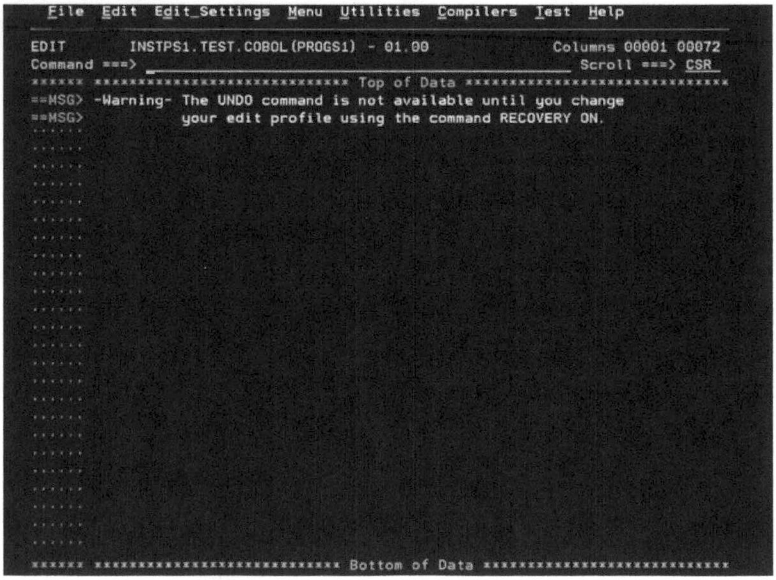

Figure 3-11. The ISPF editor for your files

The editor has three main areas. The heading area is for the two lines at the top of the screen. The first will show the name of the program, and the second is for entering edit commands.

Here's a look at some of the commands available:

SAVE
> Saves your source code to the disk.

COPY
> Copies a dataset into your editor. When you use this command, a panel will pop up, and you can indicate the lines you want to copy. This command is common because mainframe coders usually start with existing code.

CHANGE
> Similar to a find/replace command. For example, if you want to change the occurrences of the field of INVENTORY-AMOUNT to INVENTORY-TOTALS, you would do something like CHANGE INVENTORY-AMOUNT INVENTORY-TOTALS ALL. This command changes all the occurrences.

CREATE
> Creates a member in the partitioned dataset.

SORT
> Sorts the data in the dataset. Specifying SORT A indicates ascending, and SORT D indicates descending.

LOCATE
> Takes you to a certain line number in the source code.

END
> Saves the changes and then takes you back to the Edit Entry panel.

UNDO
> Reverses the most recent edits.

RETURN
> Saves the changes and brings you back to the Primary Option menu.

The line command area is the column that has the five single quotation (') marks. You can move the cursor here and enter an edit statement. One common one is I, which will add a line. Here are some others:

D

Deletes a line of code. If you want more lines, specify the number, such as d2.

R

Repeats the line of code that you are highlighting.

C/A

The C command copies a line, which you can then place somewhere else with A.

UC/LC

UC changes the text from lowercase to uppercase, and LC does the opposite.

The screen window is the open space in the middle, and you can enter your code here. You can navigate this with your arrow keys, Tab keys, or mouse. Also, pressing Enter changes the screen. On the left side, the line numbers will show up for the code and any extra lines will be taken out.

You can also scroll through the edit screen by using the F7 and F8 keys. But you can adjust the settings for scrolling, with options indicated at the top right of the screen:

CSR

When you scroll up, the cursor is displayed at the top of the window.

PAGE

Scrolls one page at a time.

HALF

Scrolls half a page at a time.

System Display and Search Facility

The *System Display and Search Facility* (SDSF) is a system within z/OS that you can access via ISPF. It helps with the management of jobs. Some of its functions include canceling and purging jobs, viewing and searching the system log, monitoring jobs that are being processed, and controlling the scheduling of jobs.

To access SDSF, go to the ISPF Primary Option Menu screen and type **SD**. This will take you to the SDSF Primary Option menu (Figure 3-12).

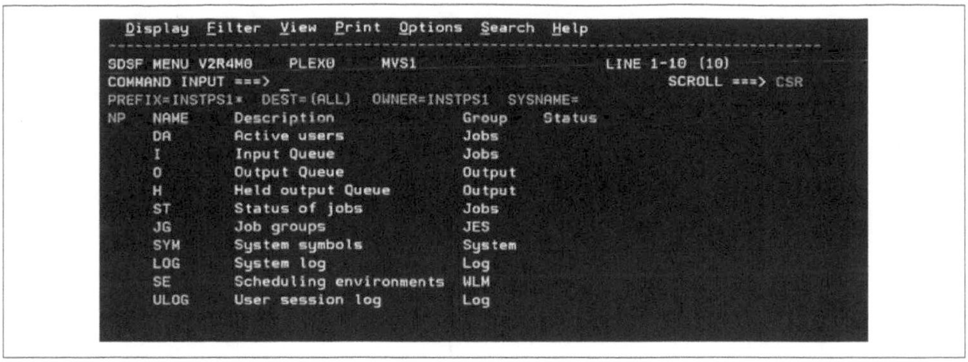

Figure 3-12. The main screen for SDSF

A useful command is Log. If you enter this, you will get the activity for the mainframe system, as shown in Figure 3-13. You can use the F10 and F11 keys to scroll vertically to see all the data.

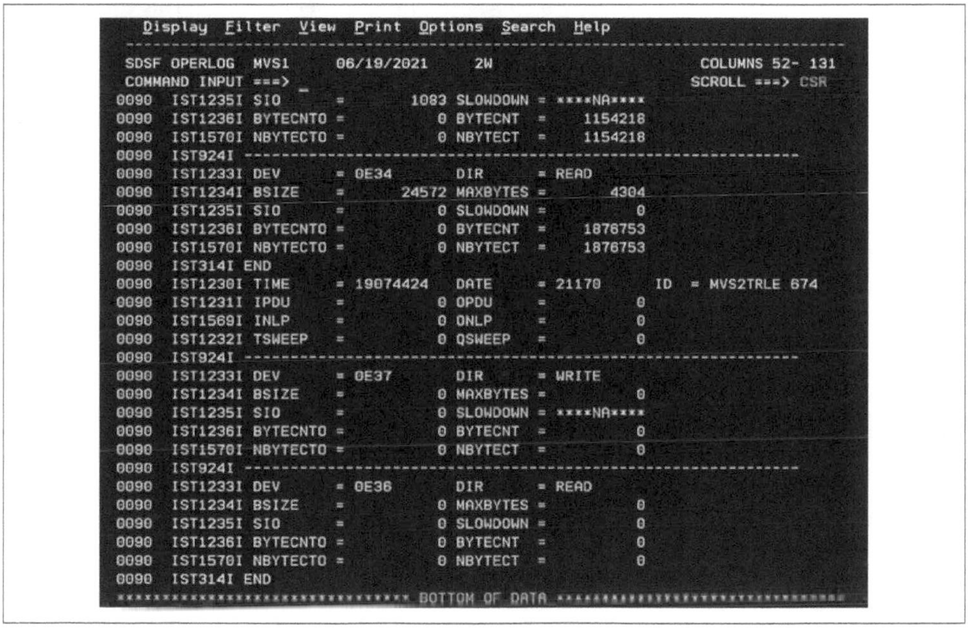

Figure 3-13. The log activity on a mainframe

Job Control Language

In a typical language, running a program is often just about pushing a button. But when it comes to mainframe applications, the process is much more complicated. You will usually need to use *Job Control Language* (JCL), which is essentially a scripting language. In this book, we'll see some examples of how to use this.

A mainframe shop usually has one core JCL script. Then when you create a new program, you can adjust the parameters for the new requirements.

Regardless, it is important to understand how to create JCL scripts from scratch. First of all, this scripting language instructs z/OS to set the parameters for running a program as well as to read and write data to a disk and output to a printer. JCL is also used for the necessary allocation of resources.

 Fred Brooks, a manager who helped create the System/360, was instrumental in the development of JCL. In an interview decades later, he noted (*https://oreil.ly/laIbU*) that developing JCL was the "worst mistake we made." He thought a better approach would have been to meld the JCL functions in a language. Regardless, JCL continued to grow and quickly became a standard for batch processing when using COBOL.

When you execute JCL, a set of sophisticated processes will be initiated, and a major part of this is the job entry subsystem (JES). This coordinates and schedules the various jobs that need to be performed by the z/OS. In other words, JCL is a batch system, and the jobs will run in the background. To help with the process, a variety of utilities are available.

For many new mainframe developers, JCL does seem complicated. But it really is not. You need to understand just a few commands.

Here's a look at a sample script:

```
//SORTJOB  JOB MSGLEVEL=1,CLASS=A,MSGCLASS=A,TIME=1,NOTIFY=&SYSUID
//MYSORT EXEC PGM=SORT
//SORTIN DD DISP=SHR,DSN=CUST.FILE
//SORTOUT DD SYSOUT=*
//*This is the JCL for a sort program ❶
```

❶ This is a comment in the code.

The first line is the job card, which is specified with JOB. The name of this script, SORTJOB, can be from one to eight characters and is usually unique. Then various parameters follow:

MSGLEVEL=1

Indicates the type of messages that will be sent to the output, such as JCL statements.

CLASS=A

Allows you to put your JCL into different classes. This helps with scheduling the jobs.

MSGCLASS=A

Assigns the output class for the job log.

TIME=1

Sets the maximum amount of time the job can use the processor. This example allows the job 1 minute of CPU time.

NOTIFY=&SYSUID

Sends a completion message to the user that submitted the job.

The EXEC statement, short for *execution*, is used to execute a program of the JCL procedure. (In this example, it has been used to execute the program called SORT). A JCL script can have more than one of these.

For each EXEC statement, there are data definition (DD) statements. These are about setting forth the characteristics for datasets for the inputs and outputs of the job. This could be for the storage and record length. In fact, when it comes to DD statements, the output may not even be a file. It could be something like SDSF memory.

In our code example, SORTIN uses a DD statement to access a dataset. As for the SORTOUT, this will use SYSOUT to display the JCL output.

Again, this is a simple script. Certainly, much more can be done with JCL, such as with procedures to execute blocks of code (with the PROC command) and the use of the INCLUDE statement to bring in outside code (this is similar to a copybook in the COBOL language). But for our purposes, we have looked at the key components of JCL.

JCL has a limit of 80 columns per line. While this is usually long enough, in some cases you may need something longer. To allow for this, you use the comma as a continuation character to go to the next line.

Unix System Services

The origins of the Unix OS go back to the mid-1960s. The creators included the Massachusetts Institute of Technology, Bell Labs, and General Electric. At first, Unix was for the GE mainframes. But over the decades, its use would spread quickly.

As a result, IBM adopted this OS for its own mainframe platforms. In fact, Unix is a built-in system that you can use alongside z/OS. This is definitely a big selling point for businesses that have extensive experience with Unix. It is also seamlessly integrated with other systems like CICS, IMS, Db2, SAP R/3, Oracle HTTP Server, and MQ.

However, the OS has a hierarchical filesystem. How is this managed on a mainframe, which relies on PDSs? IBM first created the Hierarchical File System (HFS), which was a good first version. But the next one, zSeries File System (zFS), was far superior.

Mainframe Tools

Many tools and software packages can help with mainframe development. The type you use will usually be based on the policies of the shop you work for (in Chapter 9, we'll take a more detailed look at software tools, such as for DevOps). But of course, some are widely used, such as the following:

DFSORT and Syncsort
Sophisticated tools from IBM and Precisely for sorting, merging, copying, and analyzing data.

BMC Compuware Abend-AID
Can identify, resolve, and track application and system abends.

BMC Compuware File-AID
Helps to manage files and data across platforms.

BMC Compuware Xpediter
Includes a set of debuggers and interactive analysis tools for COBOL, PL/I, C, and assembler applications.

CA Easytrieve Report Generator
A Broadcom data management system that helps create reports. It is based on an English-like language and can operate on mainframe, Unix, Linux, and Windows environments.

ChangeMan ZMF
Allows for version control for applications.

Comparex

File comparison tool that detects changes to data, text, and directory files.

Endevor

A mainframe software management system from CA Technologies, now part of Broadcom. Its name comes from ENvironment for DEVelopment and OpeRations.

Insync

Provides fast and easy access to data sources, such as from IMS and Db2.

IEBGENER

IBM tool that has been around for decades. For the most part, it helps with the copying of sequential datasets, PDSs, and HFS files.

ESP Workload Automation Intelligence

Helps with monitoring and managing scheduled and event-based workloads.

Resource Access Control Facility (RACF)

An IBM security system that manages user access to mainframe resources, such as with authentication and logging of unauthorized access attempts.

MQ (Message Queue)

IBM middleware that provides for asynchronous communication. This means that one application can send a message or data to another application even if it is not online. MQ ensures that the data is sent when the other application is available.

Modern IDEs

Even though ISPF is powerful and efficient, this system definitely has some drawbacks. You do not have features like code completion, sophisticated code highlighting, graphical interfaces, DevOps tools, and so on.

This is why many mainframe developers prefer using a modern IDE. This is especially the case for younger coders, who have learned programming with such a system. So let's look at some of the more popular IDEs for mainframe development.

IBM Developer for z/OS

This is available for Microsoft Windows and requires a license fee from IBM. The system is built on the Eclipse framework, which is a popular IDE foundation that is written in Java and has an open source software development kit (SDK). This system is built for teams and includes Git integration as well as sophisticated unit testing. IBM Developer for z/OS is available for mainframe languages like COBOL,

PL/I, High Level Assembler, and REXX. Interestingly, for those coders who are more comfortable with ISPF, there is a style editor for this.

BMC Compuware Topaz Workbench

This commercial IDE is for the Windows platform and is built on the Eclipse platform. The system provides access to not only a variety of BMC's developer tools (like Abend-AID, File-AID, ISPW, Strobe, and Xpediter) but also those that are available from other vendors. This IDE provides a full suite of software to help with testing, debugging, and tune performance. For example, it is easy to create unit tests; the Visualizer (Figure 3-14) shows the connections, files accessed, and databases used. The Code Coverage feature shows which lines are executed and even dead code. Moreover, you can integrate the IDE with popular software development systems like Confluent and Jenkins.

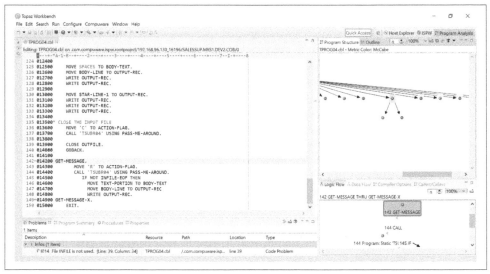

Figure 3-14. Visualization capabilities in the Topaz IDE

Che4z

This open source project, based on the Eclipse Che IDE, is built specifically for managing mainframe services. It can be hosted with a single click and has functions for editing, building, and testing code. Che4z has the COBOL Language Server Protocol (LSP) editor that allows for syntax highlighting, autocorrection, area visualizations, copybooks, and so on. There is even an editor for the assembler language.

Visual Studio Code

In 2015, Microsoft launched Visual Studio Code (VS Code). The goal was to create a lightweight open source IDE that would allow code across various platforms like Windows, macOS, and Linux. This was a big move for the company since its flagship IDE, Visual Studio, worked only on Windows.

The strategy for VS Code was spot on. The IDE has become hugely popular. According to a 2019 survey from Stack Overflow (*https://oreil.ly/z5mUn*), it was ranked number one based on feedback from over 87,000 respondents.

VS Code has support for a variety of languages, including Python, C/C++, C#, Java, Go, Dart, PHP, and Ruby. So what about mainframe languages like COBOL? You can use COBOL by installing an extension. This is a simple matter of clicking a button for the installation. VS Code also has other extensions for mainframe applications, such as Zowe (which allows for connecting to a mainframe).

Even though the editor is lightweight, it still has lots of power. It includes a rich set of interactive debugging tools—for inspecting variables, viewing call stacks, stepping through code, executing code via the console, and so on.

Here are some other features:

- There is native support for Git for source control.
- You can program in COBOL 6.3, PL/I 5.3, TSO/E REXX, and High Level Assembler for z/OS 2.4
- You can embed coding for systems like IMS 15.1.0, CICS 5.6, and SQL Db2 for z/OS 12.1.

This section demonstrates how to use VS Code and Zowe—the open source project is on GitHub (*https://oreil.ly/8vTbn*)—for mainframe development. However, this is not to imply that these tools are the standard or that you will be using them for an employer. VS Code and Zowe are still in the early stages, and their adoption will probably take time. But these tools allow fairly easy access to a mainframe environment.

Moreover, the open software systems are periodically undergoing change. Thus, the process described in this section may be different after this book is published. You can check out the Open Mainframe Project (*https://oreil.ly/x3s37*) for updates.

The first step, though, is to install the following:

Node.js (https://oreil.ly/4fPlq)
> This is an open source environment. If you already have Node.js installed, make sure it is version 8 or higher. You can check this by using node -v at your computer's terminal. On a Windows machine, you also want to make sure that the *$PATH* has */usr/local/bin*.

Java SDK (https://oreil.ly/xabTc)
> This allows you to use Java on your computer system. You want to use version 8 or higher for the SDK. You also need to set up an Oracle account for the download, which is free.

Next, install VS Code (*https://oreil.ly/JtZQH*). Once this is complete, install Zowe Explorer. To do this, click the extensions icon on the left of VS Code and then search for the extensions, which you can see in Figure 3-15. Then click the Install button to install them.

Figure 3-15. Searching and installing the mainframe extensions for VS Code

Then how do you get access to a mainframe with VS Code? IBM provides a free connection for 180 days (*https://oreil.ly/j52c9*). You will be emailed a login ID, password, and IP address.

This resource is the result of the Open Mainframe Project, a nonprofit managed by the Linux Foundation. The organization is made up of a consortium of companies like Broadcom, Rocket Software, BMC, IBM, and USE. The main goal is to provide open source software for mainframe development.

Now let's look at how to use VS Code with Zowe Explorer. On the screen, you have a new icon on the left side, which is Z for Zowe Explorer. If you click it, you will see three sections: DATA SETS, UNIX SYSTEM SERVICES (USS), and JOBS.

Make a connection to the mainframe by clicking the DATA SETS section. Then click + to create your profile, and select Click + Create a New Connection to z/OS from the pull-down. Name the connection whatever you want and press Enter. After that, click the z/OSMF option from the pull-down menu.

Next, enter the URL that you received from the Open Mainframe Project and enter your username and password. Then click "Click False - Accept connections with self-signed certificates." You will see a set of four other selections; choose the defaults.

This login process is somewhat convoluted. But the Zowe platform is undergoing development, and there are plans to launch a single sign-on system for it.

Your mainframe profile will show up in the DATA SETS section. Click > to expand this section, and select the search icon. Then type in your user ID. This will show the datasets that are available to you on the mainframe system, as shown in Figure 3-16. Note that each of the files will start with your ID.

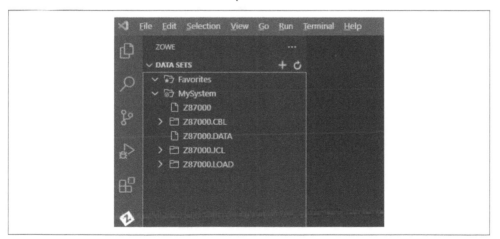

Figure 3-16. A list of the files you have access to on the mainframe

In DATA SETS, click the folder indicating .CBL. This contains the source code for various COBOL programs. Select HELLO, which has the basic code for "Hello World," as shown in Figure 3-17.

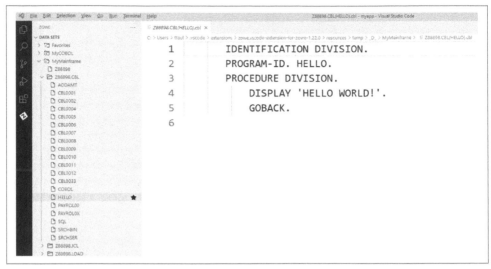

Figure 3-17. Source code for the HELLO COBOL program

You'll notice that the name of the program is the same as that specified in PROGRAM-ID. This is critical. If you do not have this same name, the program will not work.

How do you run the program? As you have seen, you need JCL. However, a typical mistake is for someone to run a job on the source file. This will result in an error.

Instead, go to the JOBS section on the left side of the screen; a list of the JCL files will appear. The names of each correspond with those from the .CBL directory.

In the JOB area, choose HELLO and then right-click it. Select Submit Job. A message will pop up that shows the name of it.

Where do you find the output? Go to the JOBS area on the left side of the screen and then select +. Choose your mainframe profile again, which will be in a pull-down. You'll then see a file for HELLO as well as the JCL code, which is in the edit screen in the middle (Figure 3-18).

In the HELLO job, you'll see CC 0000 at the end of the title. This means no errors occurred in the compilation. The *CC* stands for *condition code*, and the number is for the particular result. Anything other than 0000 indicates that the program has an issue or error. The JCL system will display this in a file called *SYSPRINT(101)*.

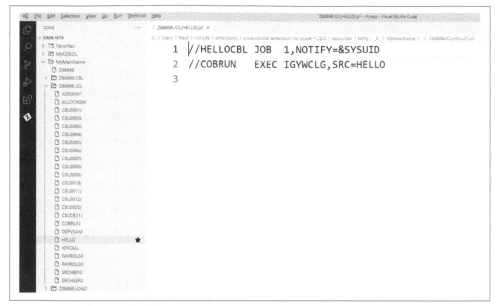

Figure 3-18. The JCL for the program

To see output of the program, select the *SYSOUT(104)* file, which will show "Hello World!" (Figure 3-19).

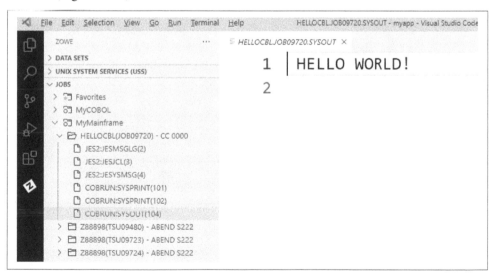

Figure 3-19. The output of the COBOL program

Zowe has a CLI as well. Therefore, you can develop your code at the terminal on your computer (Zowe has support for Windows, Linux, and Mac platforms). Using the CLI is similar to using something like Amazon Web Services (AWS), Microsoft Azure, or Google Cloud.

Standardizing on Visual Studio

Several of the top mainframe development software companies have been transitioning away from their proprietary IDEs and have ported their technologies to the Microsoft platform. One example is Micro Focus. Its system, Visual COBOL for Visual Studio, has sophisticated editing, debugging, continuous background compilation, code analysis, and code search. A rich set of tools allows for using REST and JSON calls for web services. But this is not just for COBOL. You can mix code from Visual Basic, C#, and other .NET languages.

Micro Focus has also built on Visual Studio Code. This is for its Visual COBOL IDE. And the company continues to support an Eclipse version. A nice feature is the ability to create HTML5 interfaces and to use Java and the JVM.

Next, Broadcom has been standardizing on the Visual Studio Code platform. The company has made its extensions freely available on the marketplace—although, once one of them shows that it has enterprise value, it is added to its Code4z pack for streamlined installation. Broadcom offers enterprise-grade support through the CA Brightside system.

"VS Code's 'any language, any platform' design is ideal for mainframe development and contrasts against IDEs built for specific languages like Eclipse and IntelliJ," said David McNierney, who is product marketing leader at Broadcom's Mainframe Division. "VS Code has set the standard for usability and extensibility and has experienced an explosion in popularity as a result, already reaching 14 million users."

Broadcom has become one of the biggest supporters of the open source movement for mainframe development. To this end, it has contributed to a range of free Zowe CLI extensions.

"Our team has been rethinking the entire mainframe developer experience from the ground up and designing it to be virtually identical to the experience of non-mainframe developers," said McNierney.

Broadcom has set up a Developer Cockpit simulator (*https://oreil.ly/7KKdt*) that illustrates how VS Code can be connected to COBOL as well as Db2 databases.

Simple IDEs

In some cases, you just need to run some code and not go through the typical process of a mainframe, such as with JCL. Then what to do? Some IDEs will launch a program with just a click.

One example is OpenCobolIDE, which is free. You can download the software (*https://oreil.ly/Mdb9s*) for Linux, Windows, and macOS.

OpenCobolIDE has some of the features you would find in a modern IDE, like syntax highlighting and code completion. The interface also uses the column structure for a COBOL program (you'll learn more about this in the next chapter) and has auto-indention. Then there are special features for the language, such as to compute PIC offsets. Oh, and it has a dark screen mode, which will make the environment more like what you would see for a mainframe.

Figure 3-20 shows a Hello World program in OpenCobolIDE. Note that for this book, I wrote all the COBOL code using OpenCobolIDE.

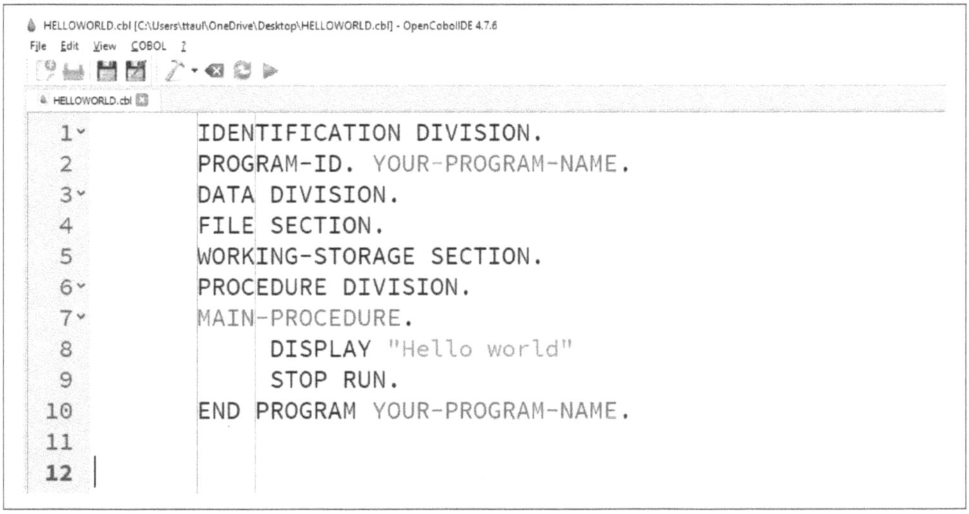

Figure 3-20. The interface for OpenCobolIDE

Web-Based Editors

A variety of web-based COBOL IDEs are also available.. They are usually good for basic coding. But they would not be a good choice if you are working with files. For this, a better alternative would be something like OpenCobolIDE.

Despite this, a web-based editor can be useful in learning the basics of COBOL. A good one to consider is Coding Ground (*https://oreil.ly/PyiKo*). It is free.

You can sign up for an account so as to save your files. There is also a Fork feature, which means you can use the GitHub repository.

But the system has some quirks. For example, if you have a program that accepts input from a user, this has to be done before the program is executed. This is handled in the STDIN section (this is an abbreviation for *standard input stream*). Figure 3-21 shows what this section looks like.

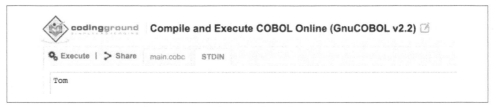

Figure 3-21. Inputting information in the web-based editor

In this case, the user input the name Tom. To see the output, click the main.cobc tab and click Execute. The output displays on the panel on the right, as shown in Figure 3-22.

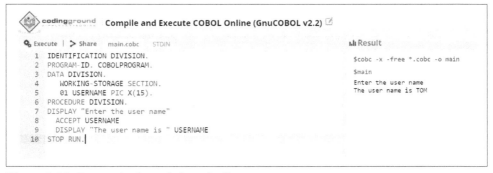

Figure 3-22. Output in the web-based editor

Development Process

It's typical for a mainframe developer to focus on maintenance of existing programs. Why? One reason is that many companies are long-term users of mainframe systems and have already developed their core applications. These organizations usually do not like to make major changes. After all, mainframe systems usually impact mission-critical functions.

Despite this, much remains to be done with the development process. A set of specifications for the code can be quite detailed. From here, the developer will begin programming on either ISPF or an IDE. The platform may also be a test LPAR.

Some projects can be extensive and involve dozens of coders. Because of this, developers use source control systems like CA Librarian, IBM Software Configuration Library and Manager, Endevor, and Micro Focus ChangeMan ZMF. When working with a PDS, an old copy of your code will be overwritten if you change the name and save it. But a version-control program will deal with this.

Once the coding is finished, it is necessary to build the source code into a program that the operating system can execute. The program, which is stored in a library on the mainframe, is often referred to as a *load module*.

But before a product is put into production, unit testing and debugging must occur. This can certainly take considerable time. Usually, this process involves using unit testing tools and creating test data.

Conclusion

In this chapter, we started with a look at how to access a mainframe. The focus was on important tools like TSO and ISPF. While they may seem archaic, they are easy to use and can get tasks done quickly.

Then we reviewed the unique file structure for a mainframe, which is based on datasets. These can be divided into different types like sequential, partition, and VSAM. There are also ways to help organize the datasets, such as with catalogs.

Next, we got an introduction to JCL. This is necessary to run many mainframe programs in COBOL.

As we've seen in this chapter, modern IDEs are available for development. We got a demo of VS Code, which has extensions for an editor and access system for a mainframe.

However, for those getting started, this may not be something to focus on. This is why you might want to start with a simple IDE like OpenCobolIDE. With this, you type in the code and click a Run button.

And finally, we got an overview of the development process. For mainframes, this process usually focuses on creating maintenance programs. There is also usually a heavy emphasis on unit testing.

In the next chapter, we will focus on the COBOL language.

CHAPTER 4

The COBOL Language

COBOL is the standard language for mainframe application development. It has the types of features that are important for business use cases, such as handling large-scale batch and transaction processing jobs.

The COBOL language has over 350 commands—and many of these you will not need to know about. This is why we'll cover a limited number in this book. But this should not imply that you will be at a disadvantage. We will focus on the core commands you need to know for real-world applications.

COBOL's Background, in Brief

COBOL is one of the oldest computer languages. Yet it has remained robust over the years and remains pivotal for business computing.

The roots of the language go back to the late 1950s, when a variety of computer languages emerged. Many of these languages were complex. This meant development was time-consuming and expensive.

A standard language was needed for data processing. To make this happen, the US Department of Defense joined with a group of computer companies—including IBM, Burroughs Corporation, Honeywell, and RCA—as well as academics and customers to form the Conference on Data Systems Languages (CODASYL) committee. Such committees have been essential for the evolution of the language.

CODASYL looked at the FLOW-MATIC language as a model for COBOL. Legendary computer pioneer Grace Hopper created FLOW-MATIC, the first language to use English-like commands for data processing and to be used for early mainframe systems, like UNIVAC I.

One of the key considerations for CODASYL was to enable COBOL to operate on different computers. It was also focused on the needs for businesses—say, for helping with accounting and customer reporting. This focus has remained the same today. In fact, you can't use COBOL to create websites or mobile apps. It's purely about business applications.

 The CODASYL committee came up with several ideas for the COBOL language. Some included Information System Language (INFOSYL), Business System (BUSY), and Common Computer Systems Language (COCOSYL). But ultimately, the CODASYL committee decided on COBOL, although it is not clear why.

COBOL Versions

The first version of COBOL, referred to as COBOL 60, came out in 1959. It certainly had its flaws, and some people predicted that the language would not last long. But the computer industry took steps to solve the problems and improve the language, especially with the development of compilers. Then new features, like tables, were added.

However, as the language grew in popularity, more incompatibilities emerged. This is why the America Standards Institute—now called the American National Standards Institute (ANSI)—took on the role of creating a standard for COBOL. This was done in 1968 and was called COBOL X3.23.

This is not to imply that the CODASYL committee was no longer a factor. The organization would continue to innovate the language.

But by the 1980s, COBOL would again have problems with compatibility. To deal with this, a new version was released, called COBOL 85.

By the 1990s, more changes were needed, and work began on a new version that would adopt more modern approaches, such as object-oriented programming. The new version of the language was called COBOL 2002.

OK then, so what is the latest version? It is COBOL V6.3, which was shipped in September 2019.

Regardless, many companies still use older versions, like COBOL 85. This is why it is important to understand the history of the language. For the most part, adoption of new approaches tends to be slower with mainframe systems. A key reason is that companies usually do not want major changes made to their mission-critical systems.

Why Use COBOL?

COBOL is not a general-purpose language. Its main focus is on data processing. But COBOL's specialization and long history have meant that the language is pervasive. Here are some stats to consider (*https://oreil.ly/L8Lcz*):

- Every day 200 times more COBOL transactions are performed versus Google searches.

- More than 220 billion lines of code are running today, or about 80% of the world's total.

- About 1.5 billion new lines of COBOL are written each year.

According to Dr. Cameron Seay, the cochair of the Open Mainframe Project COBOL Working Group and an adjunct instructor at East Carolina University, "COBOL remains an essential language for the global economy. The list of organizations that use COBOL also includes most large federal and state agencies. As of today, COBOL is irreplaceable, and there is no indication that that is going to change."

What are some of the benefits of COBOL? Why has the language had so much lasting power? Here are some of the main reasons:

Scale
> COBOL is built to process large amounts of data. The language has a broad range of functions for creating data structures and accessing them.

Stability
> The COBOL language is backward compatible. As a result, companies do not have to periodically recode their systems.

Simplicity
> Again, the original vision for COBOL was to be easy to use. You did not have to be a mathematician to learn it. It's true that the language can be wordy. But this carries an advantage. In a sense, the language is self-documenting (although it is still a good idea to provide your own documentation).

Auditability
> Even if you do not understand COBOL, you can still read its commands and get a general idea of its workflows. A key benefit is that a nontechnical auditor can review the code.

Structure

COBOL has a set of predefined ways to create programs, such as with divisions, sections, and paragraphs (you'll learn more about these in this chapter). This makes it easy for someone who did not write the code to understand it.

Speed

COBOL is a compiled language, which means that a program will be reduced to the 1s and 0s that a computer can understand. This generally speeds up performance, compared to an interpreted language (which involves an intermediate translator that converts the code during runtime).

Flexibility

The standard COBOL language is full-featured and has been well tested in intensive enterprise environments. But a myriad of extensions are available, such as for databases and transaction systems. This has made COBOL much more versatile.

Math

COBOL has a variety of features that make it easier to use currency manipulation and formatting. Other languages usually require coding for this.

COBOL Program Structure: Columns

A COBOL program has a clear-cut organization, with code arranged in 80 columns. This number harkens back to the days of punch cards. Figure 4-1 shows a visual of the layout.

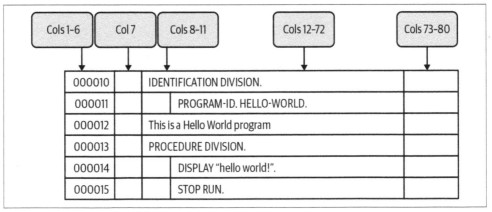

Figure 4-1. The layout of 80 columns for COBOL code

Here's a look at the columns:

1–6

This is for the line numbers. When punch cards were used, this was helpful since sometimes they would fall on the floor and get scattered. But in modern times, columns 1–6 are no longer used.

7

This can be used for several purposes. If you put an asterisk (*) in the column, you can write out a comment to document the code. Figure 4-1 shows a comment on sequence line 000012. You can also use the hyphen (-) as a continuation line for a long line of characters known as a *literal*. This is mostly for readability. This is an example:

```
'123ad53535d3506968223dcs9494029dd3393'
-  '8301sd0309139c3030eq303'
```

The literals can be either strings or numerics.

8–11

This is known as the *A margin*, or *Area A*. This is where we put the main headers for the code, which include the division, section, paragraph, and level numbers (01 and 77), which you will learn more about later. In Figure 4-1, the IDENTIFICATION DIVISION and PROCEDURE DIVISION are in Area A.

12–72

This is called the *B margin*, or *Area B*. This is where much of the code will be included.

73–80

This is no longer used in COBOL development.

COBOL Program Structure: Divisions

COBOL programs are further organized into four divisions, which need to be in the following order (each ends with a period):

- IDENTIFICATION DIVISION.
- ENVIRONMENT DIVISION.
- DATA DIVISION.
- PROCEDURE DIVISION.

Each of these can contain other levels of code. They include sections, paragraphs, and sentences. And all of these end in a period if they are in any of the divisions except for the PROCEDURE DIVISION. Otherwise, only the paragraph has a period. Granted, all this may seem kind of convoluted and inflexible. But again, in a business environment, it is important to have a solid structure. Besides, COBOL's approach is fairly intuitive once you get used to it. So in the next few sections, we'll go into more detail on the structure.

IDENTIFICATION DIVISION

The IDENTIFICATION DIVISION is the easiest division to work with. You need only two lines:

```
IDENTIFICATION DIVISION.
PROGRAM-ID. CUSTRP.
```

The PROGRAM-ID is required because the name is used for the compilation of the program. The name can be up to 30 characters and must be unique. But a mainframe shop usually has its own requirements (a typical length is up to eight characters).

Some coders may expand on the IDENTIFICATION DIVISION, such as with the following:

```
IDENTIFICATION DIVISION.
PROGRAM-ID. CUSTRP.
AUTHOR.  JANE SMITH.
DATE-WRITTEN.  01/01/2021
****************************************************************
*  This program will generate a customer report   *
****************************************************************
```

Details such as AUTHOR and DATE-WRITTEN are not common. But a comment box is often used.

COBOL is not case sensitive. You can write a command like DIVISION as Division or division or even divIsion. It does not matter. However, for the most part, the COBOL convention is to capitalize the commands.

ENVIRONMENT DIVISION

The ENVIRONMENT DIVISION is used for accessing files—say, for batch processing—which is common in COBOL. But this is usually not used if a program is for online tractions (this would be for commands like ACCEPT to get user input).

The ENVIRONMENT DIVISION is composed of two sections. One is the CONFIGURATION SECTION, which provides information about the computer and certain settings (such as for currency):

```
ENVIRONMENT DIVISION.
CONFIGURATION SECTION.
   SOURCE-COMPUTER. IBM ENTERPRISE Z/OS.
   OBJECT-COMPUTER. VAX-6400.
   SPECIAL-NAMES.
   CURRENCY IS DOLLARS.
```

Next is the INPUT-OUTPUT SECTION. This is where a program makes connections to files:

```
ENVIRONMENT DIVISION.
INPUT-OUTPUT SECTION.
FILE-CONTROL.
 SELECT CUSTOMER-FILE ASSIGN TO CUSTOMERMAST
       ORGANIZATION IS SEQUENTIAL.
```

CUSTOMER-FILE is the internal name, which is how we refer to it within the COBOL code. This name is then associated with CUSTOMERMAST, which is how the mainframe filesystem identifies the file. To make this connection, you create a Data Definition (DD) statement in Job Control Language (JCL) that will reference this file. What's more, the internal name and the filename can be the same.

Why do all this? The main reason is that if the name of the file changes on the hard drive, only the DD name needs changing in the JCL. This can avoid a lot of reworking of the source code.

Finally, the SELECT command can have various parameters. In our example, ORGANIZATION shows how the records in the file are processed (one record at a time).

DATA DIVISION

When developing in COBOL, you will usually spend considerable time creating the data structures. This is done in the DATA DIVISION, which has three main sections: WORKING-STORAGE SECTION, FILE-SECTION, and LINKAGE-SECTION.

We will cover the first two next. The LINKAGE-SECTION—which allows for the passing of data to outside programs that are called—is covered later in this book.

WORKING-STORAGE SECTION

In the WORKING-STORAGE SECTION, you create the variables, which hold the data. But in COBOL, these variables are usually referred to as *fields*.

Fields are also only global, which means they are accessible from anywhere in the program. This is in contrast with modern languages, which have both local and global variables. A local variable is available for only a particular function or block of code.

It's true that having only global variables is not ideal and can cause problems. So when developing a COBOL program, it's important to map how variables may change.

Now let's take a look at an example of a data structure:

```
WORKING-STORAGE SECTION.
      01 INVOICE-NUMBER        PIC 99          PACKED-DECIMAL          VALUE 0.
```

This is called an *elementary item* because it has only one field. The definition also has five parts: the level number, field name, PIC clause, USAGE clause, and VALUE clause. These are described next, followed by a discussion of data groups and special level numbers.

Level number. This is from 01 to 49 and refers to the hierarchy of the data. Each field has its own level number.

The typical approach is to use increments of 5 for level numbers. This is to make it easier to add new level numbers if there is a change to the data structure.

Field name. This can be up to 30 characters long. This is to allow for descriptive names.

What's more, you can have a field without a name, such as this:

```
  01            FILLER        PIC X (100).
```

This is a string of 100 characters. Why have something like this? It can be useful in creating reports.

PIC clause. Short for *picture*, this specifies the number of digits or characters a field can have. In the preceding example, PIC 99 can have two digits. But you can express it as PIC 9(2) as well. This PIC is known as a numeric and can hold only numbers. However, if you use S in front—say, as PIC S99—this will allow for + and –.

What about decimals? You use V for this. It's known as an implied decimal. An example is PIC 99V99, which provides for up to two decimal points.

A variation on numeric fields is numeric edited fields. This variation is used to format a number, such as for currencies, dates, and so on. Here's a look at some:

```
++99/99/99++
```

```
++$999.99++
```

The PIC clause can contain two other data types. One is *alphanumeric*, a string that can hold any character. It's expressed as PIC X. Yes, this will have one character. Or if you have PIC XXX or PIC X(3), it will hold three characters.

You can then use an edited field for an alphanumeric. Here's an example for a phone number:

```
++XXXBXXXBXXXX++
```

The B represents a blank.

The second is the *alphabetic* data type. It allows only uppercase and lowercase characters of A through Z. An example is PIC A(10). However, for the most part, COBOL programmers do not use alphabetic data types; instead, they code with the alphanumeric. But you still may see some alphabetics when updating older code.

No doubt, we need to learn quite a lot to understand PIC clauses completely. So it is probably a good idea to provide more examples to get a sense of the differences and how to use them; see Figure 4-2.

Data	Data Type	Code
Tom	Alphanumeric	PIC X(3)
100 Main Street, Los Angeles, CA	Alphanumeric	PIC X(30)
310-555-5757	Alphanumeric	PIC X(12)
1520	Numeric	PIC 9(4)
100.50	Numeric	PIC 9(3)v9(2)

Figure 4-2. Examples of how to use PIC clauses

In the second row, the name Tom has all letters. This is why we use an alphanumeric. We also set the length at 3. But when it comes to names, it is often a good idea to allow for more space for longer ones.

The third row has an address. Even though it includes numbers, it also has characters. This is why we use an alphanumeric.

As for the next row, the hyphens are characters. Thus, we again use an alphanumeric, and the size is 12 to accommodate the size of a phone number.

The last two rows have numbers, but different types. The first is an integer, which is why we use PIC 9(4). The second one, though, has a decimal, so we use V for the implied decimal.

USAGE clause. This specifies the kind of data to be stored. If you omit this, the default is DISPLAY (this is also known as ZONED-DECIMAL DATA). As the name implies, this is for when you want to print the data.

The PACKED-DECIMAL, on the other hand, is for when you want the data used for math purposes. Granted, DISPLAY can do this as well, but the computer will need to do a translation, which will take more time and resources.

Older IBM systems have a different naming convention. A COMP-3 is the same as PACKED-DECIMAL. There is also COMP-4, which is for BINARY. This is used for indexing data and is usually not good for math, because there could be rounding differences. Let's face it, when it comes to business transactions, every penny matters. This is why —when it comes to math for COBOL—it's usually best to stick with PACKED-DECIMAL.

VALUE clause. This is optional. But if you decide to use it, the VALUE clause will set the initial value. In the preceding example, we did this by setting INVOICE-NUMBER to 0.

You can use the VALUE clause for an alphanumeric as well. Here's an example:

```
01 FIRST-NAME   PIC X(20)      VALUE 'Jane'.
```

Notice we do not use PACKED-DECIMAL. This is because this is only for numerics.

The data group. Data in business is often put into groups. For example, you may have a customer record, which will have the name, address, phone number, credit card, and so on. COBOL has the ability to group data by using level numbers:

```
DATA DIVISION.
WORKING-STORAGE SECTION.
01 CUSTOMER-RECORD.
   05  CUSTOMER-NUMBER   PIC 9(5).
   05  CUSTOMER-NAME     PIC X(20).
   05  CUSTOMER-ADDRESS  PIC X(50).
```

Notice that CUSTOMER-RECORD does not have a PIC. That's because it is a group description, not a variable. But you can still use it to do interesting things. You can set everything to blank characters:

```
MOVE SPACES to CUSTOMER-RECORD.
```

Or you can have your own character:

```
MOVE "*" TO CUSTOMER-RECORD
```

Then how do we change the value of the fields in the group? We can do the following:

```
MOVE 111 TO CUSTOMER-NUMBER
```

Or this:

```
MOVE "125 MAPLE AVENUE, LOS ANGELES, CA" TO CUSTOMER-ADDRESS
```

You can also use MOVE to create a customer record by using one line:

```
MOVE "12345Jane Smith          100 Main Street" TO CUSTOMER-RECORD.
```

You can get more granular when using groups. Here we provide more detail for CUSTOMER-NAME:

```
01 CUSTOMER-RECORD.
   05  CUSTOMER-NUMBER PIC 9(5).
   05  CUSTOMER-NAME.
               10 FIRST-NAME PIC X(10).
               10 LAST-NAME PIC X(10).
   05  CUSTOMER-ADDRESS PIC X(50).
```

Special level numbers. COBOL has various special level numbers. Two of them, 66 and 77, are rarely used. The one that still has relevance is 88. Level 88 is actually fairly unique for computer languages, as it allows you to streamline the use of conditions in your code.

To understand this, let's consider an example. Suppose we have a customer base that has different levels of subscriptions: Free, Premium, and Enterprise. We can set this up using an 88 level number as follows:

```
01  CUSTOMER-CODE       PIC X.
    88  FREE-VERSION         VALUE 'F'.
    88  PREMIUM-VERSION      VALUE 'P'.
    88  ENTERPRISE-VERSION   VALUE 'E'.
```

In the PROCEDURE DIVISION, we can then designate the CUSTOMER-CODE by using the TRUE condition and evaluate it, as shown here:

```
SET PREMIUM-VERSION TO TRUE
IF (CUSTOMER-CODE = 'P')
DISPLAY 'The customer code is Premium'
END-IF
```

By setting PREMIUM-VERSION to TRUE, we have selected P for CUSTOMER-CODE.

Note that you can use TRUE only when it comes to designating which 88 element you want. Setting it to FALSE would be ambiguous and result in an error.

You can take other approaches with the level 88 condition. Let's suppose you have data that has multiple values, such as for the grouping of regions for customers:

```
01            CUSTOMER-REGION        PIC X(2).
    88    NORTH-AMERICA    VALUES 'US' 'CA'.
    88    EUROPE           VALUES 'UK' 'DE' 'FR'.
    88    ASIA             VALUES 'CN' 'JP'.

MOVE 'UK' TO CUSTOMER-REGION

IF EUROPE
```

```
        DISPLAY 'The customer is located in Europe'
    END-IF
```

In this case, the condition has been set to UK, and the IF condition is executed since it is in Europe.

Next, you can use ranges for the 88 conditions. Here's a look at how it is done:

```
01  COMMISSIONS PIC 9(2) VALUE ZERO.
    88 UNDER-QUOTA VALUE 0 THRU 10.
    88 QUOTA VALUE 11 THRU 30.
    88 OVER-QUOTA VALUE 31 THRU 99.

MOVE 5 TO COMMISSIONS

IF UNDER-QUOTA
        DISPLAY 'The sales are under the quota.'
    END-IF
```

This is a range for a salesperson's quota. As only five units were sold, this person was under quota.

All in all, an 88 condition can make the logic of a program easier to follow. It also usually requires less coding when changes are made.

FILE-SECTION

The FILE-SECTION may sound repetitive. As we've seen earlier in this chapter, the ENVIRONMENT DIVISION has robust capabilities for files.

So what is the FILE-SECTION all about? You can set a filename to be used for running the program via JCL and also make the necessary associations with the data structures. The storage for this will be outside the COBOL program and will not be created until you use the OPEN command in the PROCEDURE DIVISION (you will learn more about this in Chapter 5).

Here's what a FILE-SECTION looks like:

```
FILE SECTION.
FD   CUSTMAST.
01   CUSTOMER-MASTER
  05  CUST-NUM    PIC 9(2)
  05  CUST-FNAME  PIC X(20).
  05 CUST-LNAME   PIC X(2).
FD   SALES-REPORT.
01   PRINT-REPORT PIC X(132).
```

FD is an abbreviation for *file definition*, which is the internal name used in the ENVIRONMENT DIVISION. This is to make sure the correct file is being accessed.

Constants. Constants are a standard feature in most modern languages. They allow for having fixed values (say, for the tax rate or pi).

But COBOL does not have constants. You instead have to use a field, which you can change at any time. And yes, this is certainly a drawback to the language.

However, COBOL does have figurative constants. These fixed values are built into the language: ZERO, SPACE, NULL, ALL, HIGH-VALUES, LOW-VALUES, and so on.

REDEFINES command. In some cases, you might want to define a field in different ways. This is where the REDEFINES command comes in:

```
01  PHONE-NUMBER      PIC 9(10).
01  PHONE-NUMBER-X    REDEFINES PHONE-NUMBER.
   05  AREA-CODE          PIC 9(3).
   05  TELEPHONE-PREFIX   PIC 9(3).
   05  LINE-NUMBER        PIC 9(4).
```

In this example, we have two fields for the phone number—one that is an elementary item and the other a data group, which provides more granularity.

We can use the REDEFINES for an alphanumeric as well:

```
01  PRODUCT-PRICE        PIC    $ZZ9.99.
01  PRODUCT-PRICE-X      PIC    REDEFINES PRODUCT-PRICE PIC X(6).
```

We first set PRODUCT-PRICE as an edited numeric. Then we turn it into an alphanumeric so as not have the formatting information, which means it will be easier to perform calculations.

When you use REDEFINES, both fields refer to the same bytes in memory. A change in one will be reflected in the other. Also, both must have the same level numbers, and you can use the VALUE clause for only the first one.

PROCEDURE DIVISION

In the PROCEDURE DIVISION, you perform the logic of the program. True, you could just write a long list of commands, but this will make it difficult for readability. This is why it is recommended to write COBOL in a structured manner. You break up the code into chunks, which are known as subroutines, functions, or procedures. It's a good idea for each of these to perform a certain task.

Let's look at an example:

```
IDENTIFICATION DIVISION.
PROGRAM-ID.  PRINTNAME.
ENVIRONMENT DIVISION.
DATA DIVISION.
WORKING-STORAGE SECTION.
01 USER-NAME  PIC X(15).
```

```
PROCEDURE DIVISION.
100-GET-USER-INPUT.
DISPLAY "Enter the user name"
        ACCEPT USER-NAME.
200-PRINT-USER-NAME.
DISPLAY "The user name is " USER-NAME.
300-PRINT-PROGRAM-END.
GOBACK.
```

This is an easy program, but it provides a way to create a modular structure. A COBOL convention is to divide a program into paragraphs. These have a header —such as `100-GET-USER-INPUT`—that should describe the task. The order of the paragraphs does not matter. But the typical approach in COBOL is to have them in the same sequence as the workflow, and each paragraph has a number. For example, if you are using a modern IDE, it will show an outline view of the code that is based on the order of the paragraphs. As you can see in our code sample, the commands in a paragraph do not have a period except at the end. This is known as *period-less coding*. This is to help avoid problems like unintended terminations of a paragraph.

 The `DISPLAY` command is often used for debugging. It's an easy way to print out fields to see if everything is being processed correctly. An example is `DISPLAY "X field is = " X`.

It is a COBOL convention to have a paragraph that has no code (`300-PRINT-PROGRAM-END`), to mark the end of the program. The `GOBACK` command terminates the program. So for the rest of the chapter, we will look at the main types of commands and workflows for the `PROCEDURE DIVISION`.

MOVE command

A modern language has variable assignments. For example, in Python you can do something like this:

```
price = 100
```

But COBOL has no variable assignments. Then what's the alternative? How can you set the values for a field?

You can use the `MOVE` command. Instead of moving the value from right to left, the reverse is true, as seen here, which would be in the `PROCEDURE DIVISION`:

```
MOVE "SMITH" TO LAST-NAME.
```

Or you can move the value of one field to another field:

```
MOVE LAST-NAME TO LAST-NAME-2.
```

The value of LAST-NAME will be copied to LAST-NAME-2. That is, LAST-NAME will still have SMITH.

When using the MOVE statement, you can work with multiple fields. For example, this will copy 0 to COUNTER, X, and Y:

```
MOVE   0   TO   COUNTER X Y
```

But you need to be careful when using MOVE with fields that have different types. Let's first take a look when working with an alphanumeric. We will create a field as follows in the DATA DIVISION:

```
01     LAST-NAME          PIC X(7)    VALUE "COOK".
```

Then we will do the following MOVE in the PROCEDURE DIVISION:

```
MOVE   "Davis"   To   LAST-NAME.
```

LAST-NAME will now have the value of Davis. Yet there is something else to keep in mind. Since Davis has fewer characters than the length of PIC X, the compiler will add spaces to the field (the * represents a space). You can see the output in Figure 4-3.

LAST-NAME						
D	A	V	I	S	*	*

Figure 4-3. If the field has fewer characters than allocated, COBOL adds spaces at the end

This can cause formatting issues, such as with the spacing on a report. But there are ways to correct for this, which you will learn about later in this book.

What if we have a field that has more characters then PIC X? This can cause even a bigger problem. Suppose we have this:

```
MOVE   "Dumbledore"   TO          LAST-NAME.
```

This results in Figure 4-4.

LAST-NAME						
D	U	M	B	L	E	D

Figure 4-4. If a string is too big for a PIC, the extra characters are truncated

As you can see, the name is cut off—which is known as *truncation*. This is why it is critical to have well-thought-out data structures.

The same goes for numerics. Suppose we have this in the DATA DIVISION:

```
01     PRICE          PIC   9(3)V99.
```

This means we have a field with five digits, which includes two decimal places. Now let's look at some `MOVE` statements:

```
MOVE    57.2            TO      PRICE
```

Figure 4-5 shows what the compiler allocates.

PRICE				
0	5	7	2	0

Figure 4-5. If a number is smaller than allocated by the `PIC 9` declaration, 0s will be added from left to right

If a number does not fit the length provided in the `PIC 9`, 0s will be added.

We can also have truncation, such as with this:

```
MOVE    8803.257            TO      PRICE
```

Figure 4-6 shows the result.

PRICE				
8	0	3	2	5

Figure 4-6. If a number is larger than the `PIC 9` allocation, the extra numbers will be truncated

The number is first aligned along the decimal point. Since 8803 is too big for the three spaces provided, the 8 is not included. The 7 in the decimal is excluded as well, and no rounding occurs.

Truncation is common when handling math. Thus, it is important to think of the potential outliers with the calculations when putting together the data structures. The `ON SIZE ERROR` command can help avoid the problems, and we'll look at this later in this chapter.

You can use `MOVE` where there are different `PIC`s so long as the sending field is an unsigned integer. These are the options:

- Alphanumeric to numeric
- Alphanumeric to numeric edited
- Numeric to alphanumeric

Here's an example of the first one. Enter this for the `DATA DIVISION`:

```
01          ALPHA-NUM           PIC X(2)            VALUE '50'.
01          NUM-VALUE           PIC 9(2)            VALUE 0.
```

Then use this in the PROCEDURE DIVISION:

```
MOVE ALPHA-NUM TO NUM-VALUE
```

The result will be that NUM-VALUE will have the value of 50.

Math commands

COBOL has two main approaches with math. It has a set of commands like ADD, SUBTRACT, MULTIPLY, and DIVIDE. Then COMPUTE allows for more sophisticated calculations.

ADD, SUBTRACT, MULTIPLY, and DIVIDE.

To see how the ADD, SUBTRACT, MULTIPLY, and DIVIDE commands work, let's first have the following declarations for the DATA DIVISION:

```
01      WITHDRAWAL      PIC 9(3) VALUE 0.
01      DEPOSIT         PIC 9(3) VALUE 0.
01      BALANCE         PIC 9(3) VALUE 0.
```

Then with ADD, we can do this in the PROCEDURE DIVISION:

```
MOVE 50 TO DEPOSIT
ADD DEPOSIT TO BALANCE
```

BALANCE will now be 50. Or we can do this with our DEPOSIT:

```
ADD 25 TO DEPOSIT GIVING BALANCE
```

With this, we add 25 to DEPOSIT and replace the value of BALANCE with 75.

Now let's take a look at SUBTRACT:

```
MOVE 60 TO WITHDRAWAL
SUBTRACT WITHDRAWAL FROM BALANCE
```

Since BALANCE had been set to 75, the new result would be 15.

Suppose we have three checks for the amounts of 100, 125, and 395. We can use the ADD command this way:

```
ADD 100 125 359 TO DEPOSIT GIVING BALANCE
```

The numbers add up to 584, and BALANCE will be replaced with this number. You can also use GIVING with SUBTRACT. Say we have three withdrawals for 50, 125, and 200 as well as a deposit of 450:

```
MOVE 500 TO DEPOSIT
SUBTRACT 50 125 200 FROM DEPOSIT GIVING BALANCE
```

The total deposits of 375 will be subtracted from 500, giving the result of 125. BALANCE will then be equal to this amount.

Next, let's take a look at the MULTIPLY command. We'll first create two fields in the DATA DIVISION:

```
01  INCOME       PIC 9(5)V99          VALUE 500.
01  NET-INCOME   PIC 9(5)V99          VALUE 0.
```

Assume that the tax rate is 10%. Then in the PROCEDURE DIVISION, we can have this:

```
MULTIPLY .10 BY INCOME
```

The result, which is 50, will be put into INCOME. Or we can use the GIVING command:

```
MULTIPLY .10 BY INCOME GIVING NET-INCOME
```

NET-INCOME will be replaced by 50.

Division has some differences, though. You can use two main approaches: DIVIDE INTO or DIVIDE BY.

Here's a look at the first, which has this for the DATA DIVISION:

```
01  SALES           PIC 9(5)            VALUE 10000.
01  UNITS           PIC 9(4)            VALUE 500.
01  SALES-PER-UNIT  PIC 9(5)            VALUE 0.
```

Then this is for the PROCEDURE DIVISION:

```
DIVIDE UNITS INTO SALES
```

With this, SALES will now be equal to 20. Or we can use the GIVING command, which will give us the same result but put it in SALES-PER-UNIT:

```
DIVIDE UNITS INTO SALES GIVING SALES-PER-UNIT
```

Suppose we change the values to the following in the PROCEDURE DIVISION:

```
MOVE 2000 TO SALES
MOVE 192 TO UNITS
```

We can then do the calculation this way:

```
DIVIDE SALES BY UNITS GIVING SALES-PER-UNIT ROUNDED
```

The result of this formula is 10.41666. But since the PIC 9 for SALES-PER-UNIT does not have a decimal, we have instead rounded the number—which gets us 10.

We can also get the remainder of a division. In the DATA DIVISION, let's have the following:

```
01  QUOTIENT    PIC 999        VALUE 0.
01  REM         PIC 999        VALUE 0.
```

Then we have this for the PROCEDURE DIVISION:

```
DIVIDE 100 BY 9 GIVING QUOTIENT REMAINDER REM.
```

In this, the QUOTIENT is 11 and the REMAINDER is 1.

COMPUTE. The use of math commands like ADD and SUBTRACT are unique for modern languages. But the COMPUTE command looks more like what you would see in something like Python or C#.

To see how the COMPUTE command works, let's first set up some fields in the DATA DIVISION:

```
01  DISCOUNTED-PRICE    PIC 9(5)    VALUE 0.
01  RETAIL-PRICE        PIC 9(5)    VALUE 0.
01  DISCOUNT            PIC 9(2)V99  VALUE 0.
```

Now let's do the calculation in the PROCEDURE DIVISION:

```
MOVE 0.25 TO DISCOUNT
MOVE 100 TO RETAIL-PRICE
COMPUTE DISCOUNTED-PRICE = RETAIL-PRICE * (1 - DISCOUNT)
```

We set DISCOUNT for this product to 25% and RETAIL-PRICE to 100. Then with the COMPUTE formula, we subtract 1 from DISCOUNT and multiply the result by RETAIL-PRICE. This gives us the DISCOUNTED-PRICE.

The mathematical operators for COBOL are similar to what you would see in other modern languages. You can find them in Table 4-1.

Table 4-1. The mathematical operators for COBOL

Mathematical operator	Function
+	Addition
-	Subtraction
/	Division
*	Multiplication
**	Exponent

The use of an exponent is expressed like this: COMPUTE A = 2**2. This is 2 to the second power, or 2 squared.

If you use the parentheses, the calculations within them will be executed first. After this, the order of operations starts with the exponents, then multiplication, division, subtraction, and addition. For the most part, programmers rely on parentheses.

A common issue with COMPUTE arises when the fields are not large enough to hold the numbers. As we've seen, this will cause truncation, and a way to deal with this is to use the ON SIZE ERROR clause. Let's look at an example, with the following in the DATA DIVISION:

```
01          SALES       PIC 9(4)          VALUE 0.
01          PRICE       PIC 9(1)          VALUE 5.
01          UNITS       PIC 9(4)          VALUE 5000.
```

Then here's the PROCEDURE DIVISION:

```
COMPUTE SALES = PRICE * UNITS ON SIZE ERROR
DISPLAY "The amount is too large for the SALES field."
```

The result of this formula is 25000. However, the SALES field can hold up to only four digits. Because of this, the ON SIZE ERROR clause is triggered. This can be an effective way to avoid the crashing of a program.

Math Functions

COBOL comes with a rich set of 42 mathematical functions, such as for finance, statistics, and trigonometry. You use the FUNCTION command to execute them, and there may be zero, one, two, or more arguments. Table 4-2 shows a list of common functions.

Table 4-2. Common mathematical functions in COBOL

Function	What it does
SUM	Sum of the arguments
SQRT	Square root of an argument
MEAN	Average of the argument
SIN	Sine of an argument
VARIANCE	Variance of an argument
STANDARD-DEVIATION	Standard deviation of a set of arguments
RANGE	Maximum argument minus the minimum argument
MAX	Value of the largest argument
MIN	Smallest argument
LOG	Natural logarithm

Let's take a look at some examples, which are placed in the PROCEDURE DIVISION:

```
DISPLAY FUNCTION SUM (50 59 109 32 99)
DISPLAY FUNCTION SQRT (100)
```

The results are 349 and 10, respectively. You can also use the functions with the COMPUTE command.

Conditionals

The IF/THEN/ELSE construct is at the heart of all languages. It's a key part of the control of the flow of a computer program and is based on Boolean logic, which looks at whether something is either true or false.

But COBOL has its own approach—and it can be tricky. So a good way to explain conditionals is to consider some examples:

```
DATA DIVISION.
WORKING-STORAGE SECTION.
01  TEMPERATURE PIC 9(3) VALUE 0.
PROCEDURE DIVISION.
DISPLAY "Enter the temperature : "
ACCEPT TEMPERATURE
IF TEMPERATURE <= 32 THEN
  DISPLAY "It is freezing"
ELSE
  DISPLAY "It is not freezing"
END-IF

GOBACK.
```

In COBOL, this is called a *general relation condition*. Despite its long name, this condition is straightforward. The ACCEPT command takes in user input, which in this case is the current temperature. If the temperature is 32 degrees or less, it is freezing.

COBOL has English-like versions of conditionals. For example, instead of using >, you can use GREATER THAN. Table 4-3 provides a list of conditionals.

Table 4-3. Conditionals in COBOL

Shorthand	English-like version
>	GREATER THAN
<	LESS THAN
=	EQUAL TO
>=	GREATER THAN OR EQUAL TO
☐	LESS THAN OR EQUAL TO
Not>	NOT GREATER THAN
Not<	NOT LESS THAN
Not=	NOT EQUAL TO

You can write more-complex conditionals by using AND and OR, which are called *compounded conditional expressions*. To see how this works, here's an example program for the approval of invoices:

```
DATA DIVISION.
WORKING-STORAGE SECTION.
```

```
01  INVOICE-AMOUNT PIC 9(4) VALUE 0.
PROCEDURE DIVISION.
DISPLAY "Enter the invoice amount : "
ACCEPT INVOICE-AMOUNT
IF INVOICE-AMOUNT > 0 AND INVOICE-AMOUNT < 5000 THEN
  DISPLAY "No approval is needed"
ELSE
  DISPLAY "There must be approval"
END-IF
GOBACK.
```

In this code, if the invoice is between $0 and $5,000, no approval is needed.

Again, this is simple and similar to what you would see in other languages. So then what about the different types of conditionals? One is the *class condition*. However, the word *class* does not refer to object-oriented programming.

In fact, earlier in this chapter, we saw how the class condition was used. It involved the 88 level numbers to set forth a range of values or text—and a condition would be triggered if a value falls within it.

Something else we can use for a condition is the EVALUATE command. It is similar to a switch/case construct that is found in other languages. When there are a multitude of possibilities, EVALUATE can be much easier to use than a simple IF/THEN/ELSE structure.

Let's suppose we are creating an app to track customer information and want a way to designate the type of business entity:

```
DATA DIVISION.
WORKING-STORAGE SECTION.
01 BUSINESS-NUMBER          PIC 99 VALUE ZERO.
01 BUSINESS-TYPE            PIC X(20).
PROCEDURE DIVISION.
DISPLAY "Enter the business number"
ACCEPT BUSINESS-NUMBER
EVALUATE BUSINESS-NUMBER
WHEN 1 MOVE "Sole Proprietor" TO BUSINESS-TYPE
WHEN 2 MOVE "Single-Member LLC" TO BUSINESS-TYPE
WHEN 3 MOVE "S Corporation" TO BUSINESS-TYPE
WHEN 4 MOVE "C-Corporation" TO BUSINESS-TYPE
WHEN 5 MOVE "Partnership" TO BUSINESS-TYPE
WHEN 6 MOVE "Trust/Estate" TO BUSINESS-TYPE
WHEN OTHER MOVE 0 TO BUSINESS-TYPE
END-EVALUATE
DISPLAY "The business type is " BUSINESS-TYPE
GOBACK.
```

In this program, the user will input from 1 to 6, and each will correspond to a type of business. The EVALUATE statement will then go to the number selected and change the value of BUSINESS-TYPE. The last condition is WHEN OTHER, which is the default value if the user selects something that is not within the range of values.

After a user selects something, the program will go to the END-EVALUATE statement, and the DISPLAY statement will be executed.

The EVALUATE structure can involve complicated logic. Because of this, it can be a good idea to first create a decision table. For example, let's say we are creating a commission structure like the one shown in Figure 4-7.

1-10 Units	11-30 Units	More Than 30 Units
10%	15%	20%

Figure 4-7. A decision table can be helpful when creating conditionals

This will make it easier to put together the conditional logic:

```
DATA DIVISION.
WORKING-STORAGE SECTION.
01 COMMISSIONS PIC 99 VALUE ZERO.
 88 UNDER-QUOTA VALUE 0 THRU 10.
 88 QUOTA VALUE 11 THRU 30.
 88 OVER-QUOTA VALUE 31 THRU 99.
PROCEDURE DIVISION.
DISPLAY "Enter the number of units sold"
ACCEPT COMMISSIONS
EVALUATE TRUE
WHEN UNDER-QUOTA
DISPLAY "Commission is 10% and this is under the quota."
 WHEN QUOTA
DISPLAY "Commission is 15% and this meets the quota."
 WHEN OVER-QUOTA
DISPLAY "Commission is 20% and this is over the quota."
 WHEN OTHER
DISPLAY "This is the default"
END-EVALUATE.
GOBACK.
```

In the DATA DIVISION, we use a group field that has 88 level numbers. Three ranges of commissions can be earned by a salesperson. In the PROCEDURE DIVISION, we set up a structure that has EVALUATE TRUE and then specifies the three conditions for UNDER-QUOTA, QUOTA, and OVER-QUOTA. If the user inputs 15, the message for QUOTA will be executed, and so on.

With the EVALUATE statement, it's possible to include compounded conditions as well:

```
DATA DIVISION.
WORKING-STORAGE SECTION.
01 BUSINESS-NUMBER   PIC 99 VALUE ZERO.
01 VIP-CUSTOMER      PIC X.
```

```
01 UNITS            PIC 9(3).
01 DISCOUNT         PIC 9(2)V9(2).
PROCEDURE DIVISION.
DISPLAY "Enter the number of units sold"
ACCEPT UNITS
DISPLAY "A VIP customer (Y/N)?"
ACCEPT VIP-CUSTOMER
EVALUATE UNITS ALSO VIP-CUSTOMER
 WHEN 1 THRU 20 ALSO "Y"
  MOVE .20 TO DISCOUNT
 WHEN 21 THRU 50 ALSO "Y"
  MOVE .25 TO DISCOUNT
 WHEN GREATER THAN 50 ALSO "Y"
  MOVE .30 TO DISCOUNT
END-EVALUATE
DISPLAY "The discount is " DISCOUNT
```

By using the keyword ALSO, we can string together different conditions. In our example, this includes one for the units sold and whether a customer is part of a VIP program.

COBOL allows you to have nested IF/THEN/ELSE blocks. While there are no limits on how many you can have, it's usually best to not go beyond three. Otherwise, the code could be extremely hard to track.

Here is an example of a nested IF/THEN/ELSE block:

```
DATA DIVISION.
WORKING-STORAGE SECTION.
01 USERNAME          PIC X(20).
01 PASSWORD          PIC X(20).
PROCEDURE DIVISION.
DISPLAY "Enter your user name"
ACCEPT USERNAME
DISPLAY "Enter your password"
ACCEPT PASSWORD
IF USERNAME = "Tom68"
 IF PASSWORD = "12345"
  DISPLAY "Login successful!"
 ELSE
        DISPLAY "Incorrect password."
 END-IF
ELSE
 DISPLAY "Incorrect user name."
END-IF.
GOBACK.
```

The first condition is for USERNAME. If it is correct, the next condition will be triggered. If the condition is not correct, the ELSE at the bottom will be executed. The next condition checks for the password.

When putting together nested IF/THEN/ELSE conditions, it is important that you line up the code properly and terminate each block with an END-IF. If not, the code will likely give wrong results. For example, if we left out the END-IF in the nested condition, the first ELSE would be executed if the USERNAME is not correct.

Loops

The *loop* is a part of every language. As its name indicates, this structure allows you to iterate through something, such as a dataset. In COBOL, the command for a loop is PERFORM, which has several variations.

The first one we will look at is PERFORM TIMES, which is similar to a for loop in other languages. This means it is executed a fixed number of times, which can be expressed as a field or a literal:

```
DATA DIVISION.
WORKING-STORAGE SECTION.
01 COUNTER PIC 9(1) VALUE 0.
PROCEDURE DIVISION.
PERFORM 5 TIMES
ADD 1 TO COUNTER
 DISPLAY "Loop number " COUNTER
END-PERFORM
GOBACK.
```

This will loop five times, and the COUNTER field will be incremented by one for each pass. The value will be printed.

Another way to use PERFORM is to loop a paragraph or subroutine:

```
DATA DIVISION.
WORKING-STORAGE SECTION.
01 COUNTER PIC 9(1) VALUE 0.
PROCEDURE DIVISION.
100-PARAGRAPH-LOOP.
 PERFORM 200-PRINT-COUNTER 5 TIMES.
 GOBACK.
200-PRINT-COUNTER.
 ADD 1 TO COUNTER
 DISPLAY "Loop number " COUNTER.
```

This program does the same thing as the first one, but it has a modular structure. We have two paragraphs. The first one will use PERFORM to loop through the second paragraph.

 COBOL does have a GOTO command that can call a paragraph. But using it is a bad idea, primarily because the command does not return you to where you called it. Because of this, the code can get chaotic—becoming more like "spaghetti code."

Next, we can set a condition for a loop. For example, we can use PERFORM UNTIL just as we use the `while` loop in other languages:

```
DATA DIVISION.
WORKING-STORAGE SECTION.
01 COUNTER PIC 9(1) VALUE 0.
PROCEDURE DIVISION.
PERFORM UNTIL COUNTER >= 5
ADD 1 TO COUNTER
        DISPLAY "Loop number " COUNTER
END-PERFORM
GOBACK.
```

This program will count from 1 to 5 and then stop. But you have to be careful with PERFORM UNTIL. If COUNTER is already over 5, looping will not happen.

But there is an alternative: PERFORM WITH TEST AFTER. This guarantees that there will be at least one loop. This structure is similar to the `do-while` loop in other languages. So with our program, we can do the following:

```
PERFORM WITH TEST AFTER UNTIL COUNTER >= 5
ADD 1 TO COUNTER
 DISPLAY "Loop number " COUNTER
END-PERFORM
```

With this, even if COUNTER is over 5, the code will be executed and COUNTER will be incremented by 1.

Next, PERFORM VARYING is essentially a variation of the traditional `for` loop. But there are some important differences. COBOL allows the use of three counting fields for the loop, the testing of the condition can be before the loop is performed or after, and the condition for the termination of the loop does not have to be COUNTER.

That's a lot. So to get an understanding of this structure, let's look at an example:

```
DATA DIVISION.
WORKING-STORAGE SECTION.
01 YEAR PIC 9(2) VALUE 0.
01 BALANCE PIC 9(4) VALUE 1000.
PROCEDURE DIVISION.
PERFORM VARYING YEAR FROM 1 BY 1
 UNTIL YEAR > 10
 COMPUTE BALANCE = BALANCE * 1.05
 DISPLAY "Balance is $" BALANCE
END-PERFORM.
GOBACK.
```

This program shows how the value of a $1,000 investment will grow over a 10-year period. We set BALANCE to 1000 and YEAR to 0, which will be incremented by 1 until year 10. For each iteration, a COMPUTE statement will be used to add to BALANCE by an interest rate of 5%.

What if we set a PIC 9 instead for YEAR? The loop would never get to 10. In fact, this would create an infinite loop and crash the program. Again, this is why it is extremely important to think through the use of the data in your programs.

Next, with our program, we can do the looping in reverse, with the following changes to the PROCEDURE DIVISION:

```
PERFORM VARYING YEAR FROM 10 BY -1
  UNTIL YEAR <= 0
  COMPUTE BALANCE = BALANCE * 0.95
  DISPLAY "Balance is $" BALANCE
END-PERFORM
```

The value of BALANCE will be reduced for 10 years until the value gets to $595.

And you can use the PERFORM VARYING structure to call a subroutine. Let's take a variation of the prior code sample:

```
PROCEDURE DIVISION.
100-BALANCE-LOOP.
PERFORM 200-DEPOSIT-CALC VARYING YEAR FROM 1 BY 1
  UNTIL YEAR > 10
  GOBACK.
200-DEPOSIT-CALC.
  COMPUTE BALANCE = BALANCE * 1.05
  DISPLAY "Balance is $" BALANCE.
```

Finally, you can use the THRU command with PERFORM to invoke a set of paragraphs:

```
PROCEDURE DIVISION.
100-FIRST-PARAGRAPH.
  PERFORM 200-SECOND-PARAGRAPH THRU 400-FOURTH-PARAGRAPH.
200-SECOND-PARAGRAPH.
  DISPLAY 'Paragraph 2'.
300-THIRD-PARAGRAPH.
  DISPLAY 'Paragraph 3'.
400-FOURTH-PARAGRAPH.
  DISPLAY 'Paragraph 4'.
  GOBACK.
```

As you can see, PERFORM THRU will execute the 200-SECOND-PARAGRAPH, 300-SECOND-PARAGRAPH, and 400-FOURTH-PARAGRAPH—in this order.

IBM has great resources on COBOL. Check out their Programming Guide (*https://oreil.ly/J9Snd*) as well as the Language Reference (*https://oreil.ly/Ej3Ua*).

Conclusion

We have certainly covered a lot in this chapter. You've learned the main types of structures you need to know to build or edit a COBOL program. To be a successful programmer, you do not need to know the whole command set. Some commands are duplicative, and others are rarely used.

While COBOL has many similarities to modern languages, there are still some major differences. And yes, the language can be wordy, but this is by design.

In this chapter, we were able to cover the types of math you will need to know, whether through the use of commands like ADD and SUBTRACT or the use of COMPUTE, which provides more versatility. Then we covered how to employ conditionals in COBOL programs with the IF/THEN/ELSE structure. We also looked at more sophisticated decision statements like EVALUATE.

Finally, we saw how to use loops, such as with the PERFORM command. We also showed how to use this to enforce structured programming approaches.

In the next chapter, we'll look at setting up tables and creating reports.

CHAPTER 5

File Handling

A typical modern computer language may not use files often. A programming book or manual may not even cover this topic. This makes sense, as many applications do not necessarily handle data processing.

But the situation is different with the mainframe. File handling is an essential part of the process. This goes back to the early days, when businesses wanted to find ways to replace the tedious approaches of using ledgers and 3 x 5-inch cards. The mainframe and COBOL were seen as a way to automate the back office.

To this end, various types of files are available. They include sequential, indexed, and relative. In this chapter, we'll take a look at the first two and show how the COBOL language can use them. Relative files are not used much and therefore are not covered in this book.

Records and Files

A *file* for a mainframe is usually composed of a set of *records*, which is a group of related fields. An example of a record is a customer master file, which has fields for first name, last name, address, credit limit, and so on.

A mainframe initially reads the records into the real or central storage; this is similar to random access memory (RAM) for PCs. Even though the capacity is high, a file can easily exceed the storage limit. This is why a mainframe reads one or a small group of records at a time, so as not to overwhelm the real memory.

Typically, a record is fixed-length, each having the same number of characters. But in some cases, a dataset has variable-length records. These require additional COBOL coding to indicate the length of each record. We'll show how this works in this chapter.

Sequential File

A *sequential file*, also known as a *flat file*, is composed of characters. It's what you would have for Windows Notepad or TextEdit on the Mac. It is fairly simple.

To help speed up the process, a sequential file is usually blocked. This means that the records can be loaded in as groups. It is also possible to have records of fixed and variable length.

The sequential file originated when mainframes used tape drives. Essentially, the only way to store information on this type of media was to do it one record at a time. As a result, this approach would stay in effect.

True, tape drives are mostly a thing of the past. Yet sequential files still remain a major part of the mainframe world. The fact is that they are highly efficient at handling large amounts of data.

However, it is common to use sorting on sequential files, which makes it easier to process the information. This can be done by using any of the fields in the record.

There are some conventions to note. For example, the first field should be the sequence number or ID for the record. It should also be a unique numerical value, such as an employee number. Then the other fields can be in the order of importance. For a customer master file, this would be the name and address.

 When creating files, ensuring the integrity of the data is critical. Errors can cause major problems with audits, and this could lead to sanctions for businesses. This is why the code should have validation rules for user input. For example, COBOL could be used to prohibit a negative number for the units produced. This can be done using IF/THEN/ELSE conditionals.

Sequential files are used for batch processing, especially for *master files*. These are often large collections of information for the major departments in a company—say, for sales, accounts payable, accounts receivable, inventory, and payroll.

Transaction files include the activity for a certain master file. For instance, if you have a payroll master file, the transactions would be updates to salaries or hours worked. This information usually comes from user input via a terminal or computer.

After a period of time, the master file will be updated with the transaction file; this action, called a *sequential update*, creates a new master file. To do this, a COBOL program matches the unique key for the transaction and master file. If a match is found, an update occurs. If not, the program assumes an error has happened and these transactions will be put in another file, such as an error log or a print file. This provides for an audit trail.

The old master file will essentially be a backup. But it is common to have other backups as well.

To help understand this process, let's take a look at a scenario. Suppose your company has an inventory master file with five items in it. Each has a unique item number, called a stock-keeping unit (SKU), from 101 to 105. You can see the data in Table 5-1.

Table 5-1. Data for the master file

SKU	Item name	Quantity
101	iPhone 12 Pro Max	150
102	iPhone 12 Pro	30
103	iPhone 12	50
104	iPhone 12 mini	70
105	iPhone SE	90

During the past week, a variety of inventory purchases were made and then stored in the transaction file, as shown in Table 5-2.

Table 5-2. New data for the transaction file

SKU	Date	Quantity
102	02052021	30
103	02072021	30
107	02072021	90

We will match the SKUs for both of these files and create a new inventory master file with updated quantities for the iPhones (Table 5-3).

Table 5-3. The new master file

SKU	Item name	Quantity
101	iPhone 12 Pro Max	150
102	iPhone 12 Pro	60
103	iPhone 12	80
104	iPhone 12 mini	70
105	iPhone SE	90

As you can see, SKU 102 now has a quantity of 60 (this is the old quantity of 30 plus the new transactions for 30), and the quantity for SKU 103 is 80 (the old quantity of 50 plus the transactions for 30 units). But what about the purchase for SKU 107? Well, this does not match the items in the master file. This will instead be put in an error log (Table 5-4).

Table 5-4. The error file

SKU	Date	Quantity
107	020721	150

Now let's take a look at some COBOL code to work with sequential files:

```
IDENTIFICATION DIVISION.
PROGRAM-ID. CUST-FILE.
ENVIRONMENT DIVISION.
INPUT-OUTPUT SECTION.
FILE-CONTROL.
   SELECT CUSTOMER-FILE ASSIGN TO "Customers.dat"
      ORGANIZATION IS LINE SEQUENTIAL.
DATA DIVISION.
FILE SECTION.
FD  CUSTOMER-FILE.
01  CUSTOMER-RECORD.
    05   FIRST-NAME  PIC X(20).
    05   LAST-NAME   PIC X(20).
WORKING-STORAGE SECTION.
01 WS-CUSTOMER-RECORD.
    05 WS-FIRST-NAME  PIC X(20).
    05 WS-LAST-NAME   PIC X(20).
01 WS-EOF          PIC X.

PROCEDURE DIVISION.
OPEN INPUT CUSTOMER-FILE.
PERFORM UNTIL WS-EOF = 'Y'
   READ CUSTOMER-FILE INTO WS-CUSTOMER-RECORD
      AT END MOVE 'Y' TO WS-EOF
         NOT AT END DISPLAY WS-CUSTOMER-RECORD
   END-READ
END-PERFORM.
CLOSE CUSTOMER-FILE.
GOBACK.
```

If you are entering this program in a PC COBOL IDE, such as OpenCobolIDE, you need to create a data file called *Customers.dat*. Remember, this is a fixed-length record. Thus, if FIRST-NAME has George and LAST-NAME has Washington, then Washington will have to start at column 21 (the * is for a blank space). You can see this in Table 5-5.

Table 5-5. The new master file

FIRST-NAME	LAST-NAME
George*************	Washington*********

As for our program, we first make the connection to the external file through the ENVIRONMENT DIVISION. This is done by creating an INPUT-OUTPUT SECTION in

FILE-CONTROL. Then, we use the SELECT and ASSIGN TO commands to refer to the filename. In our example, we are referring to a file on the hard drive of a PC. This means you need to make sure you have the correct path (it's a common error to not do so). Or, if you have access to a mainframe, you need to find out how to access the file from your employer.

Next, you will use ORGANIZATION IS LINE SEQUENTIAL to specify that the file is sequential.

The name of the file—CUSTOMER-FILE—is also called a *ddname*. This is a type of JCL statement that is referred to as a *DD*, or data definition. It allows for connecting the dataset on the mainframe with the code in the program.

In the DATA DIVISION, we have two sections:

FILE SECTION
> The FD is CUSTOMER-FILE, which we specified in the ENVIRONMENT DIVISION for the ddname. Then we set forth the name for a record—CUSTOMER-RECORD—which has two fields: FIRST-NAME and LAST-NAME. Basically, we are making it so our COBOL program can successfully read what is in the file. It's also important to note that the number of bytes defined in the FD must match the number of bytes in a record file. This is a common area for errors.

WORKING-STORAGE SECTION
> This is similar to the FILE SECTION except we are creating fields to be used within our COBOL program. One of the records, WS-CUSTOMER-RECORD, has the fields for the first and last name.

But we have another field called WS-EOF. This is a flag that indicates whether the COBOL program has reached the end of the file.

> For each SELECT clause in the ENVIRONMENT DIVISION, there must be an FD statement in the DATA DIVISION.

The next part of the program is the PROCEDURE DIVISION. To access CUSTOMER-FILE, we only have to use the OPEN INPUT command.

But to read the contents of the file, we need to create a loop, which is done by using the PERFORM command. For each iteration, the READ command will fetch one record at a time, and each will be placed in the WS-CUSTOMER-RECORD field. The program will then test to see if the access is at the end of the file, using AT END. If not, the record will be printed, including the first and last name. And if the file is at the end, Y will be assigned to WS-EOF, and this will end the PERFORM loop. Finally, we use CLOSE to end the access to the files and then terminate the program. It is important not to forget this statement. The reason is that all the records may not be read or written if CLOSE is not used.

Finally, with the FD statement, you can add some parameters. Here's a common one:

```
FD  CUSTOMER-FILE
BLOCK CONTAINS 0 RECORDS
```

This helps optimize the handling of the data in the buffer.

File Errors

What if you try to read a file but it does not exist on the hard drive? The program will crash.

COBOL has a built-in command, called a FILE STATUS code, to avoid this. For example, if you use OPEN READ and there is no file, the code returned will be 35.

To see how to use this with COBOL code, let's continue with our example from the prior section. We need to update three areas.

In the ENVIRONMENT DIVISION, we will have this:

```
ENVIRONMENT DIVISION.
INPUT-OUTPUT SECTION.
FILE-CONTROL.
   SELECT CUSTOMER-FILE ASSIGN TO
    " Customers.dat"
       FILE STATUS IS FILE-EXISTS
       ORGANIZATION IS LINE SEQUENTIAL.
```

We create a flag, which we'll call FILE-EXISTS (you can pick what you want), for the FILE STATUS code. Then we change the DATA DIVISION:

```
WORKING-STORAGE SECTION.
   01 WS-CUSTOMER-RECORD.
      05 WS-FIRST-NAME  PIC X(20).
      05 WS-LAST-NAME   PIC X(20).
      05 FILE-EXISTS  PIC X(2).
```

This creates a field for FILE-EXISTS that will have a number with two digits. Then the next step is the following in the PROCEDURE DIVISION:

```
OPEN INPUT CUSTOMER-FILE.
   IF FILE-EXISTS NOT = "00"
      DISPLAY "File does not exist"
      PERFORM 200-END-PROGRAM
END-IF.
PERFORM UNTIL WS-EOF = 'Y'
   READ CUSTOMER-FILE INTO WS-CUSTOMER-RECORD
```

```
            AT END MOVE 'Y' TO WS-EOF
            NOT AT END DISPLAY WS-CUSTOMER-RECORD
        END-READ
    END-PERFORM.
    CLOSE CUSTOMER-FILE.
    200-END-PROGRAM.
    GOBACK.
```

After the file is opened, we check for the value of the FILE-EXISTS field. If it is not 00—which would mean that the file exists—the program will be terminated. We use the PERFORM statement to go to the GOBACK command.

You can check for many other FILE STATUS codes. Table 5-6 provides a list.

Table 5-6. FILE STATUS codes

FILE STATUS code	Definition
00	The input/output access was successful.
04	The file was read successfully, but the record length is not the same as defined in the COBOL program.
09	The directory does not exist.
10	The END-OF-FILE flag was triggered for the READ statement. This is what AT END refers to.
12	An attempt was made to open a file that is already open.
22	There is a duplicate key (this is for indexed and relative files).
34	The writing of a record is beyond the boundaries of the file, or the file is full.
37	There has been an attempt to use OPEN for a file that does not support this command.
38	An attempt was made to open a file that has been locked.
42	There was an attempt to close a file that was already closed.
44	There was an attempt to REWRITE a record that is not the same size as the record being replaced.
46	A READ command was invalid because the END-OF-FILE flag was already triggered.
48	The program tried to WRITE to a file that is not open.
49	There was an attempt to DELETE or REWRITE a file that is not open.

WRITE to a File

The WRITE statement copies records to a file (the data comes from the structures set up in the FILE SECTION of the DATA DIVISION). To see how this is used, we will continue with the prior program. We will keep the FD for CUSTOMER-FILE in the DATA DIVISION but will not keep the data in WORKING-STORAGE:

```
    IDENTIFICATION DIVISION.
    PROGRAM-ID. CUST-FILE.
    ENVIRONMENT DIVISION.
    INPUT-OUTPUT SECTION.
```

```
FILE-CONTROL.
    SELECT CUSTOMER-FILE ASSIGN TO
      "C:\Users\ttaul\OneDrive\Desktop\Customers.dax"
        ORGANIZATION IS LINE SEQUENTIAL.
DATA DIVISION.
FILE SECTION.
FD  CUSTOMER-FILE.
01  CUSTOMER-RECORD.
    05    FIRST-NAME  PIC X(20).
    05    LAST-NAME   PIC X(20).
WORKING-STORAGE SECTION.
01 WS-CUSTOMER-RECORD.
    05 WS-FIRST-NAME  PIC X(20).
    05 WS-LAST-NAME   PIC X(20).
01 WS-EOF            PIC X.
PROCEDURE DIVISION.
OPEN OUTPUT CUSTOMER-FILE
PERFORM UNTIL CUSTOMER-RECORD = SPACES
   DISPLAY "Enter the first and last name for the customer"
   ACCEPT CUSTOMER-RECORD
   WRITE CUSTOMER-RECORD
END-PERFORM
   CLOSE CUSTOMER-FILE
   DISPLAY "Output from the Customer File:"
   OPEN INPUT CUSTOMER-FILE.
      PERFORM UNTIL WS-EOF = 'Y'
         READ CUSTOMER-FILE INTO WS-CUSTOMER-RECORD
            AT END MOVE 'Y' TO WS-EOF
            NOT AT END DISPLAY WS-CUSTOMER-RECORD
         END-READ
      END-PERFORM.
   CLOSE CUSTOMER-FILE.
   GOBACK.
```

The data structures will be the same as the program we used in the prior section. The main differences are in the PROCEDURE DIVISION. First of all, we create a PERFORM UNTIL loop to allow a user to enter one or more records. When the user presses the Enter or Return key, the loop will terminate (this is when CUSTOMER-RECORD is equal to SPACES or ""). For each of the loops, the new record will be written to the file.

The next step is to read the contents of the file. This is also accomplished with the same PERFORM UNTIL we used in the program in the prior section of this chapter.

JCL for File-Handling Programs

In the prior code in this chapter, we used the following to get access to the file on the hard drive:

```
FILE-CONTROL.
SELECT CUSTOMER-FILE ASSIGN TO " Customers.dat"
```

That is what you would do when working on a PC. However, accessing a file on the mainframe would look something like the following:

```
FILE-CONTROL.
SELECT CUSTOMER-FILE ASSIGN TO CUST-FILE.
SELECT TRANFILE ASSIGN TO TRANFILE.
```

CUSTOMER-FILE is the ddname, which you will need for our JCL script. This will make it so that we can compile and run the program (or the job). TRANFILE is another ddname. This is the file to write the new sales transactions.

Notice that in the SELECT statement, the first name (FD name) and the second one (DD name) can be the same.

Here's a look at the JCL:

```
//FILEJOB JOB 400000000,'MSV1 JOB CARD   ',MSGLEVEL=(1,1),
//      CLASS=A,MSGCLASS=Q,NOTIFY=&SYSUID,TIME=1440,REGION=0M
//COMPILE1 EXEC IGYWCL,PARM=(OFFSET,NOLIST,ADV),PGMLIB='INSTPS1.COBOL.LOADLIB',↵
GOPGM= CUST-FILE
//SYSIN     DD  *
//CUSTOMER DD  DISP=(NEW,CATLG,DELETE),
//              DSN=DIV2.CUST-FILE,
//              LRECL=40,
//              AVGREC=U,
//              RECFM=FB,
//              SPACE=(40,(10,10),RLSE)
//SYSOUT      SYSOUT=*
//CEEDUMP     SYSOUT=*
```

In this script, we first create the job card, which has the name FILEJOB. This will be based on the settings of the mainframe.

Then we create a name, COMPILE1 (this can be whatever you want), for the execution statement of CUST-FILE (this is the name from the PROGRAM-ID in the IDENTIFICATION DIVISION).

Next, we use SYSIN DD *, which allows the mainframe to use the ACCEPT command. Then we specify the record for the dataset and call it CUSTOMER. With the DD statement, we connect the file on the machine with the COBOL program.

Here are some of the other parameters:

DSN
> The dataset name on the mainframe

LRECL
> The length (in bytes) for the record

AVGREC=U
> Indicates that the unit is one record

RECFM=FB
> Indicates that the record format is fixed blocked

SPACE
> A request for space on the drive

SYSOUT=*
> Used for those files that write records to the disk drive—in our code, the =* to the spool class that the output will be written to

What about `DISP`? This is a parameter for disposition. It indicates how to use the file. Here are some of the values:

SHR
> Short for *share*, this is for when a file is not being updated.

OLD
> Locks the records in your file according to your own process. However, `OLD` is not used often.

NEW
> Specifies a file to be created.

CATLG
> Creates a catalog entry for the dataset.

DELETE
> Deletes the dataset when there is an abnormal disposition of a job step.

When working with the JCL, there must be one `DD` statement for each of the ddnames. Their order is not important in the script.

The use of the ddnames may seem convoluted, but it is actually helpful: if a systems programmer makes a change to the filename on the mainframe drive, there is no need to rework the COBOL code. A change will need to be made only to the JCL script.

Inventory Update Program

Earlier in this chapter, we took a look at updates with master and transaction files, which is a common use case with COBOL. However, the code can quickly get long. Because of this, we'll look at an example that is divided into parts:

```
IDENTIFICATION DIVISION.
PROGRAM-ID. INVENTORYRPT.
ENVIRONMENT DIVISION.
INPUT-OUTPUT SECTION.
FILE-CONTROL.
```

```
SELECT INVENTORY-FILE ASSIGN TO "INVENTORY-FILE.DAT"
 FILE STATUS IS FILE-EXISTS
 ORGANIZATION IS LINE SEQUENTIAL.
SELECT TRANS-FILE ASSIGN TO "INVENTORY-TRANS.DAT"
 FILE STATUS IS FILE-EXISTS2
 ORGANIZATION IS LINE SEQUENTIAL.
SELECT NEW-INVENTORY-FILE ASSIGN TO "NEW-INVENTORY-FILE.DAT"
 ORGANIZATION IS LINE SEQUENTIAL.
SELECT ERROR-FILE ASSIGN TO "ERRORREPORT.DAT"
 ORGANIZATION IS LINE SEQUENTIAL.
```

In the ENVIRONMENT DIVISION, four files will be processed: the master inventory file (*INVENTORY-FILE.DAT*), the transaction file (*INVENTORY-TRANS.DAT*), the new inventory master file (*NEW-INVENTORY-FILE.DAT*), and the log file for the errors (*ERRORREPORT.DAT*). For the first of these, we have flags (FILE-EXISTS and FILE-EXISTS2) for the FILE STATUS to check if the files exist on the drive:

```
DATA DIVISION.
FILE SECTION.
FD INVENTORY-FILE.
01 INVENTORY-RECORD.
88 END-OF-FILE VALUE HIGH-VALUES.
  05 SKU PIC X(3).
  05 ITEM-NAME PIC X(20).
  05 QUANTITY PIC 9(3).
FD TRANS-FILE.
01 TRANS-RECORD.
88 END-OF-FILE-TRANS VALUE HIGH-VALUES.
  05 TRANS-SKU PIC X(3).
  05 TRANS-DATE PIC X(8).
  05 TRANS-QUANTITY PIC 9(3).
FD NEW-INVENTORY-FILE.
01 NEW-INVENTORY-RECORD.
  05 NEW-SKU PIC X(3).
  05 NEW-ITEM-NAME PIC X(20).
  05 NEW-QUANTITY PIC 9(3).
FD ERROR-FILE.
01 PRINTLINE.
  05 FILLER PIC X(28).
WORKING-STORAGE SECTION.
01 WS-DETAILS.
  05 FILE-EXISTS PIC X(2).
  05 FILE-EXISTS2 PIC X(2).
```

For the DATA DIVISION, we set up the FDs for the FILE SECTION to connect the files that will be accessed, and each has a data structure. The master inventory file and the inventory transaction file have the same records but with different names (this is so COBOL can differentiate between them). The first item has a level number of 88, which sets forth a condition for the end of the file. This is done by using the

HIGH-VALUES figurative constant, which is a field that stores the highest value in a byte.

Then we have a PIC numeric for the SKU, an alphanumeric for the name of the inventory item, and a numeric for the quantity on hand. The new inventory master file has the same record, except without an END-OF-FILE condition.

Then we have FILLER for the error file. This is a string of 28 blank characters where we will place items that are not matched.

In the WORKING-STORAGE SECTION, we have the triggers for the FILE-STATUS conditions:

```
PROCEDURE DIVISION.
0100-INVENTORY-PROCESSING.
  OPEN INPUT INVENTORY-FILE
  IF FILE-EXISTS NOT = "00"
    DISPLAY "Error in opening the inventory master file "
    PERFORM 9000-END-PROGRAM
  END-IF.
OPEN INPUT TRANS-FILE
IF FILE-EXISTS2 NOT = "00"
  DISPLAY "Error in opening the inventory transaction file "
  PERFORM 9000-END-PROGRAM
END-IF.
OPEN OUTPUT NEW-INVENTORY-FILE.
OPEN OUTPUT ERROR-FILE.
PERFORM 0300-READ-INVENTORY-FILE
PERFORM 0400-READ-TRANSACTION-FILE
PERFORM 0200-MATCH-INVENTORY UNTIL
END-OF-FILE AND END-OF-FILE-TRANS.
PERFORM 9000-END-PROGRAM.
```

In the PROCEDURE DIVISION, we have a variety of modules to create the different files. The first is to open the master inventory and transactions files and then test to see if they exist. If they do not, an error message will be printed, and the program will be terminated.

The next step is to create the new master inventory and error files. Then two subroutines are called: one reads the master inventory file, and the other reads the transaction file.

After this, a loop is executed to call a subroutine that performs the matching of the files. This continues until the program has cycled through the end of both files. And finally, the program is terminated:

```
0200-MATCH-INVENTORY.
EVALUATE TRUE
  WHEN SKU = TRANS-SKU
    PERFORM 0500-UPDATE-FILE
  WHEN SKU < TRANS-SKU
```

```
        PERFORM 0600-NO-UPDATE
      WHEN OTHER
        PERFORM 0700-CREATE-ERROR-RECORD
    END-EVALUATE.
    0300-READ-INVENTORY-FILE.
      READ INVENTORY-FILE
        AT END SET END-OF-FILE TO TRUE
      END-READ.
    0400-READ-TRANSACTION-FILE.
      READ TRANS-FILE
        AT END SET END-OF-FILE-TRANS TO TRUE
    END-READ.
    0500-UPDATE-FILE.
      MOVE INVENTORY-RECORD TO NEW-INVENTORY-RECORD
      COMPUTE NEW-QUANTITY = NEW-QUANTITY + TRANS-QUANTITY
      WRITE NEW-INVENTORY-RECORD
      PERFORM 0300-READ-INVENTORY-FILE
      PERFORM 0400-READ-TRANSACTION-FILE.
    0600-NO-UPDATE.
      WRITE NEW-INVENTORY-RECORD FROM INVENTORY-RECORD
      PERFORM 0300-READ-INVENTORY-FILE.
    0700-CREATE-ERROR-RECORD.
      MOVE TRANS-SKU TO NEW-SKU
      WRITE PRINTLINE FROM TRANS-RECORD
      PERFORM 0400-READ-TRANSACTION-FILE.
```

Next is the module to match the inventory. This uses an EVALUATE condition to test for three conditions. The first is to see if the SKU in the master inventory file and the SKU in the transactions file are the same. If so, the fields in the record for the master file will be copied to the new master file. Then we use the COMPUTE command to add the inventory quantities from both of these and write the new record to the new master inventory file. After this, the next record is read for both the master inventory and transaction files.

The other condition for the EVALUATE statement triggers when the master inventory SKU is less than the transaction's SKU. This means that there is no corresponding transaction and so there will be no update. Rather, the same record from the master inventory file will be copied to the new inventory file. Then the next record in the master file will be read.

The WHEN OTHER is a catchall for any other result. In this case, it means that there is no match between the SKU from the master inventory file and the transactions file. As a result, the transaction record will be sent to the error file.

In the following, we CLOSE all the open files, and then the GOBACK command is executed:

```
    9000-END-PROGRAM.
      CLOSE INVENTORY-FILE.
      CLOSE TRANS-FILE.
```

```
          CLOSE ERROR-FILE.
          CLOSE NEW-INVENTORY-FILE.
      GOBACK.
```

File with Multiple Records

In this chapter, we have been working with reading and writing files containing only one record. But this is not the typical use case. Files will have many records. And this presents a problem: when processing a file, how do you know which file you are using? Well, to deal with this, you can have a field containing a unique code in front of each record. For example, in a file of employees, the record for the compensation information could be designated as C, and the address details could be A.

What's interesting is that this code has the same address in memory. What does this mean? Let's suppose that in the DATA DIVISION, you name the compensation code COMP-CODE and the address ADDRESS-CODE. If you set COMP-CODE to C, ADDRESS-CODE will also be C.

To see how all this works, let's take a look at this program:

```
      IDENTIFICATION DIVISION.
      PROGRAM-ID. SALESRPT.
      ENVIRONMENT DIVISION.
      INPUT-OUTPUT SECTION.
      FILE-CONTROL.
         SELECT SALES-FILE  ASSIGN TO "Sales.Dat"
         ORGANIZATION IS LINE SEQUENTIAL.
      DATA DIVISION.
      FILE SECTION.
      FD SALES-FILE.
      01 SALES-REP.
         88 END-OF-FILE    VALUE HIGH-VALUES.
            05 TYPE-CODE            PIC X.
         88 SALES-REP-CODE          VALUE "R".
         88 RECEIPT-CODE            VALUE "S".
            05 SALESPERSON-NAME     PIC X(20).
      01 SALES-RECIPT.
         05 TYPE-CODE               PIC X.
         05 RECEIPT                 PIC 9(3).
      WORKING-STORAGE SECTION.
      01  CURRENCY-FORMAT           PIC $$,$$$.
      01  SALES-TOTAL               PIC 9(5).

      PROCEDURE DIVISION.
      100-MAIN.
      OPEN INPUT SALES-FILE
      PERFORM 400-READ-FILE.
      PERFORM 200-SALES-REPORT
         UNTIL END-OF-FILE
         CLOSE SALES-FILE
```

```
            GOBACK.
            200-SALES-REPORT.
               DISPLAY SALESPERSON-NAME
               MOVE ZEROS TO SALES-TOTAL
               PERFORM 400-READ-FILE.
                  PERFORM 300-CALC-SALES
                     UNTIL SALES-REP-CODE OR END-OF-FILE
                     MOVE SALES-TOTAL TO CURRENCY-FORMAT
                     DISPLAY CURRENCY-FORMAT.
            300-CALC-SALES.
               COMPUTE  SALES-TOTAL = SALES-TOTAL + RECEIPT
               PERFORM 400-READ-FILE.
            400-READ-FILE.
            READ SALES-FILE
               AT END SET END-OF-FILE TO TRUE
            END-READ.
```

In the ENVIRONMENT DIVISION, we set up access to a sequential file called *Sales.dat*. It contains two records, which are defined in the FILE SECTION of the DATA DIVISION. Here's a look at each:

SALES-REP

> This starts by using the level number 88 to set the END-OF-FILE condition. Then we have three fields for the type to designate each of the records. The R value is for names of the sales reports, and the S is for each sales transaction. Next, we have a PIC X for the salesperson's name.

SALES-RECEIPT

> This is for the sales transaction data, which will be put in the RECEIPT field.

Table 5-7 shows what the file looks like.

Table 5-7. Sales transaction data

Transaction	Name
R	Nora Roberts
S	300
S	200
R	Mary Barra
S	300
S	200
R	Elon Musk

For example, the first record is for SALES-REP, and we have the record code and the name of the salesperson, Nora Roberts. After this, we have two records for SALES-RECEIPT showing the transactions—that is, one for sales of $300 and another for $200.

The DATA DIVISION has a WORKING-STORAGE SECTION. The CURRENCY-FORMAT is a numeric edit that allows the formatting of our totals in a currency. SALES-TOTAL will be used to sum up the sales for each of the sales reps.

Now let's take a look at the PROCEDURE DIVISION. We first open the *SALES.dat* file and read it. Then there is a loop of the subroutine, 200-SALES-REPORT, which will end after the file has been read.

In 200-SALES-REPORT, the name of the salesperson will be printed out and SALES-TOTAL will be set to 0. A call to read the file follows, and a loop is performed. This goes through the transactions until the record code is equal to R, which means we have reached the next salesperson. For each iteration, the sales transaction is added to SALES-TOTAL, which will be printed.

Variable-Length Records

So far, we've been looking at fixed-length records. But you may also work with variable-length records. To use these, you need to set up the records in the FILE-SECTION of the ENVIRONMENT DIVISION. Here's an example:

```
FD TRANS-FILE
    RECORD IS VARYING IN SIZE
    FROM 20 TO 90 CHARACTERS
    DEPENDING ON RECORD-SIZE.
```

This shows that the FD clause can have various parameters. In this case, the RECORD IS VARYING IN SIZE clause indicates that we have a variable-length record that ranges in size from 20 to 90 characters. As for DEPENDING ON RECORD-SIZE, RECORD-SIZE is a name that is defined by the coder. This is referenced in the WORKING-STORAGE SECTION:

```
WORKING-STORAGE SECTION.
01 RECORD-SIZE PIC 99 BINARY.
```

The RECORD-SIZE field must be an elementary unsigned integer, and the data type is BINARY. If you are reading records, there is no need to set the value. But this is not the case when using the WRITE command.

To see how this works, let's try the following program:

```
IDENTIFICATION DIVISION.
PROGRAM-ID.  NAME-LIST.
ENVIRONMENT DIVISION.
INPUT-OUTPUT SECTION.
FILE-CONTROL.
SELECT NAME-FILE
    ASSIGN TO
    "Names.dat"
```

```
      ORGANIZATION IS LINE SEQUENTIAL.
DATA DIVISION.
FILE SECTION.
FD NAME-FILE
RECORD IS VARYING IN SIZE
DEPENDING ON NAME-LENGTH.
01 NAME-RECORD          PIC X(40).
   88 END-OF-FILE       VALUE HIGH-VALUES.
WORKING-STORAGE SECTION.
   01 NAME-LENGTH       PIC 99.
PROCEDURE DIVISION.
OPEN INPUT NAME-FILE
READ NAME-FILE
   AT END SET END-OF-FILE TO TRUE
END-READ
PERFORM UNTIL END-OF-FILE
   DISPLAY NAME-RECORD(1:NAME-LENGTH)
   READ NAME-FILE
      AT END SET END-OF-FILE TO TRUE
   END-READ
END-PERFORM
CLOSE NAME-FILE
GOBACK.
```

In the FILE-CONTROL section, we load in a file called *Names.dat*. This is just a sequential file with a list of names of famous computer programmers. But of course, each has a different size, and this is why we use a variable-length record structure. You can see this in Table 5-8.

Table 5-8. A list of variable-length records

Names
Grace Hopper
Alan Turing
Ada Lovelace
Katherine Johnson
Margaret Hamilton
Guido Van Rassum
Bill Gates
Linus Torvalds

Then in the FILE SECTION, we have an FD for the name of the file (NAME-FILE) that has the clause for RECORD IS VARYING IN SIZE. We set the maximum length for NAME-LENGTH in the WORKING-STORAGE SECTION.

In the PROCEDURE DIVISION, we OPEN the NAME-FILE and read until the end of the file. Then we use a PERFORM UNTIL loop to print each item in the record. Each has NAME-RECORD(1:NAME-LENGTH), expressing that they all have different sizes.

Indexed Files

While sequential files are used primarily for batch processing, *indexed files* are for online transaction processing. This involves ongoing user input, such as from a terminal. The indexed file can handle this since the records can be accessed directly. Functions can be used to add items, delete items, search for data, and sort the records.

A good way to understand how all this works is by using the analogy of a book. Suppose we have a digital version of *Modern Mainframe Development* and want to go to the section on file handling. If the book is a sequential file, we would have to read every word until we get to the desired section.

But if we use an indexed file, we can go directly to the section (this is also known as *random access*). This would require going to the index at the back of the book and finding the corresponding page number.

However, indexed files have some downsides. For example, the processing can be slower when compared to sequential files. This is especially the case when deleting and adding records. Higher storage levels are usually also needed. But despite these disadvantages, indexed files are still very useful and widely used.

How does an indexed file work? It has at least one key field, which is called a *primary field*. This has a unique value, which can be a number or a set of letters (or a combination of the two). This means that COBOL will be able to go directly to the record in the file.

The index essentially means that COBOL has a built-in database. In fact, this is one of the reasons the language is so powerful for businesses. This is a truly unique feature of COBOL.

Keep in mind that an indexed file can have other keys (up to 255). This is because you may not know what to search for on the primary key.

The other keys, called *alternate keys*, enable better searches. For example, these keys may indicate the customer name or business name. The alternate keys also can have duplicate items.

Creating the keys requires planning. Changing configurations can be tough, say, after the files become large. Because of this, a database administrator may help with the structure.

To create keys in a COBOL program, you first start with the FILE-CONTROL section of the ENVIRONMENT DIVISION. You then add parameters to the SELECT statement:

```
ENVIRONMENT DIVISION.
INPUT-OUTPUT SECTION.
FILE-CONTROL
    SELECT INVOICE-FILE ASSIGN TO "Invoice.dat"
    ORGANIZATION IS INDEXED
    ACCESS IS SEQUENTIAL
    RECORD KEY IS INVOICE-KEY.
```

We specify that it is an indexed file by using ORGANIZATION IS INDEXED. We then indicate how to access the file. As you can see, we do this as a sequential file. In other words, the data will be read one record at a time. But there is a difference. The order of the records will be based on the primary key.

Two other options are available for accessing a file:

RANDOM

    We read the file by randomly accessing the records.

DYNAMIC

    We can read the file as either sequential or random.

To create an indexed file, the process is similar to how it is done with a sequential file. But of course, there are some tweaks. Here's a look at a code listing:

```
IDENTIFICATION DIVISION.
PROGRAM-ID. CUSTOMERS.
ENVIRONMENT DIVISION.
INPUT-OUTPUT SECTION.
FILE-CONTROL.
    SELECT CUSTOMER-FILE  ASSIGN TO
    " CUSTOMERS.Dat"
    ORGANIZATION IS LINE SEQUENTIAL.
    SELECT CUSTOMER-FILE-INDEXED ASSIGN TO
    "CUSTOMERS INDEXED.Dat"
    ORGANIZATION IS INDEXED
    ACCESS IS SEQUENTIAL
    RECORD KEY IS INDEXED-CUSTOMER-NO.
DATA DIVISION.
FILE SECTION.
FD CUSTOMER-FILE.
01 CUSTOMER-RECORD.
    05 CUSTOMER-NUMBER          PIC 9(3).
    05 FIRST-NAME               PIC X(20).
    05 LAST-NAME                PIC X(20).
```

```
FD CUSTOMER-FILE-INDEXED.
01  INDEXED-CUSTOMER-RECORD.
    05 INDEXED-CUSTOMER-NO           PIC 9(3).
    05 INDEXED-FIRST-NAME            PIC X(20).
    05 INDEXED-LAST-NAME             PIC X(20).
WORKING-STORAGE SECTION.
01  END-OF-FILE                      PIC X VALUE 'N'.
PROCEDURE DIVISION.
    OPEN INPUT CUSTOMER-FILE
    OPEN OUTPUT CUSTOMER-FILE-INDEXED
    PERFORM UNTIL END-OF-FILE = 'Y'
        READ CUSTOMER-FILE
        AT END
            MOVE 'Y' TO END-OF-FILE
              NOT AT END
                  MOVE CUSTOMER-RECORD TO INDEXED-CUSTOMER-RECORD
                  WRITE INDEXED-CUSTOMER-RECORD
                      INVALID KEY DISPLAY 'Invalid record'
                    END-WRITE
        END-READ
    END-PERFORM
CLOSE CUSTOMER-FILE
CLOSE CUSTOMER-FILE-INDEXED
GOBACK.
```

We have already looked at how to use the ENVIRONMENT DIVISION to SELECT the file. But there is something to consider: the recommendation is to use ACCESS IS SEQUENTIAL when creating an indexed file.

Then in the PROCEDURE DIVISION, we use OPEN and OPEN OUTPUT to set up the files for reading and writing. Next, a loop assigns the record from the CUSTOMER-RECORD file to the INDEXED-CUSTOMER-RECORD, and this will be written to CUSTOMER-FILE-INDEXED. The INVALID KEY looks to see if the record has an index that is in sequence and that there are no duplicates.

Updating an Indexed File

The real power of an indexed file is in updating it. This is generally done with two files—say, one for transactions and then a master. The transactions file contains the records for input, and the processed records are saved to the master. Since the master file has an index, no sorting is needed. Still, it is a good idea to have a backup file.

Another approach also can be taken. You can have a program that gets input from a user, and the records are then updated to the master file. For a use case, consider a retail store with a customer requesting a certain part. An employee can query the part number, which will search the master file and get the number of items on hand.

In terms of the coding, our update program will look like the one we developed earlier in the chapter for sequential files. But let's take a look at the differences. For the SELECT statement in the ENVIRONMENT DIVISION, we have the following:

```
SELECT TRANSACTIONS-FILE TO "TRANSACTIONS.DAT"
    ORGANIZATION IS LINE SEQUENTIAL
SELECT MASTER-FILE ASSIGN TO "MASTERFILE.DAT"
    ORGANIZATION IS INDEXED
    ACCESS MODE IS RANDOM
    RECORD KEY IS PART-NO.
```

We first bring in the sequential file for the transactions. As for the SELECT for the master file, we indicate that it is an INDEXED file and the ACCESS MODE is RANDOM. We then set the primary key to PART-NO.

In the PROCEDURE DIVISION, the master file is read with the use of the I-O clause. We use this to allow for both reading and writing to a file:

```
OPEN INPUT TRANSACTIONS-FILE
OPEN I-O MASTER-FILE
```

The DATA DIVISION then has two FD statements for the files:

```
DATA DIVISION.
FILE SECTION.
FD TRANSACTIONS-FILE.
    05 TRANS-NO            PIC 9(9).
    05 TRANS-DESCRIPTION   PIC X(20).
    05 TRANS-QUANTITY      PIC 9(4).
FD MASTER-FILE.
    05 PART-NO             PIC 9 (9).
    05 DESCRIPTON          PIC X(20).
    05 QUANTITY            PIC 9(4).
```

In the PROCEDURE DIVISION, we can create a subroutine that gets information from a user to query for the part number. This is what it looks like:

```
DISPLAY "Enter the part number"
ACCEPT TRANS-NO
MOVE TRANS-NO TO PART-NO
READ MASTER-FILE
    INVALID KEY DISPLAY
        "This is not a valid part number"
    NOT INVALID KEY DISPLAY
        DESCRIPTION " has " QUANTITY " unit(s) in stock"
END-READ
```

This program will take the input through the field TRANS-NO and then move this over to PART-NO. Then the MASTER-FILE will be read to locate this index. If it is invalid, an error message will be displayed. Otherwise the program will print the part description and quantity available.

Notice that there is no use of the AT END condition with this. The reason is that we are only accessing one record, not going through each of them through the whole file. The INVALID KEY is instead used to test if the index exists.

Another operation for an indexed update is to change an existing record. This is done by using the REWRITE statement, not WRITE.

Here is some sample code:

```
MOVE TRANS-FIRST-NAME TO MASTER-FIRST-NAME
REWRITE MASTER-RECORD
   INVALID KEY DISPLAY
     "There was an error in writing the record to the file"
END-REWRITE.
```

Then what about deleting a record? Yes, you will use the DELETE statement. This is an example:

```
MOVE TRANS-NO TO PART-NO
   READ MASTER-FILE
      INVALID KEY DISPLAY
         "The record does not exist"
      NOT INVALID KEY
         DELETE MASTER-FILE RECORD
         INVALID KEY DISPLAY
            "The record could not be deleted"
         END-DELETE
END-READ.
```

VSAM Files

In Chapter 3, you learned about virtual storage access method (VSAM) files. IBM developed VSAM to make file processing easier but also to provide more efficiency. For the most part, this turned out to work for indexed files—but not sequential files.

A VSAM file combines data and an index (the records can have fixed or variable lengths). You can also access the data directly or sequentially. In fact, you can process information in both batch form and through transactions, such as with CICS.

The smallest number of records is known as a *control interval*. This is a minimum of 4 KB and a maximum of 32 KB in terms of the data that is transferred when accessing files on a mainframe.

Note that two or more CIs can be organized into *control areas* (CAs). What's more, a record has the following:

Record description field (RDS)

This contains an ID for each record and indicates information like the length. It is 3 bytes long.

Control interval definition field (CIDF)

This provides details about a set of records. It is 4 bytes long.

To create a VSAM file, you need to use a utility like IDCAMS, which is from IBM. With this, you create a JCL script having the following parameters:

NAME

The name of the VSAM file.

KEY

The index, which can have up to 255 characters. You refer to this as KEY (*length, offset*). The length represents the number of characters for the index, and the offset is the position you start from. For example, suppose the index is an employee number with six characters. In the VSAM key, you look at the last four. This means you have KEY (4, 2).

FREESPACE

The amount of space for each control interval. This parameter is used when you need to insert new records into the VSAM file. The syntax is FREESPACE (*CI percentage, CA percentage*), and an example is FREESPACE (20, 25). Moreover, if the FREESPACE is used up, IDCAMS will split the control interval to make more room.

RECSZ

The record size, with a syntax of RECSZ (*average, maximum*). The first parameter is the average size of the record, and the maximum is the most that will be allowed.

Dataset type

If the file is a KSDS, you use INDEXED; if it's an ESDS, you use NONINDEXED. For an RRDS, use NUMBERED, and for an LDS, use LINEAR.

VOLUMES

The serial number of the drive where the VSAM file is located.

DATA

The name of the dataset that contains the records.

Here's an example of a JCL file that uses these parameters:

```
//FILEPROG    JOB    1,TOM001,MSGCLASS = C
//STEP1       EXEC   PGM = IDCAMS ❶
//SYSPRINT    DD     SYSOUT = *
```

```
//SYSIN     DD *
            DEFINE CLUSTER (NAME(TOM001.INVENT)  - ❷
            RECSZ(90,90)            -
            FREESPACE(5,10)        -
            KEYS (5,0)                 -
            CICZ (4096)             -
            VOLUMES (XFV01)        -
            INDEXED                    -
            DATA(NAME(TOM001.INVENT.DATA))
    /*
```

❶   This brings in the IDCAMS utility.

❷   Here we specify the parameters for the new VSAM file.

As for COBOL, you can use the same types of commands for VSAM files like READ, WRITE, and DELETE. The main difference is that you specify the key if you are using direct access.

 Even though VSAM files are powerful, they can still be complex to manage and do not have rich database capabilities. As a result, there has been a trend to convert these files to modern databases. Although the process can be difficult and time-consuming, conversion may be worth the effort if more-advanced data analytics is needed.

A rich ecosystem of third-party tools can help manage VSAM files. Here are some examples:

BMC Compuware Storage Performance
This helps improve the disk performance of VSAM files. The system is an alternative to KSDS, ESDS, and RRDS. It is also significantly faster than IDCAMS reorganizations, with 20% to 60% reductions in wall-clock, CPU time, and I/O operations.

Rocket VSAM Assist
This helps improve backup, recovery, and migration of VSAM applications. Technical expertise isn't required to run the software. Only two commands are used for maintenance: DUMP and RESTORE.

CA File Master Plus
This Broadcom product helps improve the accuracy of mainframe data as well as lower the effort for test-file editing and data creation.

Conclusion

When it comes to file handling, COBOL really stands out among computer languages. The COBOL file-handling system is tantamount to a full-on database. This is the kind of application that is pervasive across all businesses.

In this chapter, we covered both sequential and indexed files. Both have their particular use cases. With sequential files, the focus is on batch processing, such as updating master and transaction files. Indexed files are primarily for handling queries and other sophisticated database transactions.

File handling in COBOL is accomplished with only a few commands, such as OPEN, CLOSE, INPUT, READ, WRITE, and REWRITE. Yet they can be used in sophisticated ways. After all, many of the world's largest businesses use these files to manage mission-critical operations.

In the next chapter, we'll look at a topic that relies heavily on files: tables and reporting.

CHAPTER 6

COBOL Tables and Reports

In the business world, Microsoft Excel is one of the most widely used applications. It allows for the easy creation of interactive reports that help with key decisions. The result is that Excel continues to generate huge cash flows, even though the software has been around for over 35 years.

But with COBOL on the mainframe, built-in features can help create tables and reports. Granted, they are not as sophisticated or seamless as Excel. But they are still powerful and can help run mission-critical business applications on a global basis. They have been one of the most important functions of COBOL and the mainframe computer.

In this chapter, we'll take a look at how to use tables and reports in COBOL. We'll also cover related topics like string manipulation.

Introduction to Tables

In a way, a COBOL table is similar to a spreadsheet. You can place numbers in certain areas, make computations, search the data, and so on. In fact, the applications are seemingly endless. You can set up a table to help compute taxes, determine the premiums for insurance, or come up with a forecast for sales.

Keep in mind that a COBOL table is the language's version of an array. In a typical language, an array stores a string of data. And each data item is referenced with an index number. For example, let's suppose we have an array, which we call Months, that is for the months in the year. But each has an index that starts at 0. So Months[0] is equal to January, Months [1] is equal to February, etc. In other words, this is a much more efficient way to work with related data, instead of having a unique variable for each one, such as Month1 and Month2.

But COBOL has its own approach. The index is instead called a *subscript*, and it starts at 1. Next, because records are about grouping hierarchical information, this must be enforced when using a table, which can get complicated.

We declare a table in the WORKING-STORAGE SECTION of the DATA DIVISION, and we use the OCCURS clause. This indicates the number of elements.

Let's suppose we want to create a table for 10 stores of a retail company. This is what we would do:

```
01   RETAIL-STORE-TABLE.
   05   RETAIL-RECORD          OCCURS 10 TIMES.
      10   STORE-ADDRESS    PIC X(20).
      10   STORE-PHONE       PIC X(12).
```

We set up a header for the table, which is called RETAIL-STORE-TABLE, and then create a data group called RETAIL-RECORD. We use OCCURS 10 TIMES to create 10 instances of it. Each has a field for the store address and phone number.

This table is called a *one-level table*. The records are dependent on one variable, which is the number of the retail stores.

In most cases, the data for a table will be populated from an external file. But if the data is relatively small and will not change much, you can place the values in the DATA DIVISION or the PROCEDURE DIVISION.

Let's take an example of a list of top-selling Nike shoes:

```
01  NIKE-SHOES.
   05   FILLER     PIC X(30)    VALUE "Nike Air Force 1".
   05   FILLER     PIC X(30)    VALUE "Nike Air Max 270".
   05   FILLER     PIC X(30)    VALUE "Nike Air Max 270".
   05   FILLER     PIC X(30)    VALUE "Nike Benassi JDI".
   05   FILLER     PIC X(30)    VALUE "Nike Flex Runner".
01 NIKE-SHOES-TABLE REDEFINES NIKE-SHOES.
   05 SHOE-NAME   PIC X(30) OCCURS 5 TIMES.
PROCEDURE DIVISION.
   DISPLAY SHOE-NAME(4)
GOBACK.
```

We start by declaring a data group called NIKE-SHOES that has five Nike brands. Each group has a FILLER since we do not need a name for the field, and then we set the name for each of the shoes with VALUE.

The next record is the name of the table, which is NIKE-SHOES-TABLE, and we link this to the prior table with the REDEFINES command. Then we create an elementary item to hold each of the shoe names and repeat this five times using the OCCURS command.

Then we display item 4, which is Nike Benassi JDI.

Yet there is a more compact way to create this type of table. For example, let's see how we can create one with the months of the year:

```
01  MONTHS-TABLE VALUE "JanFebMarAprMayJunJulAugSepOctNovDec".
   05 MONTH-GROUP OCCURS 12 TIMES.
   10  MONTH-ABBREVIATION  PIC X(3).
PROCEDURE DIVISION.
   DISPLAY MONTH-ABBREVIATION(3).
```

We set MONTHS-TABLE to a string of abbreviations for the months. Then we have an OCCURS for 12 instances, and the MONTH-ABBREVIATION is automatically filled. After this, we display item 3, which is Mar.

In a sense, these two programs are about creating a set of constants. You can create a copy of each one to be used for other programs, and this is done by using a copy member. You'll learn more about this later in the book.

So far, we have used numbers to reference the items in a table. But you can also do this with a field. Let's continue with our program for the months:

```
01  MONTHS-TABLE VALUE "JanFebMarAprMayJunJulAugSepOctNovDec".
   05 MONTH-GROUP OCCURS 12 TIMES.
      10  MONTH-ABBREVIATION  PIC X(3).
01  MONTH-SUBSCRIPT   PIC S99   BINARY.
PROCEDURE DIVISION.
MOVE 2 TO MONTH-SUBSCRIPT
DISPLAY MONTH-ABBREVIATION(MONTH-SUBSCRIPT)
```

We create a field called MONTH-SUBSCRIPT and need to make it an unsigned integer. We also set it up as a BINARY data type since this is generally more efficient than using a PACKED DECIMAL.

We next set 2 to MONTH-SUBSCRIPT and can use this as the subscript for MONTH-ABBREVIATION, which will print Feb.

Another way to use the table's subscript is with the relative subscript. This is a value that is added or subtracted from a field. To illustrate this, here's some code for the PROCEDURE DIVISION for our program about months:

```
MOVE 2 TO MONTH-SUBSCRIPT
DISPLAY MONTH-ABBREVIATION(MONTH-SUBSCRIPT + 2)
```

This adds 2 to the field MONTHS-SUBSCRIPT. Thus, the program will print Apr.

 It's important to know the size of the table's subscript. For example, if it is set at 20, and you use 21, the program will crash. This will also happen if the subscript is 0 or less.

You've seen how to set the VALUE of the data items in an OCCURS loop. But you can also use other approaches. For example, suppose you have a data item, called ITEM-PRICES, that holds various prices for a product. You can do this to initialize it:

```
MOVE 0 TO ITEM-PRICES
```

Or you can use this:

```
INITIALIZE ITEM-PRICES
```

But you need to be careful. If you have a large amount of data, the INITIALIZE command can be less efficient.

Tables and Reading Files

In Chapter 5, we took a detailed look at how to use sequential and indexed files. To do this with tables, we need to make a few tweaks.

Let's look at an example. We will use a sequential file:

```
IDENTIFICATION DIVISION.
PROGRAM-ID.  SALES.
ENVIRONMENT DIVISION.
INPUT-OUTPUT SECTION.
FILE-CONTROL.
SELECT SALES-FILE ASSIGN TO "Sales.dat"
    ORGANIZATION IS LINE SEQUENTIAL.
```

The use of the ENVIRONMENT DIVISION is familiar. It simply specifies SALES-FILE as the name, and we set it to SEQUENTIAL:

```
DATA DIVISION.
FILE SECTION.
FD SALES-FILE.
01 LOCATION-SALES.
   88 END-OF-FILE  VALUE HIGH-VALUES.
   02 LOCATION-NO       PIC 99.   ❶
   02 RECEIPTS      PIC 9(4).  ❷
WORKING-STORAGE SECTION.
   01 SALES-TABLE.
      05 SALES-TOTALS PIC 9(4)  OCCURS 5 TIMES.
01 LOCATION-COUNTER    PIC 99.
01 SALES-FORMAT        PIC $$$,$$$.
```

❶ The location number for each branch

❷ The revenues per branch

In the FILE SECTION of the DATA DIVISION, we put together a data structure for the sequential file by using an FD statement. Then we create a group item, which will have an 88 level number for the trigger of the end-of-file. Next, we have data items to describe each of the company's branches.

In the WORKING-STORAGE SECTION, we create a header for our sales table. It has a field, called SALES-TOTALS, that will be iterated five times with the OCCURS statement. Then a counter for the number of subscripts in the table and an edited PIC will put the sales numbers in a better format:

```
PROCEDURE DIVISION.
MOVE ZEROES TO SALES-TABLE ❶
OPEN INPUT SALES-FILE ❷
READ SALES-FILE
    AT END SET END-OF-FILE TO TRUE
END-READ
PERFORM UNTIL END-OF-FILE ❸
MOVE RECEIPTS TO SALES-TOTALS(LOCATION-NO) ❹
    READ SALES-FILE
        AT END SET END-OF-FILE TO TRUE
    END-READ
END-PERFORM
DISPLAY "   Monthly Sales By Location"
PERFORM VARYING LOCATION-COUNTER FROM 1 BY 1 ❺
    UNTIL LOCATION-COUNTER GREATER THAN 5
        MOVE SALES-TOTALS(LOCATION-COUNTER) TO SALES-FORMAT
        DISPLAY "Sales for location number ", LOCATION-COUNTER
        " " SALES-FORMAT
END-PERFORM
CLOSE SALES-FILE
GOBACK.
```

❶ Initializes the values for SALES-TABLE.

❷ Starts the process of accessing the file.

❸ This loop will continue until the end-of-file is reached and assign the SALES-RECEIPTS for each location to the SALES-TOTALS table.

❹ The LOCATION-NO field is the field for the subscript for the reference.

❺ The loop that will print out the information about the branches and their sales.

The last PERFORM loop uses the LOCATION-COUNTER field and sets it to 1. After this, it will be incremented for each iteration. This will continue until the value is greater than 5 (or the number of items in the table). In each loop, we print the location number of the branch and the sales.

By using the table structure, we can certainly do much more with our program—say, to track additional metrics. Suppose we want to report the total number of locations and the sales per location.

The first adjustment for the code is in the DATA DIVISION:

```
01 LOCATION-COUNTER          PIC 99.
01 LOCATION-NUMBER           PIC 99.
01 SALES-FORMAT              PIC $$$,$$$.
01 SALES-ALL-LOCATIONS       PIC 9(4).
01 AVERAGE-SALES             PIC $$$,$$$.
```

We add LOCATION-NUMBER for the total number of locations. Then we include SALES-ALL-LOCATIONS to sum the sales for all the locations and use an edited numeric for the average sales.

Now we make changes to the first PERFORM loop:

```
PERFORM UNTIL END-OF-FILE
    MOVE RECEIPTS TO SALES-TOTALS(LOCATION-NO)
    ADD 1 TO LOCATION-NUMBER
    ADD RECEIPTS TO SALES-ALL-LOCATIONS
```

Here we add one for each time a record is read for a location and then total up the sales in SALES-ALL-LOCATIONS.

Finally, after the next PERFORM loop, we add this to the report:

```
DISPLAY "Total number of locations: " LOCATION-NUMBER
COMPUTE AVERAGE-SALES = SALES-ALL-LOCATIONS / LOCATION-COUNTER
DISPLAY "Average sales per location" AVERAGE-SALES
```

We first print out the number of locations and then use COMPUTE for the average sales, which is then printed.

Multilevel Tables

It's more typical that a table will have several variables. This is known as a *multilevel table*. COBOL allows up to seven levels, but you'll likely use two to three.

Let's put together a program that shows how to use a multilevel table. In our example, we have two levels. First, we have data for five regions for a company. Then the next level is for the sales of the past four quarters.

Table 6-1 shows what this data looks like in a file.

Table 6-1. File for quarterly sales

Region number	Quarter 1 sales	Quarter 2 sales	Quarter 3 sales	Quarter 4 sales
01	100	200	210	230
02	175	250	300	270
03	182	198	254	288
04	409	380	430	397

Now let's take a look at the code:

```
IDENTIFICATION DIVISION.
PROGRAM-ID.  MULTI-LEVEL.
ENVIRONMENT DIVISION.
INPUT-OUTPUT SECTION.
FILE-CONTROL.
   SELECT SALES-FILE ASSIGN TO ❶
   "Sales.dat"
   ORGANIZATION IS LINE SEQUENTIAL.
DATA DIVISION.
FILE SECTION.
FD SALES-FILE.
01 SALES-RECORD.
   88 END-OF-FILE  VALUE HIGH-VALUES. ❷
   05 REGION-NO            PIC 99. ❸
   05 QUARTERLY-SALES      PIC 9(3) OCCURS 4 TIMES. ❹
```

❶ SALES-FILE is set to the *Sales.dat* file to get the data on the sales and the regions.

❷ SALES-RECORD has the end-of-file flag.

❸ Fields for the region number and quarterly sales.

❹ We use OCCURS 4 TIMES because we have four quarters of data.

We then need to set up more data in the WORKING-STORAGE SECTION. We include elements for the report's content, such as the table for sales and report headings. We also add fields for totals and index fields:

```
WORKING-STORAGE SECTION.
01 SALES-TABLE. ❶
05 REGION OCCURS 5 TIMES. ❷
   10 ST-QUARTERLY-SALES   PIC 9(3) OCCURS 4 TIMES. ❸
01 REPORT-HEADING.
   05  FILLER             PIC X(10)  VALUE SPACES.
   05  FILLER             PIC X(40) VALUE "Quarterly Sales Based On Region".
01  REPORT-LINE.
   05  FILLER             PIC X(50) VALUE ALL "-". ❹
01 TOTALS. ❺
   05 SALES-TOTALS        PIC 9(9).
   05 FORMAT-SALES        PIC $$$,$$$.
   05 FORMAT-AVERAGE-SALES PIC $$$,$$$.
01 REGION-INDEX           PIC 99. ❻
01 QUARTER-INDEX          PIC 99.
01 AVERAGE-SALES          PIC 9(3). ❼
```

❶ We use SALES-TABLE to create the multilevel table.

❷ An iteration for the number of regions.

❸ An iteration for the four quarters of sales.

❹ FILLER has a string of 50 hyphens for dividing the content into sections.

❺ SALES-TOTALS sums up the sales for each quarter, and FORMAT-SALES puts this in the form of a currency.

❻ The fields REGION-INDEX and QUARTER-INDEX are counters to help with the loops for the region and quarterly data.

❼ Stores the value for the average of the sales from the file data.

This part of the program highlights that the reporting capabilities can take up a lot of lines of code. With the FILLER command, you can create some space or center the text to better format the report.

The next section is the PROCEDURE DIVISION. The first part accesses the file and then initializes the values to 0:

```
PROCEDURE DIVISION.
100-START-PROGRAM.
MOVE ZEROS TO SALES-TABLE
OPEN INPUT SALES-FILE
READ SALES-FILE
    AT END SET END-OF-FILE TO TRUE
END-READ
```

The code then has nested PERFORM VARYING statements, which are used to create our multilevel tables:

```
PERFORM UNTIL END-OF-FILE ❶
   PERFORM VARYING QUARTER-INDEX FROM 1 BY 1
   UNTIL QUARTER-INDEX > 4 ❷
      ADD QUARTERLY-SALES(QUARTER-INDEX) TO
      ST-QUARTERLY-SALES(REGION-NO, QUARTER-INDEX)
   END-PERFORM
   READ SALES-FILE
   AT END SET END-OF-FILE TO TRUE
      END-READ
   END-PERFORM
   DISPLAY REPORT-HEADING ❸
   DISPLAY REPORT-LINE
   PERFORM VARYING REGION-INDEX FROM 1 BY 1
      UNTIL REGION-INDEX > 4 ❹
      DISPLAY "Region Number: " REGION-INDEX
      PERFORM VARYING QUARTER-INDEX FROM 1 BY 1
      UNTIL QUARTER-INDEX > 4
         MOVE ST-QUARTERLY-SALES(REGION-INDEX, QUARTER-INDEX)
         TO FORMAT-SALES
   DISPLAY "Quarter " QUARTER-INDEX " sales: "
```

```
            FORMAT-SALES
         ADD ST-QUARTERLY-SALES(REGION-INDEX, QUARTER-INDEX)
            TO SALES-TOTALS
         END-PERFORM
                MOVE SALES-TOTALS TO FORMAT-SALES
                DISPLAY "Total sales: " FORMAT-SALES
                COMPUTE AVERAGE-SALES = SALES-TOTALS / 4
                MOVE AVERAGE-SALES TO FORMAT-SALES
                DISPLAY "Average sales: " FORMAT-SALES
                DISPLAY REPORT-LINE
            END-PERFORM
    CLOSE SALES-FILE
    GOBACK.
```

❶ The main loop, which terminates when the end-of-file is triggered.

❷ This PERFORM VARYING cycles through the four quarters of data from the file, and the counter is QUARTER-INDEX.

❸ Displays the report headings.

❹ Loops that print out the information of the report.

In the loops in ❹, things get a bit tricky. We take the quarterly sales read from the file, which was put into a one-level table for QUARTERLY-SALES, and put the data into ST-QUARTER-SALES, which is a two-level table. The first subscript is the region, and the second is the quarter. Thus, if the region is 2 and the quarter is 3, ST-QUARTERLY-SALES (2 3) is equal to the sales. Note that you need to have one space between the different subscripts.

Once the loop is complete, we will have a two-level table filled with the data. We can then display this as a report, which will be done in the next set of PERFORM statements. But before doing this, we display the heading of the report and the report line.

Let's understand how the PERFORM VARYING statements work to print out the results. The first loop goes through the number of regions, and for each of these, sales are printed out for each of the four quarters. For each iteration, the ST-QUARTERLY-SALES field is set to FORMAT-SALES to put it in the currency format, and this data is printed. After this, the quarterly sales number is added to a counter for the sum of the sales for the year, called SALES-TOTALS. This is converted to a currency and then printed out.

Next, we calculate the average sales, which are the TOTAL-SALES divided by the number of quarters. The result is converted to a currency format and printed out.

Indexes

In this chapter, we've seen how versatile subscripts are in creating sophisticated tables. But this is not the only way to reference a value. We can also use an index, which is actually more common when using tables. You also need to use an index for the SEARCH statement in a table, which we will review in this section.

Unlike a subscript, an index is not defined as a field in the WORKING-STORAGE section of the DATA DIVISION. Instead, we specify it as part of the OCCURS statement:

```
01   INVENTORY-TABLE.
   05 INVENTORY-TRANSACTIONS OCCURS 100 TIMES INDEXED BY INDEX-1.
      10      SKU                               PIC 9(5).
      10 PRODUCT-DESCRIPTION      PIC X(30).
```

Here, INDEX-1 is the name of the index for the inventory table. Note that you can make up this name, as you can for any field.

The nice thing about the INDEXED BY command is that the COBOL compiler will handle all the details. The coder needs to do nothing else.

Also, if you want to change the value of the index, you can use the SET command:

```
SET INDEX-1 TO 2.
```

Here is something else we can do:

```
SET INDEX-1 UP BY 1.
SET INDEX-1 DOWN BY 1.
```

With this, we increase the value of INDEX-1 by 1. And yes, the use of DOWN will do the opposite.

An index is more efficient than a subscript because it points directly to the value in memory. A subscript, on the other hand, does this with an intermediate step.

So when fetching a file, do we do anything different when using index versus the subscript? The good news is the only difference is the INDEXED BY statement. If we have a one-level table, we use one of these. And if we have a two-level table, we use two, and so on.

Searching a Table

You can have a sequential search of a table. The search begins with the record that corresponds to the value of the index. After this, the search is conducted one record after another. This goes on until a match is found or the end of the file is reached.

How to do this? It's possible to create a program that uses PERFORM loops. But there is a better way. COBOL has a powerful command called SEARCH, which can handle many of the details of finding the data you are looking for.

To see how this works, let's consider a simple example: a program that searches for a letter in the alphabet. In the code, we start by setting up a table that has the letters of the alphabet and then use REDEFINES to change the structure of the table:

```
IDENTIFICATION DIVISION.
PROGRAM-ID.  SEARCH.
DATA DIVISION.
WORKING-STORAGE SECTION.
01 CHAR-TABLE.
   05 FILLER PIC X(26) VALUE
   "abcdefghijklmnopqrstuvwxyz". ❶
01 FILLER REDEFINES CHAR-TABLE.
   05 LETTER PIC X OCCURS 26 TIMES
   INDEXED BY LETTER-INDEX. ❷
01 INDEX-COUNTER  PIC 99 VALUE ZEROS. ❸
01 USER-INPUT  PIC X. ❹
```

❶ The internal data for the alphabet that will be searched.

❷ OCCURS iterates 26 times to create an index called LETTER-INDEX.

❸ A counter to identify which letter has been picked.

❹ The letter that the user will input to search.

Here's a look at the PROCEDURE DIVISION, which uses a loop to perform a basic search:

```
PROCEDURE DIVISION.
DISPLAY "Enter a letter to search "
ACCEPT USER-INPUT ❶
SET LETTER-INDEX TO 1 ❷
SEARCH LETTER ❸
   WHEN LETTER(LETTER-INDEX) = USER-INPUT
   SET INDEX-COUNTER TO LETTER-INDEX
   DISPLAY USER-INPUT, " is located at ", INDEX-COUNTER
END-SEARCH
GOBACK.
```

❶ Gets the user input and stores the letter in USER-INPUT

❷ Sets LETTER-INDEX 1 so the search will begin with the first letter

❸ The core search algorithm

In ❸, we use the SEARCH command to scan the LETTER table. The WHEN statement checks for a match by comparing each element of the table with USER-INPUT. If a match is found, we assign the position to INDEX-COUNTER and print out the value.

But what if we want a more sophisticated search, such as for a table that has multiple levels? We can certainly do this. To provide an illustration, let's set up a program that searches inventory levels at different stores for three products: the Nintendo Switch, Sony PlayStation, and Microsoft Xbox. The user will input an SKU number, and the program will search for it and provide the user with the unit levels. The program will also bring in this data through an external file.

First, let's see what the data file looks like (Table 6-2). It has three fields, for the SKU, the name of the product, and then another table for the quantity levels for four stores.

Table 6-2. The record for inventory of game consoles

SKU	Description	Store 1 units	Store 2 units	Store 3 units	Store 4 units
01	Nintendo Switch	25	51	34	29
02	Sony PlayStation	41	31	9	55
03	Microsoft Xbox	23	19	41	28

Next, here's a look at the code. We first access a sequential external file and then create an FD for INVENTORY-FILE. We have an 88 condition for the end-of-file trigger and then fields for the SKU, product description, and quantity levels, which use the OCCURS clause:

```
IDENTIFICATION DIVISION.
PROGRAM-ID.  INVENTORY.
ENVIRONMENT DIVISION.
INPUT-OUTPUT SECTION.
FILE-CONTROL.
SELECT INVENTORY-FILE ASSIGN TO
   "Inventory.dat"
   ORGANIZATION IS LINE SEQUENTIAL.
DATA DIVISION.
FILE SECTION.
FD INVENTORY-FILE.
01 INVENTORY-RECORD.
   88 END-OF-FILE  VALUE HIGH-VALUES.
   05 SKU          PIC 99.
   05 PRODUCT-DESCRIPTION PIC X(20).
   05 QUANTITY     PIC 9(3) OCCURS 4 TIMES.
```

For WORKING-STORAGE SECTION, we set up the table and use an index:

```
WORKING-STORAGE SECTION.
   01 INVENTORY-TABLE.
      05 IT-RECORD OCCURS 3 TIMES INDEXED BY IT-INDEXED. ❶
         10 IT-SKU       PIC 99.
```

```
        10 IT-PRODUCT-DESCRIPTION PIC X(20).
        10 IT-QUANTITY    PIC 9(3) OCCURS 4 TIMES.  ❷
01 REPORT-HEADING.
   05  FILLER            PIC X(10)  VALUE SPACES.
   05  FILLER            PIC X(40) VALUE "Inventory Search".
01  REPORT-LINE.
   05  FILLER            PIC X(50) VALUE ALL "-".
01 SKU-INDEX          PIC 99.
01 REGION-INDEX         PIC 99.
01 SEARCH-KEY          PIC 9(3).  ❸
01 SEARCH-FEEDBACK     PIC X(20).  ❹
```

❶ This OCCURS is for the instances of each of the SKUs.

❷ This OCCURS is to calculate the inventory levels.

❸ This is for the information input from the user.

❹ This prints the result for the user for the search.

The PROCEDURE DIVISION includes the code to search for the SKU and then display information about it:

```
PROCEDURE DIVISION.
100-START-PROGRAM.
MOVE ZEROS TO INVENTORY-TABLE ❶
OPEN INPUT INVENTORY-FILE
READ INVENTORY-FILE
   AT END SET END-OF-FILE TO TRUE
END-READ
COMPUTE SKU-INDEX = 1 ❷
PERFORM UNTIL END-OF-FILE ❸
   ADD SKU TO IT-SKU(SKU-INDEX)
   MOVE PRODUCT-DESCRIPTION TO
   IT-PRODUCT-DESCRIPTION(SKU-INDEX)
   PERFORM VARYING REGION-INDEX FROM 1 BY 1
   UNTIL REGION-INDEX > 4
   ADD QUANTITY(REGION-INDEX) TO
        IT-QUANTITY(SKU, REGION-INDEX)
END-PERFORM
COMPUTE SKU-INDEX = SKU-INDEX + 1
READ INVENTORY-FILE
   AT END SET END-OF-FILE TO TRUE
END-READ
END-PERFORM
DISPLAY REPORT-HEADING
DISPLAY REPORT-LINE
DISPLAY "Enter your search: "
ACCEPT SEARCH-KEY ❹
SEARCH IT-RECORD
   AT END
```

```
                MOVE 'Not found' TO SEARCH-FEEDBACK
                WHEN IT-SKU (IT-INDEXED) = SEARCH-KEY
                MOVE IT-PRODUCT-DESCRIPTION(IT-INDEXED)
                TO SEARCH-FEEDBACK
        END-SEARCH.
        DISPLAY REPORT-LINE
        DISPLAY "Inventory information for: " SEARCH-FEEDBACK
        PERFORM VARYING REGION-INDEX FROM 1 BY 1 ❺
           UNTIL REGION-INDEX > 4
           DISPLAY "Region Number " REGION-INDEX " quantity: "
           IT-QUANTITY (IT-INDEXED REGION-INDEX)
        END-PERFORM
        CLOSE INVENTORY-FILE
        GOBACK.
```

❶ Initializes INVENTORY-TABLE.

❷ Sets the SKU-INDEX counter to 1 to start at the first record for the search.

❸ This loop brings in the data.

❹ The program asks for the information to search.

❺ The loop that searches for the SKU.

Again, for this we use the SEARCH structure. The WHEN clause evaluates the data to see if there is a match; a match occurs if the SKU is equal to the SEARCH-KEY input from the user. If the match attempt is successful, we move the product description from the table to the SEARCH-FEEDBACK field. After this, we display a small report that shows the product that the SKU refers to as well as the inventory levels for each store.

Binary Search

A sequential search is certainly effective. However, it can still be inefficient because it has to search one record after another.

But COBOL provides a better way: a *binary search*. This is an algorithm that has multiple steps. First, the table is sorted. Next, the data is split, and the two nearest items are compared. The algorithm then goes to the half that has the value that is closer to the search query. This part of the data is split again and again until there is a match. This process usually has fewer steps than a sequential search.

So how do you do this with COBOL? It's really easy: the language provides the SEARCH ALL command.

In our inventory search program, we would just do the following: SEARCH ALL IT-RECORD. Then we need to make the following changes to the WORKING-STORAGE SECTION:

```
01 INVENTORY-TABLE.
   05 IT-RECORD OCCURS 3 TIMES ASCENDING KEY IS IT-SKU
   INDEXED BY IT-INDEXED.
```

By using ASCENDING KEY IS IT-SKU, we can sort the data to allow for the binary search.

Reports

With the reading of files and the creation of tables, you can certainly put together sophisticated reports with COBOL. In fact, we have already gone through much of the coding you will need to know.

But you need to deal with extra considerations when creating a report. One is that you have to spend considerable time developing the report's structure.

A typical report has a heading at the top, with the title of the report, the date, the report number, and the page number. After this is a detail line. This lists certain information—say, the products, sales by region, inventory available for each store, and so on. Then a footer may have totals. Figure 6-1 is an example of a report.

INVENTORY REPORT					
DATE: 2/1/2022 TIME: 02:30PM				PAGE: 1 RPT100	
SKU	PRODUCT DESCRIPTION	QTY	SUPPLIER		
111	iPhone 12	123	Apple		
112	iPhone SE	85	Apple		
113	iPhone 12 Pro	72	Apple		
211	Galaxy S21	34	Samsung		
212	Galaxy Note20	133	Samsung		
213	Galaxy Z Flip	56	Samsung		
214	Galaxy Z Fold2	77	Samsung		
Totals		580			

Figure 6-1. An inventory report for smartphones

To help with the process of creating a report, some coders make a print chart. This can be with a spreadsheet or even a piece of paper. The print report has one square for each location on the screen.

Figure 6-2 shows what a few lines of our inventory report would look like.

															I	N	V	E	N	T	O	R	Y		R	E
D	A	T	E	:		9	9	/	9	9	/	9	9													
T	I	M	E	:		9	9	:	9	9	X	X														
				P	R	O	D	U	C	T																
S	K	U			D	E	S	C	R	I	P	T	I	O	N											
9	9	9			X	X	X	X	X	X	X	X	X	X	X	X	X	X	X	X	X	X	X	X		

Figure 6-2. An example of a print chart to help create a report

When you do this, try to map the data items to their respective PIC equivalents. For example, the SKU has three 9s, which would be a PIC 9(3). Then the Product Description has room for 20 characters. So this would be a PIC X(20).

For a report, the tradition is to develop it for a printer. For a typical line printer, each line would have 132 characters, and the height would be 66 lines. However, the practice is to leave a few extra lines at the top and bottom.

For a mainframe, a printed report is considered an external file. Actually, most printed files are saved to the disk.

In today's digital world, the use of a printer may seem archaic. But printed reports are still common for mainframe shops.

Once we have the format requirements for the report, we can start the coding with the DATA DIVISION. And this can be quite extensive.

One set of fields is to help manage multiple pages:

```
01 PRINT-MANAGEMENT.
    05  PAGE-NUMBER         PIC 9(3)        VALUE 0.
    05  PAGE-LINES              PIC 9(3)        VALUE 54.
    05  LINE-COUNT              PIC 9(3)        VALUE 100.
    05  SPACE-CONTROL       PIC 9.
```

The first field, PAGE-NUMBER is a counter for the current page number. This is set to 0 since the PROCEDURE DIVISION has a PERFORM that adds 1 to the field.

PAGE-LINES indicates the total lines per page. We set this to 54, which is lower than the length of the page. This is to provide for some space to allow for better formatting.

Then the LINE-COUNT page is a counter for the number of lines that have been printed on a page. Why is the VALUE of this at 100? We want it to initially be larger than the PAGE-LINES field.

And finally, the SPACE-CONTROL field indicates the number of lines that will be advanced before another line is printed.

Next, we want to set up data items for the total of the inventory, and we also want fields for the date and time for the report:

```
01 TOTAL-INVENTORY          PIC 9(7)              VALUE ZERO.
01 DATE-AND-TIME.
   05 INVENTORY-DAY          PIC 9(2).
   05 INVENTORY-MONTH        PIC 9(2).
   05 INVENTORY-YEAR         PIC 9(4).
   05 INVENTORY-HOUR         PIC 9(2).
   05 INVENTORY-MINUTES  PIC 9(2).
```

Note that we set TOTAL-INVENTORY to ZERO because we will use this to add up the number of the inventory. In the next part of the DATA DIVISION, a variety of group items provide the formatting for the different sections of the report, such as the heading, detail items, and footers.

Let's first work on the heading. Actually, there may be several. For example, in our inventory report, we have a heading for the title of the report, the date and time, and the titles for the columns.

Here's a look at the first heading:

```
01  HEADING-LINE-1.
    05 FILLER PIC X(2)   VALUE SPACES.
    05 FILLER PIC X(16)   VALUES "INVENTORY REPORT".
01  HEADING-LINE-2.
    05 FILLER PIC X(6)    VALUE "DATE: ".
    05 DATE-MONTH PIC 9(2).
    05 FILLER PIC X(1)    VALUE "/".
    05 DATE-DAY        PIC 9(2).
    05 FILLER PIC X(1)    VALUE "/".
    05 DATE-YEAR      PIC 9(4).
    05 FILLER  PIC X(2) VALUE SPACE.
    05  FILLER PIC X(7)  VALUE "PAGE: ".
    05  CURRENT-PAGE   PIC 9(3).
```

For each data group, we have a description per line. As a result, HEADING-LINE-1 indicates the content for the first line, and so on. Moreover, as you can see, we use a mix of FILLERs and PICs to provide the right spacing for the report.

It is important to provide a VALUE for a FILLER, and it should be either an alphanumeric literal or a SPACE. The reason is that old data could be put inside the fields, which would result in a report that may not make much sense.

The PROCEDURE DIVISION for Reports

In the PROCEDURE DIVISION, we generate the report. Some of the coding involves reading the files and then mapping the records to an internal data structure. Then there will likely be several PERFORM statements that print the headings as well as loop through the details for the report. There may also be calculations, such as for the totals.

Here's some sample code:

```
OPEN INPUT INVENTORY-FILE
OUTPUT INVENTORY-REPORT
PERFORM PRINT-REPORT-HEADING
PERFORM PRINT-REPORT-DETAILS
    UNTIL END-OF-FILE = "Y"
PERFORM PRINT-TOTALS
CLOSE INVENTORY-FILE
CLOSE INVENTORY-REPORT
GOBACK.
```

Notice that we write the report to a file called INVENTORY-REPORT, which is the print file. Then we call the PRINT-REPORT-HEADING module to print the heading of the report and then go through a loop to print the details. After all this, we print out the totals.

Next, we need to write code to WRITE each line of the report to the file and to make sure the spacing is correct. Here's a look:

```
ADD 1 TO PAGE-NUMBER
PRINT-REPORT-HEADING.
WRITE HEADING-LINE-1 AFTER ADVANCING 1 LINES
WRITE HEADING-LINE-2 AFTER ADVANCING 2 LINES
```

PAGE-NUMBER is incremented by one, which allows us to track the page number the program is on. Then we print out the two headings. But after each of these, we advance the printer by a certain number of lines.

Testing a Report

Testing a report program can be more challenging than with a typical COBOL program. First, you need to come up with your own set of test files, which need to account for outliers and potential problems. Second, more runtime errors usually occur because tracking the workflows of a report can be difficult. Essentially, this involves trial-and-error by running the program.

Yet some approaches can help out. For example, it is a good idea to have different phases for the testing. The first phase could be to use the files you have created to evaluate the main parts of the report. Is the spacing correct? Are the pages advancing properly? Are the totals right?

The next phase could be to look at the outliers. What if a number is too large or too small? Is there a division by zero? In other words, you should test files that are more advanced.

For both of these phases, you do not need a large amount of data. The goal is to make sure that the overall structure of the program can account for potential problems.

Finally, you can then run the report with actual data. You can do several tests to get a sense of whether the numbers are correct.

Reporting Tools

While COBOL has a robust system for creating reports, it can be tedious. To deal with this, you might want to create a set of predefined report formats that you can copy and paste into your code and then make adjustments.

But COBOL does have a system to help streamline the process: the Report Writer. For example, while a report could take over 100 lines of regular code in the PROCEDURE DIVISION, the Report Writer might be able to do the same thing in 10 to 20 lines. This is because much of the code is in the DATA DIVISION. Moreover, the Report Writer is based on the idea that most reports have a general structure. They have headers at the top, for example, a list of data items, and then a footer. With the Report Writer, each report has a REPORT DESCRIPTION, or RD, in the REPORT SECTION of the DATA DIVISION. Here's sample code for this:

```
REPORT SECTION.
RD INVENTORY-REPORT
        PAGE LIMIT 70 LINES
        HEADING 1
        FIRST DETAIL 5
        LAST DETAIL 65
```

This provides the sections of a report to print. We first set the maximum length for the lines of the report. Then we put the header at the first line and have a set of details lines for the data.

Next, we provide more definitions for the sections. For example, in this code, we set forth the heading text and the column locations:

```
01   TYPE REPORT HEADING.
LINE 1.
   10    COLUMN 44       PIC X(16)
                         VALUE 'Inventory Report'.
```

The `PROCEDURE DIVISION` contains minimal code to display the report. It might look something like this:

```
INITIATE INVENTORY-REPORT.
PERFORM 100-PRINT-INVENTORY-REPORT
   UNTIL END-OF-FILE.
TERMINATE INVENTORY-REPORT
CLOSE INVENTORY-FILE
GOBACK.
100--PRINT-INVENTORY-REPORT.
   GENERATE DETAIL-LINE.
   READ INVENTORY-FILE
     AT END SET END-OF-FILE TO TRUE
   END-READ
```

The `INITIATE` clause starts the report generation process, which looks at what we have already set up in the `DATA DIVISION`. Consequently, there is no need to use various `PERFORM` loops and counters. This is all handled by Report Writer.

`GENERATE DETAIL-LINE` prints out the individual data items for our report, such as the different products from the inventory. Again, there is no need to use any loops or counters or to handle the pagination.

Besides the Report Writer, various third-party report software systems exist for mainframes. One is Crystal Reports, which is currently owned by SAP. It uses drag-and-drop features to create professional reports that can connect to a myriad of databases.

Business intelligence (BI) systems can access mainframe systems. This type of software can create interactive dashboards and visualizations and even provide data-driven insights for business managers. Some examples of BI software include Cognos, SAP BusinessObjects, Domo, Qlik, and MicroStrategy.

Working with Characters and Strings

One of the challenges of developing reports is the data, which may be in formats and structures that do not translate well for presentation purposes. For example, the dates may be in the form of MM/DD/YYYY even though you want something like June 12, 2021.

Because of this, you will likely need to do some wrangling with the data. COBOL has a variety of functions that can help out.

One is the reference modification. This allows you to parse a string of characters.

This is done by using two values: the offset and the length. The offset indicates where you start in a string, and the length is the number of characters you want to extract. Let's use some code to see how this works:

```
IDENTIFICATION DIVISION.
PROGRAM-ID.  REFMOD.
DATA DIVISION.
WORKING-STORAGE SECTION.
01 TODAY-DATE   PIC X(10) VALUE '01/01/2021'.
01 TODAY-DATE-PART  PIC X(10).
PROCEDURE DIVISION.
MOVE TODAY-DATE (4:2) TO TODAY-DATE-PART
DISPLAY TODAY-DATE-PART
GOBACK.
```

The DATA DIVISION contains two fields. TODAY-DATE is an alphanumeric that has a date in a traditional format. TODAY-DATE-PART holds the part that we specify.

For the PROCEDURE DIVISION, we use the MOVE command to do the parsing. The format for it is offset:length. That is, for the TODAY-DATE field, we go to location 4 of the string, which has a value of 0, and take two characters. These are 0 and 2.

In our case, this is 02, which is the numerical representation for February. We could then have an IF/THEN conditional or EVALUATE structure to print out the month.

No doubt, we could have done this another way, such as by using a data group that breaks down the different parts of the date field. But of course, this would have taken much more space. For the most part, the reference modification is an easy and efficient way to parse text.

What about using the reference modification for a table? You can do this as well. However, the format is different.

Suppose we have a table called INVENTORY-TABLE that has 50 entries. If we want to change the content in entry 15, and select the three characters that have an offset of 7, we would have this:

```
INVENTORY-TABLE (15) (7:3)
```

Another way to help with the formatting of text in a report is to use intrinsic functions. Let's go through some examples.

Suppose you have accounting data that has transaction numbers ending with CR (for credits) and DB (for debits). But we want to convert these to numerics so we can make calculations. We have this:

```
DISPLAY FUNCTION NUMVAL ("  591.32CR")
```

This strips out the two leading blank spaces and then gets rid of CR.

What if some of the numbers have commas and the currency sign? We can use the following intrinsic function:

```
DISPLAY FUNCTION NUMVAL-C ("$1,234.50CR")
```

The result is 1234.5.

Next, two intrinsic functions convert a string to uppercase and lowercase:

```
DISPLAY FUNCTION LOWER-CASE ("ADA LOVELACE")
DISPLAY FUNCTION UPPER-CASE ("Ada Lovelace")
```

This gives us ada lovelace and ADA LOVELACE.

In some cases, you might want to determine the length of a string. This is easy to do:

```
DISPLAY FUNCTION LENGTH ("ELON MUSK")
```

The length is 9.

STRING

A *string* in many languages is the name of a data type for more than one character set to a variable. But as you've seen, COBOL has no such data type. Instead, you would use an alphanumeric, such as a PIC X(10).

But COBOL does have a STRING command that helps break down a set of characters into different component parts. This is common for such tasks as interpreting the records from an external file.

Basically, STRING allows for combining one or more strings. Here's a simple code example:

```
IDENTIFICATION DIVISION.
PROGRAM-ID.  STRING.
DATA DIVISION.
WORKING-STORAGE SECTION.
01 FULL-NAME PIC X(30).
PROCEDURE DIVISION.
STRING "Jane" " " "Murphy" DELIMITED BY SIZE Into FULL-NAME
DISPLAY FULL-NAME
GOBACK.
```

We start with STRING and then list the strings we want to combine. In our example, these include Jane, a space, and then her last name, Murphy. We use DELIMITED BY SIZE since we want to use the full length of the sending fields. They are then set to FULL-NAME, which we print out to get Jane Murphy.

If the receiving field is too small, an overflow error occurs, and the text will be truncated. This would happen if we set the FULL-NAME to PIC X(3).

We can use ON OVERFLOW to guard against this, though:

```
STRING "Jane" " " "Murphy" DELIMITED BY SIZE Into FULL-NAME ↵
ON OVERFLOW DISPLAY "There is an overflow error"
```

When using the STRING command, various DELIMITERs allow for combining strings:

```
IDENTIFICATION DIVISION.
PROGRAM-ID.  DELIMITER.
DATA DIVISION.
WORKING-STORAGE SECTION.
01 FIRST-NAME PIC X(15) VALUE "Jane".
01 LAST-NAME  PIC X(15) VALUE "Murphy".
01 FULL-NAME PIC X(30).
PROCEDURE DIVISION.
STRING FIRST-NAME DELIMITED BY SPACE " " DELIMITED BY SIZE
   LAST-NAME DELIMITED BY SPACE INTO FULL-NAME
DISPLAY FULL-NAME
GOBACK.
```

The STRING statement may seem somewhat convoluted. So let's explain it. We first take FIRST-NAME and take the text until there is a space or the end of the string. Then a space is added to this, and the use of DELIMITED BY SIZE means we will use the whole space. Then the LAST-NAME text is used until there is a space or there is an end to the string.

UNSTRING

The UNSTRING command may sound kind of strange. But it is useful and easy to use. For the most part, the command allows you to separate a string into parts. To do this, you use delimiters, which could be a space, a comma, and so on.

Note that the receiving field for the UNSTRING command is not initialized. Thus, to avoid having stray characters, you should initialize the field.

When using the UNSTRING command, one sending field has the complete text, and one or more receiving fields contain the parts. You also cannot have a reference modification for the first field.

Here's a simple example:

```
IDENTIFICATION DIVISION.
PROGRAM-ID. UNSTRING.
DATA DIVISION.
WORKING-STORAGE SECTION.
01 FIRST-NAME PIC X(15).
01 LAST-NAME  PIC X(15).
01 FULL-NAME PIC X(30) VALUE "Grace Hopper".
PROCEDURE DIVISION.
UNSTRING FULL-NAME DELIMITED BY SPACE INTO FIRST-NAME LAST-NAME
DISPLAY FIRST-NAME
DISPLAY LAST-NAME
GOBACK.
```

In the DATA DIVISION, FULL-NAME is the sending field (which we initialize), and then the receiving fields are FIRST-NAME and LAST-NAME. The UNSTRING command separates the sending field by a space and then prints out the results.

But let's suppose that FULL-NAME instead has Grace Brewster Murray Hopper as its value. If we use the DELIMITED BY SPACE clause, we will get only the first two names. So what to do? We instead use the DELIMITED BY ALL SPACE statement:

```
IDENTIFICATION DIVISION.
PROGRAM-ID.  UNSTRING.
DATA DIVISION.
WORKING-STORAGE SECTION.
01 NAME-1 PIC X(15).
01 NAME-2 PIC X(15).
01 NAME-3 PIC X(15).
01 NAME-4 PIC X(15).
01 FULL-NAME PIC X(30) VALUE "Grace Brewster Murray Hopper".
PROCEDURE DIVISION.
UNSTRING FULL-NAME DELIMITED BY SPACE INTO NAME-1 NAME-2 NAME-3
    NAME-4
DISPLAY NAME-1
DISPLAY NAME-2
DISPLAY NAME-3
DISPLAY NAME-4
GOBACK.
```

To make this work, we had to create two more fields.

Another feature for the UNSTRING command is the TALLYING statement. This indicates the number of receiving fields that are changed. You can increment the instances with TALLYING IN.

To see how this looks, let's make some adjustments to our code sample. First of all, we need a counter:

```
01 INSTANCE-COUNTER PIC 9.
```

Then we make the following changes to the UNSTRING statement:

```
UNSTRING FULL-NAME DELIMITED BY SPACE INTO NAME-1 NAME-2 NAME-3
    NAME-4 TALLYING IN INSTANCE-COUNTER
```

INSTANCE-COUNTER has the value of 4, which is the number of receiving fields. Next, the UNSTRING command has the COUNT IN clause that will show the number of characters that have been moved over to the sending fields (the delimiters are not included). This code shows how to use this:

```
IDENTIFICATION DIVISION.
PROGRAM-ID.  UNSTRING.
DATA DIVISION.
WORKING-STORAGE SECTION.
01 FIRST-NAME PIC X(15).
```

```
01 LAST-NAME PIC X(15).
01 FULL-NAME PIC X(30) VALUE "Grace Hopper".
01 FIRST-NAME-COUNTER PIC 9.
01 LAST-NAME-COUNTER PIC 9.
PROCEDURE DIVISION.
UNSTRING FULL-NAME DELIMITED BY SPACE INTO
    FIRST-NAME COUNT IN FIRST-NAME-COUNTER
    LAST-NAME COUNT IN LAST-NAME-COUNTER
DISPLAY FIRST-NAME
DISPLAY "Length: " FIRST-NAME-COUNTER
DISPLAY LAST-NAME
DISPLAY "Length: " LAST-NAME-COUNTER
GOBACK.
```

This is the variation of the program we used to parse the name of Grace Hopper. But in the DATA DIVISION, two new fields hold the length for each of the receiving fields, which are FIRST-NAME-COUNTER and LAST-NAME-COUNTER.

Then, in the UNSTRING statement, we use a COUNT IN statement for each of the receiving fields.

INSPECT

The INSPECT command allows for the counting of characters as well as their replacement in strings. This is done by using clauses such as TALLYING and REPLACING.

Let's first start with TALLYING. As we've seen earlier in this chapter, this allows us to count text. But this is more sophisticated when using INSPECT. For example, this counts the number of periods in a string:

```
INSPECT TEXT-INFO TALLYING PERIOD-COUNTER FOR ALL "."
```

The field PERIOD-COUNTER has the number of instances.

Or suppose you have text that has leading characters, such as ***234 for privacy. You can use INSPECT to find the number of these:

```
INSPECT TEXT-INFO TALLYING PERIOD-COUNTER FOR LEADING "*"
```

You can also count the number of a certain character that appears before another character (say, a space). This is how it works:

```
INSPECT TEXT-INFO TALLYING PERIOD-COUNTER FOR CHARACTERS BEFORE " "
```

With this, the number of characters are summed up in PERIOD-COUNTER, and the CHARACTERS BEFORE " " will do this before the first instance of a space.

Now let's see how we can use the REPLACING clause. Suppose we have dates that are in the format of 99-99-9999 but we want to replace the hyphen (-) with a forward slash (/). We can do this as follows:

```
INSPECT DATE-ITEM REPLACING ALL "/" BY "-"
```

Maybe you have input text that is for a password. But you want to change each letter to an asterisk (*). This can be done easily with the INSPECT command:

```
INSPECT PASSWORD-TEXT REPLACING CHARACTERS BY "*"
```

It's important to keep in mind that you cannot insert or delete characters by using REPLACING. For example, you can replace two characters with only two characters, not one or three.

Conclusion

In this chapter, we started with a look at tables, which are the foundation for data structures for reports. We saw how to create different types, such as with various levels. A key to this is the use of the OCCURS clause, which is a looping structure.

We can reference tables in different ways, including with subscripts and indexes. However, indexes are usually used because of the speed and versatility. This is especially the case if you want to search a table. And speaking of searching, we have looked at two main approaches: sequential and binary. The latter is generally more powerful and quicker.

We also looked at constructing reports. All in all, it can be a tedious process, but we have looked at strategies to help out, such as by using print charts.

Reports need to be tested, which can be a challenge. This is why it's recommended to have different phases of testing.

Finally, we reviewed the myriad ways to change text. This is essential as it is common for the data to be in different formats. In this chapter, we looked at commands like INSPECT, STRING, and UNSTRING.

The next chapter covers concepts like copy members, subprograms, and sort/merge functions.

CHAPTER 7

Other Languages and Programming Techniques

We have focused on the COBOL language. This is definitely the standard for mainframe development. But a myriad of other languages are available. These include C++, C, Java, assembler language, PL/I, REXX, and CLIST.

You do not necessarily need to know all these languages, but having a general understanding of them is a good idea. This will be our focus in this chapter.

We'll also look at some of the programming techniques to help speed up your development. For this, the focus will be on COBOL.

What Language to Use?

Despite the strong capabilities of COBOL, sometimes you really need to use another language. When making this decision, you should consider a variety of factors:

- Is speed important?
- What are the skills sets of the developer?
- Does your employer have certain preferences?
- Are there functions that are much more efficient in other languages?

It's also important to have an understanding of the categories of computer languages. For example, most are *high-level*. This means that they use English-like statements and the structures are fairly straightforward. This is the case with COBOL.

A *low-level language*, on the other hand, is much closer to the machine and its capabilities. Because of this, the instructions and logic can be much more complex and tedious. The good news is that you will likely not need to use a low-level language. Still, this chapter provides an overview of one of them: assembler.

Older languages like COBOL use procedures and modules for structured programming. But object-oriented platforms, such as C++ and Java, use more versatile classes and objects.

Next, modern languages have rich visual interfaces, which allow you to drag and drop components. This is the case with Visual Basic and Visual C++.

Scripting languages are much more limited and focus on certain use cases. Examples include JCL, REXX, shell scripting, Perl, and PHP.

And finally, a new type of language is emerging. It goes by the name of either *low-code* or *no-code*. As the names indicate, the language is extremely easy and involves a LEGO-like approach, such as with templates and drag-and-drop.

Low-code and no-code languages are focused primarily on enterprise environments. They provide a nice balance between custom coding and out-of-the-box solutions.

We'll start with a discussion about assembler and then move into discussions of other languages.

Assembler Language

In the early days of computers, developers used *machine language*. This meant stitching together long lines of 0s and 1s. No doubt, this was extremely complicated and prone to errors. Creating even the simplest applications took a long time.

To help improve things, programs were created with *hexadecimal code*, which uses a numbering system that is much more compact. Yet it was still tough to use.

So yes, another evolution of computer languages occurred, and the result was the introduction of *assembler language*. It uses more understandable commands like IN, MOV, ADD, and so on.

True, it is still complex and requires deft programming skills. But assembler language did wind up becoming a staple in mainframe development.

But there are some things to note. For example, assembler language often varies from one platform to the next. The language is highly tuned to a particular machine. So if you take a course or buy a book for the assembler version for the Raspberry Pi or x86, it will have many differences from a mainframe.

Let's take a look at the process of an assembler language program (Figure 7-1).

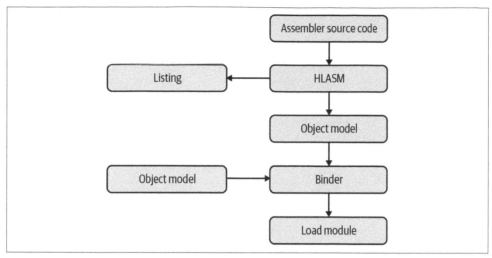

Figure 7-1. The general process for creating a program in assembler

First you write the assembler language source code and do some basic debugging. Then the compilation process includes a myriad of steps. The code is sent to the High-Level Assembler (HLASM), which produces a listing of the 0s and 1s, and this is moved over to the Object module. After this, the binder will see if there are any other object modules to combine. The final file is called the *load module*, or the *executable*. You can then run this program on the mainframe system.

Memory

Assembler language involves manipulating the memory of a machine. Thus, you need to know how it works.

The most basic unit of memory is the *bit*, which is short for *binary digit*. Think of it as the atom of a computer system.

The bit can store either 0 or 1, and 8 bits constitute a byte. But interestingly enough, the IBM mainframe has a hidden ninth bit to help with parity checking (this process checks that data transmission is accurate). But it is fine just to focus on 8 bits per byte. After all, a programmer cannot use the ninth bit.

The number of combinations of 0s and 1s available for a byte is 256. This is calculated as 2 × 8. Table 7-1 shows a few examples of the combinations.

Table 7-1. Conversion of binary to decimal

Binary	Decimal
00000000	0
00000001	1

Binary	Decimal
00000010	2
00000011	3
00000100	4

How do we convert binary to decimal? You multiply the binary number by 2 to the power of the position of the binary number. Then you sum all of them.

A little confusing? To clarify things, let's consider an example. Suppose we have the binary number 01101100. The conversion would be as follows:

$$(0 \times 2^7) + (1 \times 2^6) + (1 \times 2^5) + (0 \times 2^4) + (1 \times 2^3) + (1 \times 2^2) + (0 \times 2^1) + (0 \times 2^0) = 108$$

Converting a binary number to decimal or vice versa is tedious. But you can use an online calculator (*https://oreil.ly/jOJmu*).

For the IBM mainframe, EBCDIC is a system that assigns a binary number to a character. Table 7-2 shows some examples.

Table 7-2. Conversion of binary to decimal

Binary	Character
11000001	A
01101011	,
01100001	/
01100000	-
01001110	+

You can use an online conversion calculator for EBCDIC (*https://oreil.ly/8H83r*).

Keep in mind that a byte can be divided into two equal sections (each is called either a *nibble* or *nybble*). The first one, which has bits from 0 to 3, is the high-order nibble, and the other one is the low-order nibble. The combined number is known as an *address*, which is used to access memory.

The bytes can then be linked together in *fields*. A *halfword* is a two-byte field. And yes, there is a *fullword*, and this has a 4-byte field. What about one for 8 bytes? This is called a *doubleword*.

For an IBM mainframe, though, the memory addressing system can get tricky. The original machines, like the System/360, were based on 24 bits. This means that it could address a total of 16 megabytes of memory. Over the decades, this has increased to 64 bits, so a modern IBM mainframe can address up to 16 exabytes (1 exabyte is 1 billion gigabytes).

However, the *above and below line* is at 16 GB. Because the early mainframes had 24 bits for addresses, some older programs can operate only in this region.

Registers

A *register* can serve several purposes with the hardware CPU. For example, it can allow for high-speed math, access to the OS, and the addressing of memory. Each register is numbered from 0 to 15, which is to indicate the type of instruction.

The IBM Z mainframe has the following registers:

General purpose registers (GPRs)
> For math instructions, logical operators, the calling of subroutines, and the passing of operands.

Access registers (ARs)
> Identify an address or data space. This can help with providing more virtual storage.

Floating point registers (FPRs)
> Used for instructions that have floating-point numbers (they are 64-bits in length), in either binary or hexadecimal. If you want to use decimal, the math is done with GPRs. Also, floating-point numbers are usually large and are for scientific calculations. These are not widely used for business purposes.

Control registers (CRs)
> Used to control the processor operations, although CRs are not available for a developer.

Program status word (PSW)
> Shows the status of the processing. Flags indicate what the processor is doing when instructions are being executed and the next instruction that will be executed.

The one you will likely spend time on is the GPR.

> On the IBM Z mainframe, the data and programs share the same memory. Therefore, data can be executed like an instruction, and a program can be handled like data.

Base Displacement Addressing

Addressing is the process of specifying the location of a byte in memory. This is critical for assembler language because, for many instructions, you need to know the locations of the fields.

For the IBM mainframe, you use the addressing for the GPR, which has 64 bits. Yet there may be different modes. The addressing could actually use 24 bits or 31 bits. This is because the IBM mainframe has backward compatibility.

To deal with this, the machine will truncate the values of the register. If you have a 24-bit address, the leftmost 40 bits will be set to 0s. And for 31-bit addressing, this will be 33 bits. This is also the common mode for assembler programming.

A typical way of handling this is with *base displacement addressing*, which uses the address in the object code (this is what the compiler creates). The address has two bytes, and the first four bits are the base register, and the remaining are the displacement. Note that the displacement ranges from 0 to 4,095.

But with 16 bits, how can we address a large mainframe system? The 16 bits will represent a pointer to a larger address in memory. Figure 7-2 provides a visual.

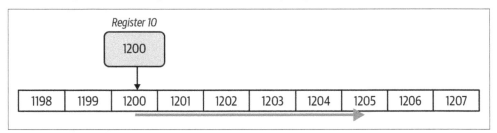

Figure 7-2. The workflow for base displacement addressing

Suppose our address is the hexadecimal of A005. The A is the value of 10, which is for the register. The 005 is the value of the displacement, which moves the execution of the program from memory location 1200 to 1205. In other words, the address is 1205.

A benefit of this approach is that you do not have to change A005 in the code. Instead, you can change the value of register 10.

And there is another advantage. The base displacement addressing makes the linkage processing easier for the compilation.

In terms of coding in assembler language, you would use something like D(B). The B would be the base register, and the D would be the displacement.

Sample Assembler Language Code

The original IBM System/360 had about 140 instructions. But over the decades, this has increased to over 1,200. This has certainly added to the complexity of assembler language. However, many developers will focus on a small subset of the instructions. In fact, many developers will not even have permission to use them.

Let's take a look at assembler code, which shows how to do a simple loop:

```
              LA    R4,10
LOOPIT        WTO   'Hi'
              BCT   R4,LOOPIT
```

The LA is the load address instruction. The first number is the base register, and the second is the displacement value.

Next, we have a header for the loop, which is LOOPIT, and the WTO (write to operator) instruction will print out *Hi*. The BCT instruction, which is short for *branch on count*, is the counter for the loop. It knows where to start since we have indicated the register, which is 10, and this will then be decremented by one. If it is not at the end of the loop, the program will go back to LOOPIT.

As you can see, this is quite compact but also tedious. The coding is much more detailed when compared to most languages.

Why go through all this effort? What are the advantages? First of all, assembler is extremely fast (this is why games are often developed in this language). What's more, at times you may need to manipulate the system on a byte level. This is the case when you need to utilize special areas of a mainframe.

This concludes the introduction to assembler. Next, we'll take a look at a more modern language for the mainframe, Java.

Java

Launched in the mid-1990s, *Java* became a must-have language for the fast-growing internet market. It was based on modern principles, such as object-oriented programming, and allowed for servlets. These provided for web-based programs that run on a server, not the browser.

But perhaps the biggest advantage for Java is its cross-platform capabilities arising from its underlying compiler architecture. Note that a different platform, called a Java Virtual Machine (JVM), is used for each system.

Yet this is not to imply that Java is an interpreted language like BASIC, in which a program translates the source code into machine language as it is run. Rather, Java is compiled into byte code, and then this is run on the JVM.

In theory, you can "write once and run anywhere." But of course, the reality is not as tidy. Compatibility issues still exist, especially when it comes to lower-level applications like graphical interfaces. The compatibility can definitely vary.

Regardless, Java has proven to be versatile and powerful. In fact, IBM has been a long-term supporter of the language and has built its own services for the z/OS. For example, it supports all the Java APIs, and custom ones exist for the unique filesystems on the mainframe. The Java Native Interface (JNI), which is part of the Java Development Kits, enables Java to interoperate with other languages like COBOL and PL/I. The technology is also available for 31-bit and 64-bit addressing.

Of course, Java is not without its drawbacks. The language is more complex than COBOL and other mainframe scripting languages like REXX. Java also has more than two thousand APIs, and they can be difficult to manage.

Despite all this, Java has remained one of the most popular languages for the mainframe. This is definitely the case for the purposes of migration. When a company wants to move legacy COBOL code to a cloud platform like Microsoft Azure, Google Cloud, or AWS, Java is usually the language of choice. It has strong enterprise and networking functions.

But this is not to imply the migration is easy. It is not. The process can be quite complex and require specialized software tools.

 Your employer will likely restrict you to certain languages. This may be for security purposes. After all, languages like Java can have powerful capabilities that can damage data.

C and C++

The *C language* is another widely used language for the mainframe. There are several reasons for this. First of all, it has roots in the Unix operating system, which is embedded on the mainframe. Next, the C language has been around for a long time and has many existing code sets that can be reused. C also has a rich set of features like exception handling, dynamic memory management, data structures, and so on. Finally, it can be used across many platforms (although it does not have the same level of compatibility as Java).

How does C differ from C++? The main difference is that C++ is an object-oriented language, whereas C is based on procedures and functions. In other words, if you are looking to create your own complex data structures or types, C++ is the better option. Also, C++ is less verbose and compact.

PL/I

In the 1960s, mainframe computers had two types of programming languages: FOR-TRAN and ALGOL for writing scientific applications, and COBOL for business programs. However, IBM wanted to develop something for both, and the result was *PL/I*. For the most part, it was meant to be a general-purpose language.

PL/I was quite sophisticated and had many modern features. Just some included bit string handling, recursion, exception handling, pointers, and linked data.

IBM had a variety of goals with PL/I. It needed strong compilation (the original compiler could work on only 64 KB of memory), had to support structured programming, and needed to work on different machines and operating systems.

The original name for PL/I was MultiPurpose Programming Language (MMPL). But IBM changed it in 1965. *PL* is for *Programming Language*, and the *I* is the Roman numeral for one. So you pronounce PL/I as "P L one."

In terms of coding with PL/I, it is structured the same way as COBOL. Therefore, you need to know the setup of columns on the screen:

Column 1
> This is reserved for the OS.

Columns 2–72
> This is where you put the PL/I statements. Unlike COBOL, this is free-form. There is no need to put the code into certain columns.

Columns 73–80
> This is where the OS puts the sequence numbers.

Now let's take a look at sample code:

```
ADDITION: PROCEDURE OPTIONS (MAIN);
   GET LIST(X,Y);
   THEOUTPUT = X + Y;
   PUT LIST(THEOUTPUT);
```

Each statement ends with a semicolon (;). Then when you start a program, you include its name and end it with a colon (:). The first procedure is always called OPTIONS(MAIN).

The GET LIST command gets the user input for the two variables X and Y and then adds them up for the variable THEOUTPUT. After this, we print out the result.

To run a program on a mainframe with PL/I, you need to create a JCL script. You use the same commands that we did when using COBOL code.

 PL/I is not used much anymore, and finding tutorial materials for the language can be tough. Despite this, a considerable amount of legacy code still exists. PL/I is most prevalent in Europe.

CLIST and REXX

Command List (CLIST, pronounced "sea list") is an interpreted language that allows for improving TSO. This means there is no need to go through the link-edit process for compilation. All you have to do is run the program, which means that the testing process is fairly quick.

CLIST programs tend to be focused on discrete tasks, such as creating a custom panel on ISPF, allocating for a dataset, or invoking a program from another language. Note that most of the code is a list of TSO commands. But basic programming structures like IF/THEN/ELSE statements and loops are also used.

While CLIST is still used today, the preference is often to use REXX instead. It's not clear why. In the world of languages, adoption is far from predictable.

IBM employee Mike Cowlishaw developed REXX as a side project during the early 1980s. He wanted to create a language that was easier than PL/I.

The result is a language that's similar to Python, as both are fairly easy to use but have powerful features. For example, REXX has extensive math functions and supports procedures, which allow for structured programming. In fact, REXX has only about two dozen instructions and more than 70 built-in functions. Note that REXX is not just for the IBM mainframe. It is also available on platforms like Linux, Windows, and macOS.

Here are some of the other important characteristics of the language:

- You do not have to enter the code statements in certain columns.
- The commands are not case sensitive.
- The variables are not typed. For example, a variable can be used to store a number or a string.
- There is a command to drop a variable. This takes it out of memory.
- There is no need to use JCL to run it.

- You can use REXX to create macros in z/OS.
- REXX provides for a double-byte character set (DBCS), which means that it can support national languages that have many unique characters or symbols (like Chinese or Japanese).

Here's a look at sample code:

```
/***************************/
/**********Rexx************/
/***************************/
SAY 'Enter a number'
PULL first_number
SAY 'Enter another number'
PULL second_number
SAY (first_number,second_number)
```

We use /* and */ for comments, and REXX needs to be specified. This is to indicate to z/OS that we are using the language.

The `PULL` command accepts user input, and we do this twice. Then we add the two inputs up using `ADD` and print out the result using `SAY`.

For the next few sections, we'll take a deeper look at the core elements of REXX because it is widely used in mainframe environments. And to try out the code, you can use the Coding Ground online REXX IDE (*https://oreil.ly/xsvRA*).

REXX Variables

All variables in REXX are strings. The language essentially handles all the management of the different types of data.

So what happens when there is a comparison, such as for an `IF/THEN/ELSE` statement? REXX will first see if the two variables have numbers only. If so, then the comparison is treated as a numeric. Any space and leading zeros are ignored.

But if the variables have any letters or special characters, a string comparison will occur, and this will be case sensitive.

Here are the rules for naming variables:

- A variable name can have letters, digits, and special characters like !, ?, . and _.
- A variable cannot start with a digit or a period.
- If a variable has a period, it is a compound variable and is used for such things as creating tables and arrays.

To assign a value to a variable, you simply use the equal sign. Here's an example: `my_name = 'Tom'`.

If you do not assign a value, the variable is uninitialized and will have the value NO_VALUE_YET. This is an example:

```
If number_value = 'NO_VALUE_YET'  then
    Say 'The variable has not been set.
```

Another nice feature of REXX is that you can easily manipulate hexadecimal and binary numbers. Here's a look:

```
Hex_value = 'CB5A4'x
Binary_value = '001101'b
```

REXX Comparisons

The comparison operators in REXX, which are in Table 7-3, are similar to those in typical languages. But some differences exist.

Table 7-3. Comparison operators for REXX

Comparison operator	Definition
=	Equal
\= ¬=	Not equal
>	Greater than
<	Less than
>= \< ¬<	Greater than or equal to
<= \> ¬>	Less than or equal to

The backslash (\) symbol is short for "not equal to." But what is this strange character, ¬? It also means "not equal to" but is for the mainframe. This symbol is mapped to the keyboard, and you will not find it on a PC.

To get a sense of how the comparison operators work, let's look at the examples in Table 7-4.

Table 7-4. Examples of comparison operators in REXX

Comparison statement	Result
'Jane' = ' Jane'	True
'Jane' \= ¬= ' jane'	False
'12' \> ¬> ' 54'	True

REXX provides for strict comparisons. This means that the leading and trailing spaces will not be ignored. To make this type of comparison, you double the comparison character. For example, an = will be ==, or a > will be >>. These are only for string comparisons.

You can make multiple comparisons by using & for *and* and | for *or*. Here are some examples:

```
if first_name = 'Jane' & last_name = 'Smith' then
        say 'Hi' || first_name || last_name
if first_number > 2 and second_number > 4 then
        say 'You meet the requirements.'
```

Note that in the first statement, we use the || to concatenate the strings.

Next, REXX has mathematical operators as shown in Table 7-5.

Table 7-5. Mathematical operators in REXX

Mathematical operators	Definition
+	Addition
-	Subtraction
*	Multiplication
/	Division
**	Exponent

You can use parentheses to manage the order of mathematical operations. This is no different from most languages. Here's an example:

```
say (9 / 2) + 4 + 2**2
```

Control Structures

We've already seen how to use IF/THEN/ELSE statements. But so far, we have looked at those that execute one statement. What if we want more?

This requires changing the code. You will have to use the do and end commands. This is how it works:

```
If variable_1 > 10 then do
   Say 'The number is greater than 10'
   Switch_value = 2
   end
else do
   say 'The number is not greater than 10'
   Switch_value = 3
end
```

REXX allows for nesting of IF/THEN/ELSE statements. But since the language is free-form, it does not matter where you line up the statements. In other words, you need to make sure that each of the IF/THEN/ELSE statements is in the right order.

Let's see an example of a nested structure:

```
Say "Enter your user name"
Pull user_name
Say "Enter your password"
Pull password

If user_name = "tom" then ❶
   If password = "t123" then ❷
      Say "Login successful"
   Else
      Say "Incorrect password"
Else
   Say "Incorrect user name"
```

❶ The first condition checks for whether the user_name is a match. If it is, the nested IF/THEN/ELSE will be executed.

❷ The nested IF/THEN/ELSE checks for a match for the password.

An IF/THEN/ELSE structure can be unwieldy when three or more conditionals are evaluated. An alternative is to use the SELECT statement. This is similar to the EVALUATE command in COBOL, which we covered in Chapter 5.

We'll use the same example, which is a selection of the different types of business entities available:

```
Say " Enter the business number "
Pull business_number
Select ❶
   When business_number = '1' then ❷
      Say 'Sole Proprietor'
   When business_number = '2' then
      Say 'Single-Member LLC'
   When business_number = '3' then
      Say 'S Corporation'
   When business_number = '4' then
      Say 'C-Corporation'
   When business_number = '5' then
      Say 'Partnership'
   When business_number = '4' then
      Say 'Trust/Estate'
   Otherwise ❸
      say 'The number does not exist'
End ❹
```

❶ We begin the evaluation of the different conditions for the business_number variable.

❷ The WHEN statement is used to see whether business_number is equal to a certain value. If it is, a message will be printed.

❸ If there is no matching value for `business_number`, this is the default condition.

❹ The `End` command is needed after all the conditions for the `Select`.

For a loop in REXX, you use the `Do` and `Do While` commands. Here's some code for the first one, in which we have a counter that goes from 1 to 5:

```
Counter = 1 ❶
Do  5 ❷
   Say Counter ❸
   Counter = Counter + 1
End
```

❶ Counter is set to 1.

❷ The `Do` command loops five times.

❸ This prints out the counter and then increments it by one. `End` is needed to terminate the loop.

Now let's go over how the `Do While` loop works. This code also has a counter from 1 to 5:

```
Counter = 1
Do While Counter <= 5
   Say Counter
   Counter = Counter + 1
End
```

Instead of setting a fixed number for the loops, we set a condition for when to terminate the program. This is when `Counter` is less than or equal to 5.

The `Do` loop also allows for more parameters. For example, you can set the increment, as shown here:

```
Do Counter = 1 to 10 by 2 ❶
   Say Counter
End
```

❶ This counts to 10 but in increments of 2.

Calling Functions

REXX allows for calling functions from within your code, for built-in functions and those that are available from external code. If you're using external code, the function can be written in any language so long as the correct interface is used for the data.

For REXX, a function returns a value, and a subroutine does not. And for both, you use the Call command:

```
Say "Enter the first number"
Pull First_number
Say "Enter the second number"
Pull Second_number
Call MultiplyNumbers first_number, second_number ❶
Exit ❷
MultiplyNumbers: ❸
PARSE ARG a,b ❹
Say a * b ❺
```

❶ This invokes the MultiplyNumbers subroutine. It has two arguments, which are the first_number and second_number variables.

❷ You use Exit to terminate the program.

❸ This is the header for the subroutine.

❹ Parse takes the arguments and puts them into internal variables. In this case, they are a and b.

❺ The multiplication of the two numbers is printed out.

We can now make some adjustments to this code to make MultiplyNumbers into a function that returns a value:

```
Say "Enter the first number"
Pull first_number
Say "Enter the second number"
Pull second_number
Say MultiplyNumbers(first_number, second_number) ❶
Exit
MultiplyNumbers:
PARSE ARG a,b
Return a * b ❷
```

❶ We do not use the Call statement. Instead, we print out the result of the MultiplyNumbers function and put the arguments within parentheses.

❷ The Return statement takes the multiplication of the two numbers and then returns this to the function.

Arrays

The array capabilities in REXX are powerful. Consider that there are no limits on the number of dimensions. However, in terms of practical coding, it's probably best to limit arrays to no more than three dimensions.

REXX arrays do not have to contain values. It is OK to have empty positions or variables that are uninitialized.

Like traditional arrays, a REXX version is referred to with subscripts. However, the language does not have other features that can help with the management of data, such as lists and record structures.

The syntax for an array is to use one or more periods in the variable name. The first part of the name is called the *stem*, which ends with the first paragraph. Then one or more tails are separated by periods.

To initialize the values of an array, you set the value of the stem. For example, you can do the following:

```
Employee_numbers. = 0
First_name. = ''
```

Now here's a look at sample code using arrays:

```
First_name. = ''          ❶
First_name.0 = 'Jane'     ❷
First_name.1 = 'Joe'
First_name.2= 'Alice'
do  Counter = 0  to 2     ❸
    say  'Name: 'First_name.counter
end
```

❶ We initialize the array for `First_name`.

❷ The next three statements assign values of 0 to 2 to the array. This is done by creating a numerical subscript after the period.

❸ This loop uses `Counter` for the subscript, and the names will be printed out.

What if we set the loop to go to 3 instead? For a traditional array, an error would occur. But this is not how REXX works. It will instead print out the value for subscript 3, which is a null.

Keep in mind that REXX does not have a function that shows the maximum number of subscripts in an array. You need to create your own code to test for this, as shown here:

```
First_name. = ''
First_name.0 = 'Jane'
```

```
First_name.1 = 'Joe'
First_name.2= 'Alice'
do  Counter = 0  while first_name.Counter <> ''  ❶
   say  'Name: 'First_name.counter
end
```

❶ This counts from zero until `first_name.Counter` is equal to an item that has a null value.

This approach does have a limitation. It will terminate if the dataset has an empty value. So what to do? Perhaps the best approach is just to count out the number of items in the dataset and then set this to a variable for the condition.

 A typical language starts arrays with the subscript of 0. But this does not apply to REXX. In fact, you can use whatever value you want. Yet it is common for programmers to start with 0.

Object-Oriented COBOL

As we have seen, COBOL has major limitations. Some include the use of only global variables and the paragraphs for dividing the code into modules. The result is that managing and maintaining large programs became extremely complicated.

Because of this, the COBOL language adopted object-oriented capabilities during the 1990s (it was called *OO COBOL*). This has allowed for more modern approaches for programming and has made it easier to work with systems like Microsoft's .NET. OO COBOL has the typical features for an object-oriented language like inheritance, interfaces, abstraction, and polymorphism.

But despite this, this language has not caught on. Perhaps the main reason is that coders will instead use another language like C++ or Java.

Programming Techniques

The rest of this chapter covers these programming techniques:

- Copy members
- Subprograms

These help improve the speed of your coding and allow for more functionality.

Copy Member

As a COBOL programmer, you will notice that you use certain tasks and functions frequently. Of course, you can create a file of these routines and then copy and paste them when needed.

But COBOL does have a more sophisticated approach for this: the *copy member* or *copy book*. On an IBM mainframe, you can save source code as a member of a portioned dataset (called a *copy library*). This can save you lots of time.

To access a copy member in your COBOL application, you use the Copy command, which is easy to work with. The format is as follows:

```
COPY [the member name]
```

You also need to indicate the copy library in your JCL that runs your COBOL applications with a DD statement:

```
//SYS1     DD    DSN=USER1.DATA1,DISP=SHR  ❶
//SYS2     DD    DSN=USER1.DATA2,DISP=SHR
//SYSIN    DD    *
               COPY INDD=(SYS1),OUTDD=SYS2  ❷
               SELECT MEMBER=B
```

❶ SYS1 and SYS2 identify the datasets.

❷ The SYS1 dataset is copied to the SYS2 dataset.

Why is this better than copy and paste? One big reason is that the code is actually not copied over with the COPY command. There is instead a pointer to it. This means that you need to change the code only once. As for cut-and-paste, you would have to change all the instances, and this would certainly be time-consuming.

Moreover, when you use the COPY command, you do not see the code that it refers to. You see only the command.

Another advantage for the copy member is that it provides for more standardization. This can help improve productivity and reduce the time for debugging.

Copy members should have strong governance. If changes are made, it could adversely impact other programs. Copy members should also have detailed documentation so as to make the customization process easier.

Some of the typical areas for copy members include the following:

Record descriptions
> As we've seen in some of the examples in this book, this part of COBOL programming can be verbose. But record descriptions are often static. In fact, they are often the most common for copy members.

SELECT *statements*
> These provide access to external files, which can often be similar among many programs. And another popular area for copy members is the FD statements in the FILE SECTION.

You can add other capabilities to the COPY command, such as the REPLACING command. This can replace text and spaces in the source code. However, this command is not recommended. It can add more complexity and lead to more errors in the code.

You can use the COPY command in the PROCEDURE DIVISION. But this is not common because subprograms are usually more effective for this.

Subprograms

There is a big difference between a copy member and subprogram. A subprogram is already compiled, whereas you need to compile a copy member, which is done as part of the whole application. You then use the CALL command to invoke the subprogram, and you can use the USING command to include parameters.

This is some sample code:

```
CALL "TaxRate" INCOME-AMOUNT FILING-STATUS.
```

This accesses a program called TaxRate and then uses two parameters for the tax calculation. A critical part of this is making sure you use the right sequence for the parameters. If not, you will likely get the wrong results or even an error.

The PIC definitions for the parameters also need to match those for the subprogram. You might be able to find the definitions from the code. But in many cases, it may be in another language. In this case, you need to rely on the documentation.

The program that calls the subprogram and the subprogram itself need to have their object modules linked. This puts them into a load module that can be executed on the mainframe. For this to work, you need to make the connection in the JCL. Here's an example of the DD statements for this:

```
//LINK.SYSLIB        DD
//                             DD DSN=USER1.PROG.OBJLIB,DISP=SHR ❶
```

❶ USER1.PROG.OBJLIB is the library that contains the subprogram.

Some of the usual subprogram use cases include the following:

- Error and exception handling
- Calculations, such as for finance
- Edit routines
- Handling of formatting—say, for currencies
- The processing of totals for columns

Besides improved speed and productivity, subprograms provide other advantages. One is that a programmer can specialize in certain areas. Given the difficulties of attracting technical talent, this is extremely important.

Next, a subprogram can be written in a myriad of languages. This means you can take better advantage of the core capabilities of the mainframe. Granted, subprograms also have drawbacks. If an error occurs, it can be difficult to root out. Is it in the calling program or the subprogram? Answering this question can take a lot of time. This is why it is important to have stringent testing for subprograms. If an error occurs, it will probably be an issue with the connection with the calling program.

Another best practice is for the subprogram to focus on one function. This can help reduce the potential for errors and integration problems.

 When you start a mainframe coding project, a good first step is to see what subprograms are available. And if there are none, the project could be a good prospect for creating one.

Conclusion

A common misperception about mainframe programming is that it is mostly about IBM COBOL. True, this language is critically important, and you need to have a good understanding of it. But the mainframe environment allows for many other languages.

In this chapter, we have taken a look at the main ones. The first one is assembler, which came before COBOL. This low-level language has deeper connections to the byte level of the mainframe. The language can also create fast applications.

But assembler is not easy to learn. The instruction set is cryptic, and you need to have a strong understanding of the core capabilities, memory, and registers of a mainframe.

Another popular language for the mainframe is Java. It is based on object-oriented principles and is generally portable from one system to another. Often when companies look to migrate their mainframe applications from COBOL, they will use Java. It certainly helps that the language works well with the internet.

The IBM mainframe also has strong Java capabilities, including access to all the APIs. It also has special integration with other languages, like COBOL and PL/I.

In this chapter, we took a brief look at C and C++. These languages are often used as modules that are called in from a COBOL program. They have the advantage of many available applications and integration with the Unix platform.

Then we covered PL/I. Although this general-purpose language isn't used as much, a large amount of legacy code remains in mainframe environments.

Next, the mainframe has scripting languages like CLIST and REXX. We took a much deeper look at the latter. REXX has proven to be effective in creating programs that can automate mainframe functions like the creation of datasets.

The last part of the chapter covered techniques to speed up mainframe development. The two main approaches we looked at are the copy member and subprograms. They allow for reusing existing code, which can speed up the development process.

In the following chapter, we will look at how to use databases in a mainframe environment.

CHAPTER 8

Databases and Transaction Managers

The worldwide database software market is enormous. According to research from ReportLinker, the spending was over $142 billion in 2020 (*https://oreil.ly/IFPLK*). Of course, the major players include companies like Oracle, SAP, and Microsoft. But Amazon has become a major factor in the market, and a variety of startups, such as MongoDB, Couchbase, and Trino, have been quickly gaining traction.

Since the early days of mainframe computers, the database has been critical. Businesses need efficient ways to store huge amounts of data on customers, inventory, payroll, and so on. In fact, databases have been essential for economic growth since there is less need for paper-based files.

But until recently, the innovation in the industry has been generally slow. The rise of AI and analytics has created a surge in demand for new types of databases, such as NoSQL platforms.

In this chapter, we'll take a look at the two traditional databases for the mainframe: IMS and Db2. We'll also look at transaction systems, such as CICS, which handle huge amounts of data in near real time.

Information Management System

The origins of IBM's *Information Management System* (IMS) go back to the mid-1960s. The development of this database was spurred by the Apollo space program, which needed to create a system that could manage the accounting for the construction of space modules, which each had over two million parts.

IBM joined a team of other companies, which included North American Rockwell and Caterpillar. They would launch the first version of IMS in 1967. But IBM saw that

163

the technology was more than just about the space program. Instead, the company saw that IMS would be a successful commercial product.

The marketing motto for the application was "The world depends on it." And this was not typical tech hype. IMS quickly became a standard in the corporate world. Even today, the database is widely used among Fortune 500 companies. IMS processes more than 50 billion transactions per day (*https://oreil.ly/s8Gst*).

Before IMS, a mainframe application would meld the coding and data into one. But this proved to be unwieldy because of duplicate data and the lack of reusability. A key innovation for IMS was to separate both of these parts. This was accomplished through the development of the Data Language/Interface (DL/I), which is what an application uses to access and manipulate the data. This technology is still in use today in IMS.

This database is essentially three products, illustrated in Figure 8-1.

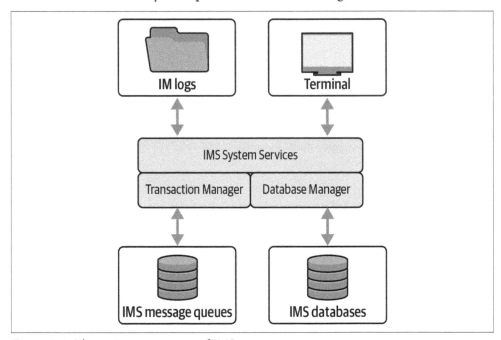

Figure 8-1. The main components of IMS

The IMS Database Manager handles the core database functions, such as storing and retrieving the information. The IMS Transaction Manager is an online system that processes large amounts of transactional data from terminals and devices. This is handled by using a system based on queues. IMS Systems Services coordinates the transactions and provides a log.

In the next sections, we'll take a closer look at the IMS Database Manager and the IMS Transaction Manager.

IMS Database Manager

The *IMS Database Manager* is known as a hierarchical database. It has different levels of data, which go from more general to more specific.

For example, suppose you want to put together a hierarchical database for the departments in a company. Figure 8-2 shows a simple design.

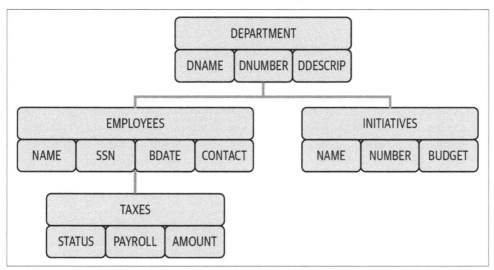

Figure 8-2. An example of a hierarchical database

At the top of this chart is the *root segment*, which provides the general information for the department. Only one root segment is allowed per database record.

After this, all other segments are called *dependent segments*. However, there are different levels. In our example, the EMPLOYEES segment is the child segment for the DEPARTMENT segment and the parent to the TAXES segment. The INITIATIVES segment is only the parent segment to the DEPARTMENT segment. INITIATIVES has no dependent segment.

Each segment has fields. DEPARTMENT has three fields: DNAME (the name of the department), DNUMBER (the unique number for the department), and DDESCRIP (the description of the department). In other words, this is where the data resides.

It's true that hierarchical databases can be complicated to set up. Another issue is that it is difficult to make changes after the initial structure is created. This is because remapping of the relationships is then required, and this can be time-consuming.

Then why use a hierarchical database? Perhaps the biggest reason is that it is fast. Keep in mind that IMS is the only database environment that can run over 117,000 database update transactions per second.

One of the main reasons for the speed is that relationships don't need to be created, because they already exist by the nature of the hierarchy. As a result, no extra processing is needed.

Speed is certainly important when it comes to handling large numbers of simultaneous instructions from disparate sources. IMS also has the benefits of a long history of reliability, security, scalability, less use of disk space and CPU power, and a relatively low cost per transaction.

The IMS Database Manager has a myriad of types of databases, such as the following:

Full-function databases
> You access the data with DL/I calls, in which you can query, replace, delete, or add segments to the database. This system can use approaches including message processing, batch message processing, and Java message processing. Primary and secondary indexes help speed up the operations. Data is stored in the VSAM format. A variety of access methods can be employed, with hierarchical direct access method (HDAM) and hierarchical indexed direct access method (HIDAM) being the most widely used.

Fast path databases
> These are for workloads that require high rates of transaction speed. This type of database has different flavors, such as data entry databases (DEDBs), which provide for more efficient storage and strong availability, and main storage databases (MSDBs), which are good with frequently used data. A fast path database also does not have any secondary indexes.

High availability large databases (HALDBs)
> IBM developed this for improved availability as well as for managing huge amounts of data. A HALDB can store over 40 terabytes of data.

Note that IMS data is stored only once. This means there is a high degree of efficiency for the database. Data integrity is another key factor. Even when an IMS database is not running, the data will remain consistent. Finally, the IMS database has its own systems to allow for backups and recoveries.

 Using XML with an IMS database is seamless. Because both rely on a hierarchical approach, IMS can be much easier when it comes to working with API calls.

IMS Transaction Manager

The *IMS Transaction Manager* is a comprehensive platform for handling large numbers of transactions. This system is integrated not only with IMS but also with the Db2 database. Three main types of actions are available:

Transactions
> This is the most common form. It is incoming data from an external source, such as a point-of-sale system, ATM, credit card device, website, or mobile app. If the transaction comes from an application, it is called a *program switch*.

Commands
> These are messages that come from system channels. Examples include TSO, z/OS, Zowe, or a user terminal. Commands are used to help with the management of the IMS platform.

Message switch
> These are transactions sent between two or more machines.

IMS operates on the z/OS subsystem and accesses some of the address spaces. This allows for much higher speeds and security. The address spaces are often called *regions*, and they include the following:

IMS control region
> Think of this as the "brain" of the system. This region handles the managing and scheduling of the transactions and messages, provides for the allocation of data to the users, and keeps track of the activity logs. You can invoke this through the START command in z/OS. The messaging is also for the Db2 database.

IMS environments
> This involves a variety of hardware and software configurations, depending on what needs to be done. For example, you might set up the environment to have the IMS Transaction Manager and the IMS Database Manager. Or you could just have one of these. You can also specify certain functions, such as for batch processing.

IMS separate address spaces
> These can activate services for recovery control, batch processing, and so on.

Message processing region
> This is to handle the processing of transactions in real time.

Java processing region
> This allows Java apps to use special processing messages.

IMS fast path
> This is for messages that require higher priority.

It's not uncommon for an organization to have multiple IMS Transaction Managers. In addition, data may come from a myriad of sources like CICS, MQ, and WebSphere Application Server. Of course, this can create lots of complexity in the management of transactions. A sophisticated message queue system is used to deal with this.

Another important benefit for the IMS Transaction Manager is that it is part of an integrated system. There is no need to switch between different LPARs or systems. All in all, this can be key for better performance and productivity.

IMS Services and Tools

While it's true that IMS can be operated on only the z/OS system, this is not much of a problem. IBM has made the technology extensible so that other platforms like Linux, z/VM, and z/VSE can call that database or initiate transactions. One common way to do this is through Java Database Connectivity (JDBC). It's even possible to make a connection via TCP/IP. On the other hand, IMS can make calls to external systems, which is a process called *call out*.

Over the years, IBM has developed a wide array of tools that work with IMS. Here are some:

IBM Z Application Performance Management Connect
This is a connector for transaction tracking.

IBM Z Service Automation Suite
This automates hardware and software resources in a sysplex, which is a clustering technology that provides for high levels of availability.

IMS Database Solution Pack for z/OS
This helps with the management of full-function databases and provides for 24/7 availability. It also helps reduce the impact of database reorganization.

IMS Cloning Tool for z/OS
This simplifies the cloning process for IMS subsystems and databases, resulting in lower costs and less downtime.

IBM Security Guardium Data Encryption
This is a sophisticated encryption system for databases like IMS but also for files and applications. It has tokenization, data masking, and key management. The system complies with a myriad of laws, including the General Data Protection Regulation (GDPR), the Health Insurance Portability and Accountability Act (HIPAA), and the Payment Card Industry Data Security Standard (PCI DSS).

Another important system for IMS is the IMS Enterprise Suite. This has a modern user interface and provides a wide assortment of tools. All IMS customers get this software for free. Some of its main features are as follows:

IMS Explorer for Development

This is a development environment that is based on the Eclipse framework. You can easily display and edit databases, segments, and fields.

IMS Data Provider for Microsoft .NET

Many database professionals do not know the proprietary language for IMS databases. But with this tool, you can use Structured Query Language (SQL) for queries. This has certainly been a key feature and has allowed for much broader use of IMS. This tool also provides for development in .NET languages like C# and Visual Basic.

IMS SOAP Gateway

The SOAP gateway server connects external web services and IMS applications. With this tool, there is no need to make changes to the existing business logic in the code.

IMS Connect API for Java

The simplifies application development using Java on z/OS, Linux, and Windows.

Besides IBM tools and systems, many offerings are available from independent software developers. For example, BMC AMI Data is like a self-driving system for managing IMS databases. To do this, it leverages the power of AI and machine learning (ML). Some of its benefits include higher availability, better backup and recovery options, and agility for development with teams.

This type of automation is becoming much more important because it is getting tougher for companies to hire IMS database administrators and systems programmers. According to a BMC blog post (*https://oreil.ly/00Oc0*), BMC AMI Data is "like having a modern mainframe data scientist at hand to keep your data accurate, organized, and backed up so it's always available to the right people at the right time. For newer DBAs, it's the ultimate in mentorship and professional development, helping them add value like seasoned pros right from the start."

A customer that has used this tool is PT Bank Central Asia Tbk (BCA), the largest commercial bank in Indonesia. The company wanted to modernize its IT infrastructure, but the IMS databases were difficult to reorganize because of the downtime—having even a few minutes of downtime was too much because of the adverse impact on customers.

The bank selected BMC AMI Data (*https://oreil.ly/u9vcU*) because it allowed for zero downtime. The process to copy the IMS databases while still capturing updates was seamless.

Here are some examples of third-party IMS tools from other vendors:

Broadcom Database Management Solutions for IMS for z/OS
This system helps optimize database performance, such as with faster data retrieval, lower backup and recovery times, more data availability, conservation of CPU resources, and quicker creation and rebuilding of indexes.

CONNX DB Adapter for IMS
This provides for seamless joins with databases by using connectors like JDBC, ODBC, .NET, and OLE DB. This tool can create a single metadata model that can span all enterprise data sources and applications.

DataVantage for IMS
This tool protects personally identifiable information (PII) and private company data. This is done by using a sophisticated masking process in IMS.

IMS Programming Language

As mentioned earlier in this book, IMS has its own programming language and can support various others. This allows for much better processing of the incoming and outgoing messages and transactions with the databases as well as the queries, sorts, and so on.

Figure 8-3 illustrates the workflow.

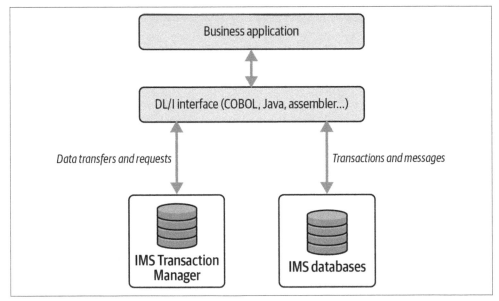

Figure 8-3. The workflow of the IMS system and languages

The DL/I interface is the language you use to access the IMS databases and connect to the communications system. Each language has its own version of code. For example, it's `CBLTDLI` for COBOL. Table 8-1 shows the codes for other languages.

Table 8-1. The DL/I codes for other languages

DL/I code	Language
ASMTDLI	Assembler
PLITDLI	PL/I
PASTDLI	Pascal
CTDLI	C

Let's see how we can create some code for an IMS database by using COBOL. This is a look at the `WORKING-STORAGE SECTION` of the `DATA DIVISION`:

```
DATA DIVISION.
WORKING-STORAGE SECTION.
01 DLI-FUNCTIONS.
   05 DLI-GU      PIC X(4)    VALUE 'GU  '.
   05 DLI-GN      PIC X(4)    VALUE 'GN  '.
   05 DLI-GHN     PIC X(4)    VALUE 'GHN '.
   05 DLI-GHU     PIC X(4)    VALUE 'GHU '.
   05 DLI-GNP     PIC X(4)    VALUE 'GNP '.
   05 DLI-REPL    PIC X(4)    VALUE 'REPL'.
   05 DLI-GHNP    PIC X(4)    VALUE 'GHNP'.
   05 DLI-ISRT    PIC X(4)    VALUE 'ISRT'.
   05 DLI-DLET    PIC X(4)    VALUE 'DLET'.
   05 DLI-PCB     PIC X(4)    VALUE 'PCB '.
   05 DLI-CHKP    PIC X(4)    VALUE 'CHKP'.
   05 DLI-XRST    PIC X(4)    VALUE 'XRST'.
   05 DLI-XRST    PIC X(4)    VALUE 'ROLL'.
01 IMS-PARAMS.
   05 TWO         PIC S9(9) COMP VALUE +2.
   05 THREE       PIC S9(9) COMP VALUE +3.
```

The preceding example lists the codes for IMS calls. We use `PIC X(4)`, as each code has four characters. Inputting this information is usually a matter of cut-and-paste, as they are standard codes. We won't cover all of them, but here are samples:

ISRT *(insert)*

   For loading a database and adding one or more segments

DLET *(delete)*

   For deleting a segment and any of the dependencies

GU *(get unique)*

   For getting segments in a database and setting a starting position for sequential processing

In this code section, we also set variables that specify the number of parameters for the IMS call. We use this in the PROCEDURE DIVISION.

Next, we need to create data items in the LINKAGE SECTION:

```
LINKAGE SECTION.
01  DB-PCB-MASK.
    05 DB-NAME              PIC X(8).
    05 SEGMENT-LEVEL        PIC XX.
    05 STATUS-CODE          PIC XX.
    05 PROC-OPTIONS         PIC X(4).
    05 FILLER              PIC S9(5) COMP.
    05 SEGMENT-NAME         PIC X(8).
    05 KEY-LENGTH           PIC S9(5) COMP.
    05 NUM-SENSEGS          PIC S9(5) COMP.
    05 DB-KEY-AREA.
       10  CUSTOMER-KEY     PIC X(4).
       10  CUSTOMER-DB-KEY  PIC X(8).
```

In IMS, the program communication block (PCB) provides a view of the database. In our COBOL code, we have created a mask for this. It has the parameters of the database, such as the name, the segment level, the segment name, and the keys.

However, the status code is often the most critical. This two-character alphanumeric shows the outcome of the database call. You can use status codes in the COBOL code to test for conditions like whether the program has reached the end of the database, or a segment was not found, or a segment already exists—just to name a few.

Next, here's the code for the PROCEDURE DIVISION:

```
ENTRY 'DLITCBL' USING DB-PCB-MASK.  ❶
CALL  'CBLTDLI' USING TWO ❷
      DB-PCB-MASK.
GOBACK.
```

❶ The ENTRY statement must refer to the PCB mask.

❷ We specify two parameters.

 IMS 15 is the latest version of the database. A key part of this new system allows for cloud-computing capabilities as well as access to DevOps tools and Zowe. Enhancements for the use of Java have also been added.

Db2 and the Relational Database

In 1983, IBM launched its Db2 database. The strategy was to have different versions for its different operating systems. But by the 1990s, IBM made Db2 into a common code base for Linux, Unix, and Windows. Yet there was still a different version for z/OS.

Db2 was a major development in the market because it was a relational database. Before this, databases comprised flat files or were based on models like hierarchical relationships. But these systems could be complicated and difficult to change.

It was an IBM researcher, Edgar F. Codd, who came up with the original theoretical foundations for the relational database and SQL in 1970. But interestingly enough, the company was initially resistant. One reason was a perception that a relational database would not scale for enterprise environments. Another reason was that IBM did not want to disrupt its existing products.

However, Silicon Valley software developer Larry Ellison read Codd's papers and saw the huge potential for relational databases. He went on to create Oracle in 1977. Ellison would be critical in making relational databases a massive business and a standard for businesses.

Despite this, IBM would continue to innovate Db2, which has also become a major business. In the 1990s, the company made it possible for this database to store multimedia data as well as to access web documents. Since then, upgrades to the performance, security, and reliability of the platform have been ongoing.

How does a relational database work? The data is stored in different tables and linked together to form relationships. A table has two dimensions, columns and rows. Figure 8-4 is an example of a table containing employee data.

EmployeeNo	FirstName	LastName	Address	City	State	Zip
10001	Jane	Thomson	123 Maple Ave	Irvine	CA	92602
10002	Fred	Smith	243 Green Street	Los Angeles	CA	90001
10003	Mary	Wang	349 Lemon Street	Irvine	CA	92602
10004	Larry	Hartford	200 California Street	Pasadena	CA	91001
10005	Zeek	McDonald	100 Mission Avenue	Los Angeles	CA	90001

Figure 8-4. A table in a relational database

This table has seven columns for the employee information and then five rows, which are records for individual employees. The conjunction of the column and row is called a *value*, or a *field*. For example, FirstName in row 3 has the value of Mary. A value can be alphanumeric, numeric, or null.

EmployeeNo is a unique number for each employee. Because of this, it is used as the primary key. This allows for searching, updating, and deleting of information. A relational database may also create an index for the primary key, which will help speed up operations. It is possible to create your own index.

With the keys, you can also create relationships with other tables. In our Employee table, for instance, we can make a connection to the Dependents table, shown in Figure 8-5.

FirstName	LastName	Relationship	EmployeeNo
Harry	Thomson	Husband	10001
Lisa	Thomson	Child	10001
Bill	Wang	Husband	10003
Lisa	Wang	Child	10003
Steven	Wang	Child	10003

Figure 8-5. A table for employees' dependents

The connection between the Employee table and the Dependents is with the field EmployeeNo. This is when one column—the *foreign key*—points to the primary key.

There are three types of table relationships:

One-to-many
> One primary key corresponds with one or more foreign keys in the other table. This is what we have for our example with the Employee and Dependents tables.

One-to-one
> Only one field connects the two tables. This is not used much, because you can convert the data into one table.

Many-to-many
> More than one field connects to a table with more than one field. This is also not used as much because the relationship can get complicated. Rather, you can create two one-to-many relationships for the tables.

Benefits of Relational Databases

While innovations have emerged in the database market during the past decade or so, the fact remains that relational databases remain quite durable. They definitely have many advantages, and this technology will likely remain a key part of enterprise environments for many years to come.

Let's take a look at some of the main advantages of relational databases:

Intuitiveness

The underlying concepts are straightforward and easy to understand. It is not difficult to structure databases—even for nontechnical people—and to use SQL to perform operations on the tables.

Structure

The core elements of a relational database, like tables, views, and indexes, are separated from the physical storage. As a result, renaming a database, for example, does not impact storage of the files. This means that a database administrator can focus on the management of the infrastructure, while a coder can spend time on the development of the databases.

Reports

With the ability to organize databases into tables and create relationships with SQL, it is possible to create sophisticated reports. It is also possible to do basic analytics.

Data integrity

Built-in systems ward against potential problems with a database. For instance, a primary key must be unique and not null so as to allow for accurate searches and functions on the data.

Recovery

In the event of a problem, backing up and restoring a database is seamless. These actions can be taken even when a database is in operation and handling transactions in real time.

Stored procedures

Managing databases involves many common tasks. A stored procedure can automate these and allow for more efficient operations.

Less redundancy

A well-structured relational database minimizes instances of duplicate data. Employing best practices is a big part of this, such as having a table handle data for one category. Another technique is normalization, which involves finding ways to make the tables and relationships clearer.

Commitment

It's common for a business process to have multiple steps, and if one is missing, none of the steps will be committed.

Concurrency

This system allows for simultaneous transactions with the database. It essentially permits the appropriate users to get access, and allows functions to be performed that are in accordance with policies.

Using Db2

You do not need to have a mainframe or pay a hefty fee to use the Db2 database. IBM has a free version called the IBM Db2 Community Edition, which has three options:

Db2 Docker Container

You can run the database in a container, which uses OS-level virtualization on your desktop. This means you can operate it in isolation from the applications on your system.

Db2 Standard Download

Available for Mac, Linux, and Windows systems, this is an executable that you can download and run on your computer. The Db2 instance has 16 GB of memory, and the database size is 100 GB.

IBM Db2 on Cloud

This is accessible from your web browser, and the database size is 200 MB.

For the purposes of this chapter, we'll take a look at the cloud version (*https://oreil.ly/ Z5hQq*). To try the service for free, you need to create an IBM ID and provide your credit card information. You will not be charged if you do not use the database extensively. Also, if you do not use the service for 30 days, your database will be deleted. To maintain the service, you need to extend it via email every 90 days.

When you log in, you will be taken to the dashboard for the IBM Cloud (Figure 8-6).

Figure 8-6. The dashboard for the IBM Cloud

Click Catalog at the top of the screen and then search for Db2. Select the first option to access the screen shown in Figure 8-7, where you will configure your database.

Figure 8-7. Configuring the new database

Select the Lite option, which is the free version, and then click the Create button. Your database will appear on your dashboard, under "Resource summary." If you click this, you will see Services and then the name of the database. You can click this and then select Console, which is where you can perform operations.

Next, choose Load Data. Here will you bring in a file for your table. It must be a CSV file, and each field needs to be separated by a comma. Also, at the top, you need a name for each of the fields. Table 8-2 shows an example.

Table 8-2. Data for a table

user_name	email	first_name	last_name	subscriber
jsmith	jsmith@gmail.com	John	Smith	1
lisa99	lisa99@yahoo.com	Lisa	Herndon	
harry45	harry49@gmail.com	Harry	Lindon	0

Note that this file can come from your computer or even from cloud object storage or Amazon Simple Storage Service (S3). After this, you will be asked to use an existing schema or create one. In Db2, a *schema* is a collection of tables. So we will create our own, which we will call `SocialNetwork`.

The next screen asks us to either use an existing table or create one. The system will then generate a table with the data and also come up with the data type for each field. Many data types are available in Db2. Here are some of the common ones:

TIMESTAMP
> Shows the current time, which is accurate to the microsecond.

DATE
> Shows the month, day, and year.

CHAR
> A string that has a fixed length. The length is specified in parentheses like CHAR (20), which allows for 20 characters.

BOOLEAN
> Is either true or false, which is represented as either 1 or 0.

VARCHAR
> A variable-length string. `VARCHAR (20)`, for example, indicates that 20 is the maximum length of the data type. It can be as long as 32,740 characters.

BLOB
> Holds a large amount of varying-length data.

Structured Query Language

Structured Query Language (SQL, pronounced *ess-que-el*) is a way to take actions with a database. It is a standard language, so you can use SQL with a myriad of databases other than Db2. Some systems have their own proprietary extensions.

Db2 uses these categories of SQL:

Data manipulation language (DML)
    For reading and modifying data

Data definition language (DDL)
    For defining a new database, making changes, or deleting it

Data control language (DCL)
    For granting and revoking permissions for the database

This chapter focuses on DML. The other categories are mostly for administrative purposes, not for developers.

One common SQL command is CREATE, which creates a new database table. As an example, we will create a table with data for customer invoices. Here's a sample of the data:

InvoiceNo
    The invoice number

CustomerNo
    The customer number

InvoiceDate
    The date of the invoice

Amount
    The outstanding amount owed on the invoice

Now let's put together the SQL statement for this:

```
CREATE TABLE CustomerInvoices (
InvoiceNo INT NOT NULL PRIMARY KEY,
CustomerNo INT,
InvoiceDate:  TIMESTAMP,
Amount:  MONEY
);
```

CREATE TABLE is the command to make the table. Then we specify the name of the table, which is CustomerInvoices. Next, we define the names of the columns and the data types. InvoiceNumber will be an INT and also the primary key. We indicate NOT NULL because there cannot be an empty value.

InvoiceDate uses TIMESTAMP for the current time and day. For Amount, we use the MONEY data type. This is for handling currency numbers.

With this new table, we can use a myriad of SQL commands. For example, we can use SELECT to retrieve data from the table:

```
SELECT * FROM CustomerInvoices
```

The asterisk (*) means that all the columns of the table will be captured and put into a result table. This is a temporary holder that allows for viewing the information or manipulating it within in application.

But we usually want to see a portion of the data, and we can do that by making qualifications to the SELECT statement:

```
SELECT * FROM CustomerInvoices WHERE Amount > 1000
```

This will bring in information only for those invoices in excess of $1,000. We can further limit the information by specifying the columns to include:

```
SELECT CustomerNo, InvoiceNo WHERE AMOUNT > 1000
```

With this, we will get the information for the customer and invoice numbers. This could then become the basis of a report that is created by using a COBOL program.

Another useful command is INSERT, which inserts a record in a table. Here is sample code:

```
INSERT INTO CustomerInvoices
    (InvoiceNo, CustomerNo, InvoiceDate, Amount)
VALUES (1100,3202,'2021-10-31 10:15:01', 300)
```

We start with the INSERT command for the CustomerInvoices table. Then we specify the names of the columns and provide the details for the row in the VALUES section.

Or we can update an existing record:

```
UPDATE CustomerInvoices SET InvoiceDate = '2021-10-31 10:15:01'
    WHERE InvoiceNo = 392
```

This changes the value of the InvoiceDate field for invoice number 392.

We can also use DELETE:

```
DELETE FROM CustomerInvoices
    WHERE InvoiceNo = 490
```

This deletes the record for invoice number 490.

Joins

In certain cases, you will want to combine the data from two tables based on a relationship. You can do this in SQL by using the JOIN command.

The most widely used version of this is known as an *inner join*, or *equi-join*. For example, suppose we have a table for vendors, called VendorList, that has Company Name, CompanyNumber, and CompanyAddress fields. An inventory table, called Parts, has `CompanyNumber`, `OrderNumber`, and `Amount` fields. We can use these with the following SQL statement:

```
SELECT VendorList.CompanyNumber, VendorList.CompanyName, Parts.CompanyNumber, ↵
Parts.PartNumber, Parts.OrderNumber
FROM VendorList
INNER JOIN Parts On VendorList.CompanyNumber = Parts.CompanyNumber
ORDER BY Parts.OrderNumber
```

This takes a subset of both tables. The result table will have only those records where the company number is the same in both tables (if there is no match, the result table will be empty). The results will also include data for the part number, order number, and company name. All in all, this would be the basis for a report.

In an *outer join*, the result table includes the records from the inner join but also rows where there are no matches.

Outer joins come in three flavors. A *left outer join* gets all the data from the first table but only the matching data in the other table. A *right outer join* does the opposite.

You can also have a *full join*. This brings in the data from both tables, regardless of whether any similarities exist among the fields.

Finally, when it comes to joins, you can use more than two tables.

Database Administrator

As a mainframe developer, your handling of the databases will likely be limited. Instead, this role will be mostly for the database administrator (DBA). Some of the typical duties include the following:

- Creating and managing the data definitions and the free space. Db2 has tools for this, such as the Administration Tool and Db2 Estimator.
- Helping test the systems, optimize the performance, and provide for the upgrades.
- Assisting with the backups and other jobs.
- Providing support to the developer for application development with the databases.
- Documenting root cause analysis (RCA).

Because databases often handle sensitive information, security requirements are onerous. It's not uncommon for a DBA to be limited to certain databases or functions.

Application Development with Db2

When you write a program that accesses a Db2 database, you will be using the SQL language. You can embed this by using a variety of languages, say with C, C++, Java, PL/I, COBOL, assembler, or REXX.

For this, two kinds of SQL statements are available. With *static* statements, you create the SQL in Db2 and then implement it in your code. There is no need to make any changes.

When using *dynamic* SQL, the structure will change. In fact, a mainframe has a program called SPUFI that is based on dynamic SQL. Essentially, you can run any SQL in your Db2 database.

How can you integrate a Db2 database in your code? This is done by using embedded SQL statements. It's common to use COBOL and have the statements in either the A or B margin. The SQL is then placed between the EXEC SQL and END-EXEC statements.

There are two kinds of embedded SQL. One is included in the WORKING-STORAGE SECTION of the DATA DIVISION and is called a *nonoperational* SQL statement. Here's an example:

```
EXEC SQL
    INCLUDE INVENTORY
END-EXEC.
```

This command brings in the INVENTORY table from the Db2 database. This is similar to the COPY command in COBOL.

The second SQL command helps with the management of tables:

```
EXEC SQL
        INCLUDE SQLCA
END-EXEC.
```

SQLCA is short for *SQL communication area*, an interface between the Db2 database and the COBOL program. It provides status codes about each SQL statement that is run. For these to work, you need to define them in the DATA DIVISION. Here's a sample:

```
01 SQLCA.
        05 SQLCABC          PIC S9(9) BINARY.
        05 SQLCODE          PIC S9(9) BINARY.
        05 SQLWARN.
                10 SQLWANR01        PIC X.
                20 SQLWARN02        PIC X.
```

You can then have an IF/THEN statement to test for these codes. For example, if SQLCODE returns 0, the SQL was successful. A positive number indicates a warning. A negative number indicates the SQL has an error.

```
EXEC SQL
DECLARE CUSTOMERCURSOR CURSOR FOR
           SELECT CUSTOMERNO, FIRSTNAME, LASTNAME, EMAIL
        FROM DB2002.CUSTOMER
        ORDER BY CUSTOMERNO DESC
END-EXEC.
```

The preceding SQL statement brings in the data from the customer file. However, since COBOL cannot read a database table, a cursor needs to be created. This is a visual pointer that allows for scrolling through the rows of data. To create one, you use DECLARE and then provide a name for it, which is CUSTOMERCURSOR. Then we specify CURSOR FOR, which will relate the SQL statement.

The next type of embedded SQL is called *operational* SQL. This SQL is included in the PROCEDURE DIVISION. Interestingly enough, the structure is similar to what we've seen when loading in a sequential file using COBOL.

The first step is something like the following:

```
EXEC SQL
        OPEN CUSTOMERTABLE
END-EXEC
```

This provides access to the Db2 database. But we now need to read the rows. To do this, we usually use a PERFORM loop and then end it when the end of the table is reached:

```
PERFORM 200-GET-DATA
        UNTIL SQLCODE NOT EQUAL TO ZERO.
...
200-GET-DATA.
EXEC SQL
            FETCH CUSTOMERTABLE INTO
            :CUSTOMERNO, :FIRSTNAME, :LASTNAME, :EMAIL
END-EXEC.
```

In this code, we use the SQLCODE variable to test when the loop will stop. Iteration of the 200-GET-DATA module follows. This uses the FETCH command to get data—one row at a time.

What about the colon in front of each field? These fields are known as *host variables*. This is a data item we have created in the DATA DIVISION of our COBOL program. It will essentially be mapped to the table. In other words, by doing this we bring the data into variables that we can use in the program.

Finally, we have to close the database connection by using the CLOSE command:

```
EXEC SQL
        CLOSE CUSTOMERTABLE
END-EXEC
```

After you finish writing your source code, the process for compiling the program will have some extra steps. They are usually handled on the Db2I panel or JCL (so long as DCLGEN, or declaration generator, is not involved). First of all, you may use DCLGEN. This mainframe utility maps the database columns to the data in a program, such as the DATA DIVISION of a COBOL program.

But you are not required to use DCLGEN. Then what would happen? You would need to do the mapping manually.

Next is the precompile stage. This is required because a mainframe compiler cannot process SQL. So with precompilation, the SQL is commented out and CALL and MOVE statements are created to connect with Db2.

Then there is the BIND stage. Here the mainframe system validates the SQL for the Db2 catalog. If no problems occur, a package is built that will have the best access path to your Db2 data.

The next step is for the compilation and link-edited process to create the executable load module. This will be like any other mainframe application.

Db2 Ecosystem

Like IMS, Db2 has an extensive ecosystem, with various conferences, user groups, and educational programs. IBM has also developed tools to help boost productivity:

IBM Data Server Manager
A set of management tools to make things simpler for the setup, use, monitoring, and management of Db2 databases.

IBM Db2 Advanced Recovery Feature
Even though Db2 has powerful data backup and recovery, this system adds even more layers of capability.

IBM Data Studio
An open source integration for Db2 for z/OS, db2 for i, IBM Informix, and Db2 Big SQL.

IBM Lift
A self-service system that provides for sending data over the internet from private, on-premises data sources.

IBM Db2 Augmented Data Explorer
A web-based platform that connects to Db2 databases, whether they are on premises or on the cloud.

A case study of one of these tools (*https://oreil.ly/6bw9f*), IBM Data Server Manager, was created by Nordea Bank. The firm is one of the largest financial services organizations in Europe's Nordic region and provides services to millions of customers. It has a sophisticated setup of Db2 databases that span operating systems and physical data centers.

When it came to tracking performance, the company used scripts. But this proved unwieldy, especially because of the need for updates. To help with this, Nordea Bank implemented IBM Data Server Manager. Information has been centralized, and transparency with the database has increased across the organization. The change has meant less downtime, stronger performance, and fewer tedious tasks for DBAs.

Third-party software companies also offer many Db2 tools and utilities. Here's a look at some of the top ones:

Broadcom's Database Management for Db2 for z/OS
This suite of software tools helps improve the service levels, data availability, and application performance of Db2 databases for z/OS.

Quest's Toad for IBM DB2
This helps automate routine administration tasks for Db2 databases. This is for both the cloud and on-premises systems.

BMC AMI Data
This helps with the accuracy, organization, and availability of data. The software has been shown to reduce data management costs by up to 65% or more.

BMC AMI SQL Performance for Db2
This can shift left the quality control of Db2 through a Jenkins plug-in to prevent SQL from violating company requirements.

An example of the use of one of these tools—BMC AMI SQL Performance for Db2—is for retailer Dillard's. The company's Db2 databases had difficulties handling real-time online and in-store sales, especially during the holidays and busy times. But with BMC's software, the company's staff was able to quickly identify poorly performing SQL. A 35% reduction in CPU utilization also helped lower costs. Dillard's used other software tools from BMC, like AMI Ops Monitor for Db2, AMI Ops Monitor for CICS, and AMI Apptune for Db2, to enhance the performance of the IT infrastructure.

Customer Information Control System

IBM began development of its *Customer Information Control System* (CICS) in 1966 and launched it in 1969. The project was similar to IBM's creation of the Sabre system for processing American Airlines reservations. CICS addressed the problems of batch processing by allowing for near real-time transactions.

The initial focus of this software was on the utility industry. But interestingly enough, IBM almost eliminated the CICS effort because there was much more interest in IMS. Key advocates in the company kept it going, as they saw that the system could be more than just for the utility industry.

These efforts proved to be spot on. CICS would go on to be one of the most successful software systems ever. It still processes huge numbers of transactions for banks, insurance companies, and other large enterprises.

 In the early days, CICS was bundled with IBM hardware. This became the first example of open source software. Programmers from companies such as Standard Oil of Indiana would contribute code to the platform.

Working with the CICS Platform

Currently, the CICS platform is quite robust. It supports a myriad of platforms like Multiple Virtual Storage (MVS), Enterprise Systems Architecture (ESA), Unix, OS/390, and of course, z/OS. Programmers can also use languages like COBOL, REXX, C, C++, Java, and PL/I to build applications for it.

CICS is similar to a subsystem, much like JES and IMS, as it does not have all the features of a standalone OS. It manages complicated tasks, controls user access and permissions, handles memory allocation, and provides for simultaneous access to data. However, the z/OS is still the final point of decision within the mainframe system.

It's common for an organization to run several instances of CICS. To manage this, z/OS will create address spaces, which are called *multiregion operations* (MROs).

Another critical part of CICS is its speed. It is incredibly fast. After all, if a customer is using an application to process a credit card, it's important that there be no delays. Even a few extra seconds can cause apprehension from customers.

Originally, CICS was used for processing input from terminals. But the technology has evolved to integrate other devices and interfaces. For example, CICS works seamlessly with smartphones and web services. If anything, the platform is quite unique in the technology world, in terms of its scale, speed, and capabilities.

When it comes to working with CICS, there are some terms to keep in mind, such as the following:

Transaction

> This is the data for one request to CICS. This is usually from a terminal but could be from the web or a smartphone. Regardless of the source, a transaction has a name or transaction identifier (`trans-id`) that's up to four characters long and is part of the program control table (PCT).

Task

> Any request for CICS initiates one or more tasks. These tasks help execute a transaction.

Unit of work or unit of recovery

> This is a complete operation that is recoverable. That is, CICS can commit it, or undo it if a major problem occurs.

In a CICS transaction workflow, a user logs on to the system and enters some data. For example, this could be information to inquire about the price of a ticket or the status of an insurance claim. These actions are the transactions.

CICS has applications to process the transactions, which are stored on a DASD. The system loads them when needed, so as to ensure enough storage for other operations.

Since many similar transactions often hit the system at the same time, CICS uses multithreading. Although there is one copy of the application, it is running various transactions simultaneously.

Programming in CICS

Because of the large numbers of incoming and outgoing transactions, programming in CICS requires a different approach than what is typical. After all, if you use traditional conversational programming, you will lose much efficiency and agility. When a user is at a terminal, a screen is presented and the application waits for a response. After information is input, a function is performed. While this will get the job done, resources are wasted due to the wait time.

A better approach is to use pseudo-conversational programming. When a program is launched, a screen is sent but no waiting is involved. The program ends instead. If a user inputs something, the program is restarted. By doing this, there is much less idle time with mainframe resources.

To build a CICS program, you also need to create the different screens for user input and output. This is done by using basic mapping support (BMS), which is based on assembler. Specific lines of code define the different maps. When you compile this, you get a physical mapset and a symbolic mapset. CICS uses the first one to draw the screen. The symbolic mapset is a copy member you insert into your COBOL program.

You use assembler macros to code the mapsets. These macros include the following:

DFHMSD
> Defines the mapset

DFHMDI
> Defines a particular map

DFHMDF
> Defines a field within a map

Let's look at an example of the DFHMSD macro:

```
INVPROG1      DFHMSD    TYPE=&SYSPARM, X  ❶
              LANG=COBOL,X  ❷
              MODE=INOUT,X  ❸
              TERM=3270-X, X  ❹
              STORAGE=AUTO,X  ❺
              MAPATTS=(COLOR,HILIGHT)  ❻
```

❶ The name of map is INVPROG1. This cannot be more than eight characters.

❷ We interface with this macro using a COBOL program.

❸ The map allows for both input and output.

❹ The macro is for a 3270 terminal.

❺ This provides for automatic storage capabilities.

❻ Color is supported on-screen.

For this program, there are three main parts, or visual columns. Columns 1 to 9 are for the names of the maps, columns 10 to 16 are for the macros used, columns 17 to 71 are for the parameters, and column 72 is used if there is a continuation character (this is indicated by X).

The CICS language has over 100 commands. But you usually need to use only a small portion, and they will be bracketed by EXEC CICS and END-EXEC. The commands are APIs that execute the services.

Here is some code to illustrate this:

```
EXEC CICS SEND
     MAP ('INVMAP01')
     MAPSET ('INVMAPS2')
     FROM (INVMAP02)
END-EXEC.
```

This takes the map, `INVMAP01`, that is stored in the `INVMAPS2` mapset and includes the data from `INVMAP02`. The screen is then displayed on the user's terminal.

And if a user enters information? You can use this code:

```
EXEC CICS RECEIVE
    MAP ('INVMAP01')
    MAPSET ('INVMAPS2')
    INTO (INVMAP02)
END-EXEC.
```

This just scratches the surface of what the CICS language can do. Some of its capabilities include authentication, diagnostics, file control, exception handling, monitoring, security, and web services.

When it comes to data management, CICS has two approaches. First of all, you use VSAM files for processing. The CICS commands allow for reading, updating, and browsing data.

Next, CICS provides seamless integration with Db2 databases. For this, you use `EXEC SQL`.

Conclusion

We started this chapter with one of the oldest databases: IMS. IBM created this to help with the Apollo space program, and the system proved quite versatile. IMS continues to be widely installed among large companies and powers huge numbers of transactions.

This system is really three products: a database for managing data, a transaction system to handle near-real-time requests and inquiries, and a services platform that helps with scheduling and keeping track of logs.

The IMS is a hierarchical database. Data is segmented into parts, from general to specific. The relationships are then implied by this structure.

It's true that hierarchical databases can be complicated and rigid. But their main advantage is speed of operations. This can be particularly important when using transaction systems.

In this chapter, we also took a look at the Db2 database, which is based on the relational model. Data is separated into tables, and relationships are created among them. This is done by using unique columns of data, called primary keys, that connect to foreign keys in other tables.

A relational database also uses the SQL language. This is fairly intuitive and allows for functions that insert, update, and delete data in tables. There are also sophisticated tasks like the joining of tables and the use of procedures.

A relational database has a myriad of advantages. It has less redundancy, built-in backup and recovery, and the ability to handle many concurrent users and systems, allowing for data integrity.

As for Db2, IBM has continued to innovate the platform—for example, with web features and integrations. The database is the most common within mainframe environments.

Finally, in this chapter we looked at CICS, a sophisticated system for managing transactions at scale. It is another platform that is widely used across mainframe environments. IBM has also continued to invest heavily in CICS, providing integrations and access to multiple platforms.

In the next chapter, we'll take a look at DevOps.

PART II

Modern Topics

CHAPTER 9

DevOps

DevOps is a combination of the words *development* (coders, front-end developers, and quality assurance) and *operations* (systems, network, and database administrators). Traditionally, these two teams have been siloed in organizations, and this has resulted in slower software development, less quality, and more errors. So the goals for DevOps are to allow for better communication, transparency, collaboration, and agility in the process.

But this usually takes time, and cultural resistance often arises, especially from larger organizations that rely on mainframe systems. Despite this, DevOps has become a growing trend and has shown standout results.

As should be no surprise, this category has undergone much evolution during the past decade. This is typical with any tech category, as dynamic change is ongoing. DevOps is a journey.

In this chapter, we'll take a look at the main concepts of DevOps as well as its various approaches. We will also look at the different automation tools to help with the DevOps process.

Advantages of DevOps

Perhaps the biggest trend in mainframe development is DevOps. The industry is in much need of rethinking its approaches, such as in terms of faster development. The traditional ways are essentially making it more difficult for organizations to compete against nimbler startups.

DevOps certainly has many advantages. Here's a look at some of the top ones:

Speed and quality

These two concepts may seem at odds with each other. But they are not. As shown by companies such as Amazon and Google, it is possible to quickly build high-quality software applications. But mindsets need to change. In the context of DevOps, a variety of approaches exist, like Agile. In fact, when it comes to mainframes, the benefits of speed and quality are perhaps the most important.

Innovation

This is often the main reason for adopting DevOps. Companies need to find ways to create applications that customers want and drive results. But this can be extremely difficult for large organizations as bureaucratic processes can stifle creativity. An effective DevOps strategy can break through this.

Improved customer satisfaction

Customers expect easy-to-use and quick applications. After all, they have become accustomed to standout offerings from companies like Uber and Airbnb. Through DevOps, feedback loops help improve customer satisfaction. Fewer disputes occur because objective data about the application is available.

Less unplanned work

Unplanned work can be a time sink. But with a DevOps program, unplanned work is lessened because there are better processes in place and clear goals set.

Higher productivity

DevOps helps reduce the needless waste of programmers who have nothing to do. In fact, idle time is a big reason developers get frustrated and leave their employers.

Lower costs

Software release costs should be lower because of the leveraging of automation systems that allow for higher efficiencies. Next, fewer bugs in the codebase will likely occur, and this means less time devoted for fixes. One estimate is that a bug costs about $2,000 (*https://oreil.ly/rkhGR*). Finally, DevOps can help improve the mean time to recovery (MTTR) for adverse incidents and outages. Later in this chapter, we'll take a look at this metric as well others.

For an example of the benefits of DevOps, we can look at Liberty Mutual Insurance, which has a large footprint of mainframes. "With the implementation of DevOps, our team is now deploying code 200 times faster, creating more stability, enabling us to experiment more, and allowing us to launch new products and features on a much faster timeline," said Justin Stone, senior director of Secure DevOps Platforms at Liberty Mutual Insurance. "When done right, DevOps should speed up the development process, enabling companies to cut costs and work faster. It allows developers to drive down the lead time it takes to make changes based on customer's needs, reducing the overall failure rate as they mature and the time to recovery from incidents and outages."

 According to a DevOps Research and Assessment (DORA) study, one firm that had over 4,000 developers was able to generate more than $8 million in value by adopting DevOps (*https://oreil.ly/ 5VsKk*). Some of the benefits included reduced MTTR and less maintenance for legacy tools.

Waterfall Method Model

The traditional method for software development is the *waterfall method*. Professor Herbert D. Benington came up with this concept in 1956 to help streamline the development of Semi-Automatic Ground Environment (SAGE) during the 1950s. This sophisticated computer system was designed to provide defenses against a potential air attack on the United States from the Soviet Union. At the time, it was the largest IT project and led to innovations in memory, real-time processing, networking, tape storage, graphics, and the creation of the FORTRAN language. Using the waterfall method allowed for a more disciplined approach to software management.

Keep in mind that the waterfall approach would quickly become a must-have for mainframe development. Even today, it is still used.

How does the waterfall method work? It is essentially a linear approach to software development that includes various phases. These phases do not overlap; they cascade like a waterfall. Moreover, each phase must be completed before another is started.

Here's a look at the key steps for the waterfall method:

Conception
> This idea stage of the project involves workshops for the team to brainstorm. The team looks at the goals to achieve and the general costs.

Initiation
> The team begins looking at the resources needed for the project. This may include hiring new coders or reassigning existing ones.

Requirements
> With the information gathered from the first two stages, a detailed requirements document is developed. This shows the timeline for the milestones.

Design
> This stage looks at the requirements for the IT infrastructure. Will other hardware, services, or applications need to be purchased?

Implementation
> Coding starts. This typically involves rigorous project management to keep things on track.

Testing and debugging
> This can easily take the most time among all the stages. If a lot of bugs exist, the project could easily miss its deadline.

Deployment and maintenance
> The application is put into production, and employees track the performance. Updates and patches usually need to be provided.

It's understandable why the waterfall method has been popular with mainframe development. It is highly structured, which is a benefit when it comes to creating mission-critical applications. Even a small error can have an adverse impact, such as with a miscalculation of payroll or inventory on hand. It's also important to note that—back in the mid-1980s—the US Department of Defense required the waterfall method for its software development contractors. As a result, this approach became a standard for mainframe development.

However, the waterfall method is risky. It is not uncommon for major changes to be needed after the application is finished, and this can prolong the project. What's more, complex projects—which are often the case for mainframe development—can be extremely difficult to manage. And the rigid structure can often make it difficult for innovation. In fact, because of the disadvantages, the waterfall method has even been blamed for expensive failed mainframe development projects (we will look at examples of these later in the chapter).

Because of this, there has been a move away from the waterfall method for mainframe development. This does not necessarily mean having daily release cycles. But then again, if a mainframe project will take more than a year, there's a good chance that it will not be approved.

In the next few sections, we'll take a look at alternatives to the waterfall method and how they can allow for better mainframe development.

Agile Method

The rise of the Internet in the 1990s led to a need for a software development approach that was more flexible than the waterfall method. If anything, the association with mainframes was not seen as a positive. Fast-growing companies like Yahoo! and Amazon saw themselves as a new breed of innovators, and they were focused on frequent release cycles. There simply was not enough time for the waterfall method's structured approach.

But interestingly enough, the development teams of these startups were coming up with their own approaches, and this caused fragmentation. Some of the methods that emerged included rapid application development (RAD), extreme programming (XP), and the dynamic systems development method (DSDM).

But a set of guidelines was needed, and in 2001, a group of noted software developers met at Snowbird, Utah, to sketch them out. This became known as the Manifesto for Agile Software Development (*https://oreil.ly/gIbUZ*), which is based on the following values:

- Individuals and interactions over processes and tools
- Working software over comprehensive documentation
- Customer collaboration over contract negotiation
- Responding to change over following a plan

The *Agile method* is meant to be open. There are no must-haves or rigid requirements. Instead, the Agile method is a philosophy of development, and this means there are varying interpretations. For example, some development teams may not stress documentation. This may ultimately be part of the existing UI. But if an application is for enterprise environments, such as with mainframe environments, documentation will probably be critical.

Now the word *agile* can be misleading. This does not imply that it is about having a free-form environment, in which coders can do whatever they want. Even though autonomy and speed are important, Agile still demands a plan of action and concrete deliverables. Consider that the planning is often ongoing. As user feedback comes in and the product changes, so will the planning.

Then how does Agile really work? It has several major themes. One is the importance of priorities. A project often involves a set of features, and then a chunk of them are accomplished in a short period of time (say, a couple of weeks). After each of these, a demo may be presented. This could instill pride in the development team, or could create peer pressure if a lack of progress is experienced.

For Agile, the product owner or project manager takes a customer-focused approach to the application. This usually involves coming up with "user stories" of how the product should work and the problems to be solved. But this does not imply that the product owner is merely engaging in "throwing it over the wall" to the development team. The process also means collaboration and buy-in to get better results.

Another responsibility of the product owner is the backlog, which is the list of remaining tasks and features that need to be completed. But this is not static, as the backlog will evolve based on the customer feedback.

Even though the Agile method generally increases the pace of development, it is still not perfect. Rushing the process can easily lead to adverse results.

Moreover, there is a temptation to quickly staff up resources. The irony is that this will likely slow the project even more. This phenomenon is known as the *mythical man month* (which is based on a book written by Frederick Brooks in the 1970s). According to this, the development time is hampered because of the challenges of onboarding new coders as well as the added complexities of having a larger number of people on the team.

This is why effective development teams are typically small. It harkens to what Amazon's Jeff Bezos calls the *pizza rule*: a team should be no bigger than two pizzas can feed.

Note that Agile can be combined with other approaches, such as Scrum, Lean, and Kanban. Each of these is presented in the following subsections.

 Perhaps one of the worst ways to measure the productivity of a coder is based on the number of lines per day. This incentivizes for bloated code bases and often results in a delayed project. As Bill Gates once noted (*https://oreil.ly/mbcFc*), "Measuring programming progress by lines of code is like measuring aircraft building progress by weight."

Among the various approaches, Agile is generally the most popular for mainframe development. It helps that it has usually been used across other departments in the organization, which means there is less of a learning curve. But Agile's focus on faster release cycles is much needed for mainframe development. For larger companies to remain competitive and be innovative, this is absolutely critical.

Scrum

The origins of *Scrum* go back to the mid-1980s when professors Hirotaka Takeuchi and Ikujiro Nonaka published a groundbreaking article in the *Harvard Business Journal*. In it, the authors noted that the traditional rigid approach to product development was failing. In light of the rapid rise of global competition, companies had to act quicker and be more responsive to customer needs.

The authors looked at case studies of companies like 3M, Xerox, Honda, and Canon. They showed how they implemented systems to promote teamwork. In fact, the word *scrum* came from rugby and described the formation of players.

Here's how the authors described the approach (*https://oreil.ly/2ZGsn*): "Under the rugby approach, the product development process emerges from the constant interaction of a hand-picked, multidisciplinary team whose members work together from start to finish. Rather than moving in defined, highly structured stages, the process is born out of the team members' interplay."

While the authors did not look at software development, the principles were still applicable. Scrum was about how to manage projects in dynamic environments, in which it was difficult to come up with the initial requirements.

By the 1990s, engineers like Ken Schwaber and Jeff Sutherland applied Scrum to software development. They wrote several papers on the topic and promoted the concept at conferences. They also were contributors to the Agile Manifesto.

With Scrum, the product owner manages the backlog. In addition, a Scrum master provides the overall management of the project.

A Scrum team is small, about 5 to 10 members. This helps provide for agility as well as less hierarchy. The project is divided into multiple sprints, which could last from one week to a month.

In a book called *Scrum: The Art of Doing Twice the Work in Half the Time* (Crown Business), Sutherland provides various examples of the benefits of Scrum and how to effectively implement the system. Interestingly enough, one of its most notable case studies is about mainframe systems. The FBI, which wanted to digitize its records, initially used the waterfall method but failed, wasting over $400 million. After implementing Scrum, the FBI project took less time and cost about $40 million.

According to the author: "It wasn't that these weren't smart people. It wasn't that the Bureau didn't have the right personnel in place, or even the right technology. It wasn't about the work ethic or the right supply of competitive juices. It was because of the way people were working. The way most people work. The way we all think work has to be done, because that's the way we were taught to do it."

Kanban

Toyota helped create the Kanban system in the 1940s for its factory floors. *Kanban*, which means *visual design* in Japanese, was a revolutionary approach that helped propel the company's success.

But Kanban has proven to be versatile in terms of its applications. For example, professor David J. Anderson used the system for software development for companies like Corbis and Microsoft in 2004. He saw it as an easier approach since it required less cultural change.

Kanban uses a physical or virtual display board. The idea is to provide a visual way of understanding a project. This can be particularly important since software projects can sometimes be difficult to conceptualize, as is the case with mainframe applications. The board also allows for collaboration and a quick way to get a sense of a project's progress.

A board is divided into five parts:

Visual signs
These are the cards or stickies (they may be Post-it notes, for example). Each has a particular task or a part of the user story. As the team accomplishes the task, the cards are removed from the board.

Columns
These show the timeline and workflow of the project. The cards are distributed along the columns.

Work-in-progress (WIP) limit
This is the maximum number of cards that can be placed on a column. This limitation encourages the team to finish tasks. Also, if a column is getting close to the WIP limit, this is an alert that the project may be going sideways.

Commitment point
This is the backlog. With this, the team can select the next tasks.

Delivery point
This is the final point of the Kanban workflow. This is usually when the application is being used by the customer.

A myriad of apps are used for Kanban boards. They usually provide broader project management capabilities, as with Gantt charts, and templates for other approaches. These tools are also usually for more than just IT purposes. They can be used across departments such as sales, HR, and finance.

Here are some of the top apps:

Trello (https://trello.com)
This sophisticated collaboration platform is fairly easy to use. But it has no features for progress reporting or time tracking.

monday.com
This has a wide array of integrations with apps like Jira, Dropbox, Slack, and even Trello. It also has a low-code system that allows for the creation of helpful automations.

Wrike (https://www.wrike.com)
This easy-to-use project management system offers customizable Kanban boards and a sophisticated reporting system.

Of course, the Kanban method is not without its drawbacks. For example, the boards can get cluttered and complicated. In addition, clear lines of responsibility are usually lacking for the teams. It's even difficult to get a sense of the timelines.

Lean

Lean is a process methodology based on the Toyota Production system, which is focused on lowering waste and defect rates. In 2003, management consultants Mary and Tom Poppendieck wrote *Lean Software Development* (Addison-Wesley Professional), which showed how this approach could be applied to coding.

The authors set forth a framework that includes seven main principles:

Eliminate waste
> At the heart of Lean is avoiding the use of anything that does not bring value to the customer. In terms of software development, this means eliminating needless features, engaging in relearning, reducing the number of needless handoffs, and minimizing bugs. Tools are used to help out, such as value stream mapping, which provides visualizations for the development process.

Amplify learning
> Coding is a dynamic process, so it can be a mistake to have too many requirements or extensive documentation, especially in the early stages. Also, having short periods for releases helps developers learn from user feedback.

Decide as late as possible
> This may seem counterintuitive. Doesn't this go against the goal of being Agile? Actually, this is really not the case. You need to be sure that the software has been sufficiently vetted before it is deployed. This is especially the case for features that would be extremely difficult to fix once the software is in production.

Deliver fast
> This may seem contradictory to the prior principle. But it isn't. To deliver fast means that a product should not be weighed down by too many features. The focus is on building a minimum viable product (MVP). Then, as user feedback is received, this can be incorporated into new versions of the software.

Empower the team
> If you want high performance, the team members must be empowered to make decisions and have their input be seriously considered. Effective approaches are required to resolve conflicts and encourage constructive feedback. Although, the "deliver fast" principle can get in the way, the approaches need to be balanced.

Integrity built in

Quality code should be a constant. It's not something that is left to the testing process. If anything, there should be much quicker assessments. Another strategy is to use pair programming, in which a task is coded by two developers. This leverages the experience but also helps provide different perspectives. Test-driven development (TDD) enables tests to be developed before programming begins.

Optimize the whole

In software development, the tendency is to over-focus on certain areas of the process. But this usually results in a suboptimal product. As much as possible, we need to have a holistic view of the development process.

As is the case with any software development framework, Lean has pros and cons. On the positive side, this approach helps streamline processes and lower costs. Empowerment of the development team is another positive factor.

As for the negatives, Lean is generally not as scalable as other software development frameworks, as true teamwork is required (and yes, this is difficult to achieve across an organization). Having flexibility in the requirements carries risk. Requirements can become too loose and result in a software that is not very effective.

OK then, among the various approaches—Agile, Scrum, Kanban, Lean—which is preferred for mainframe development? There is no clear-cut answer. Again, each method has its own pros and cons. Selection is really about what works for an organization. Mixing aspects of the various methods is common. What's important is to have a set of principles focused on improving the productivity and quality of the development.

Agile: It's Not All About Speed

While speed is critically important, it should be not be taken to extremes. The result could be a code base that is unmanageable.

This happened to Amazon. By 2000, the company wanted to leverage its ecommerce platform into other categories. But this proved extremely difficult because the code base was a mess. Since its inception, the company had experienced breakneck growth, and the developers often did not spend as much time planning.

CEO Jeff Bezos realized that Amazon's approach to development and the underlying architecture required significant rethinking. This meant creating a highly scalable service platform that could essentially allow for ecommerce as service. At the heart of this was developing modular components via APIs, which would make it easier for developers to build new applications and not have to spend as much time on backend operations.

This strategy turned out to be a big success. The technology infrastructure would ultimately become the basis for AWS, which is the world's largest cloud platform and the biggest source of profits for Amazon. It is also one of the world's most agile system, with 50 million software updates each year (*https://oreil.ly/fYkqw*).

Mainframes and the Challenges for DevOps

When it comes to mainframes, DevOps provides a lot of opportunity to make a big difference in the success of development. Even an improvement of a month or two in development cycles can be significant.

But, realistically, the transition to DevOps will not be quick. Time is needed for cultural change. But there will also be the many nagging issues that remain with mainframe environments. For example, mainframe development usually involves different specialized areas. This presents problems with cross-training because of the complexities of the domains.

The other problem is that the code bases can involve millions of lines and usually work with mission-critical processes. So even a small mistake can have devastating consequences. Even worse, little documentation and few resources may be available to understand the code. And as more mainframe developers retire, less talent will be ready to help with the transition.

While legacy mainframe code is generally structured, complicated structures and archaic approaches still exist. With ongoing maintenance of the code base, the refactoring can lead to lower quality. Pockets of dead code will exist.

But the code structure is just one of the problems. Manual processes—such as for JCL, macros, and scripts to run the programs—can add needless time to the development process.

All this sounds daunting, right? It certainly is. It is why modernization efforts have not been easy, even for those organizations that want to be more innovative.

But despite this, DevOps efforts are well worth it. We just need realistic expectations about what can be done.

> In the 2020 study "State of Mainframe DevOps" from IDC and Broadcom, respondents indicated that these are the top five benefits of DevOps for mainframe environments: improved developer productivity, a more relevant digital business strategy, better regulatory and compliance reporting, improved configuration compliance, and enhanced collaboration.

DevOps Best Practices

Perhaps the most important best practice for DevOps is to find ways to change the culture. It's about "changing the hearts and minds" of the development team. Unfortunately, this can be difficult with mainframe departments. They are often isolated from the other parts of IT. They also have specialized requirements that are often not understood by those who use modern tools and systems.

What to do? It's critical to make DevOps a clear priority—and this should come from the highest reaches of the organization. Ideally, this means the chief information officer (CIO) or chief technology officer (CTO). This will definitely help inspire change.

What are some of the other best practices to consider? Let's take a look:

Embedding
> Embedding means that a member of one team joins another. This could be someone from the database team who goes to the mainframe development team and vice versa. This provides different views and insights. Even better, investment in training should occur. The embedding will bring forth a better understanding of the day-to-day activities of the other team. Given that changing culture is vitally important with DevOps, having embedding can be a great way to help this along.

Authority and responsibilities
> A common phrase in DevOps is "You build it, you own it." This certainly helps provide accountability and should lead to better results. However, clear lines of authority need to be established. If there is a lack of empowerment, a breakdown in DevOps will likely occur. Keep in mind that some tools, like OpsLevel, can help track the roles and responsibilities of the team.

Chaos monkey
> Reliability is table stakes for Netflix. If the user experiences degradation of the service, the company could easily lose subscribers. To prevent outages or degradation of services, Netflix built a sophisticated DevOps system that relies heavily on automation. But the company also looks to practice failure. This is done by having *chaos monkeys*, automated scripts that randomly shut down certain systems. No doubt, this seems risky and almost diabolical. But it has been a critical factor in helping maintain the reliability of the Netflix platform. The developers are more mindful in creating robust systems. Having chaos monkeys also provides more opportunities to test the infrastructure.

Blameless postmortems
> In complex IT environments, failure is inevitable. When failure does happen, a *postmortem* (an examination of what went wrong and why) should be arranged—

ideally, within 48 hours of the incident so that the team can best learn from the situation. This postmortem should not be about blaming people. The goal is to focus on the root cause of the problem, come up with the timeline that led to the breakdown, and then put together recommendations. According to Etsy, a practitioner of blameless postmortems (*https://oreil.ly/8yuf1*), "Our intention is not just to learn from our mistakes, but also to cultivate a mindset where everyone is continuously unearthing new opportunities for improvement. We're building scalable internal processes, training more facilitators, and implementing practices that encourage a healthy and just learning culture."

Everything is code
Concepts like source control and integration have been common for many years for software development. But why not apply this to operations, such as for IT infrastructure? This is becoming more common. By applying Software Development Life Cycle (SDLC) practices, notable improvements should occur in agility, quality, and costs.

Security
A team of developers may develop an effective application that meets the needs of customers. But they may not necessarily have much of a background in security. As a result, the application could be vulnerable to threats. If a breach occurs, costs could be substantial in terms of damage to a company's reputation and coffers. Thus, when it comes to DevOps, security should be a focus from the early stages.

Shadow IT uses software, devices, and services to solve a problem. But there's a hitch: the users do not have the permission of the IT department. This has become increasingly common, especially since technologies are much cheaper and accessible (such as from the cloud and smartphones). But shadow IT is often a sign of a lack of effective DevOps. For the most part, these activities would not be needed if the organization were more agile. Besides, shadow IT can be costly because it could increase security threats and fragmentation of applications.

Configuration Management

Configuration management is about using tools to help automate hardware, the operating system, services, and network connectivity. The software will upgrade the software and deploy it, and orchestration allows the tasks to be coordinated across systems. The main goal of configuration management is to ensure that the infrastructure maintains a consistent state as changes are made over time.

So let's take a look at some of the approaches for configuration management:

Declarative or functional
> You set forth a desired end state, and an automation tool tries to achieve it. Then once this has been accomplished, changes are ignored. Puppet is an example of a software tool that uses the declarative approach.

Imperative or procedural
> The user comes up with the exact steps to reach the end state. This could include installation, database creation, and so on. One of the popular tools for the imperative approach is Chef.

Idempotent
> You can run the configuration scripts multiple times on the same infrastructure, and the results will be exactly the same. Thus, if an artifact does not meet the requirements, a change will be made.

In a typical mainframe environment, configuration is critical. Small changes can add up and bog down the system, which can also lead to more failures and outages. Configuration management provides more control and discipline for the process. However, for a mainframe environment, configuration management can be a bottleneck for DevOps because the systems tend to be walled off. The process is also usually manual and based on legacy systems.

Yet things are starting to change. Some vendors in the configuration management space have been adding capabilities for mainframes. For example, the Red Hat Ansible Automation Platform allows for storing and managing the current state for IT systems. Ansible is an open source platform that Red Hat acquired in 2015 (IBM owns Red Hat).

With the software, you can automate z/OS applications as well as the IBM Z hardware infrastructure. Seamless integration occurs with tools like JCL, REXX, and z/OS Management Facility (z/OSMF). The result is that it is easier to have a holistic approach to configuration management, which can extend to cloud assets and other on-premises installations.

Another tool to help with configuration management is a configuration management database (CMDB). This standard database has all the necessary information of an organization's hardware and software assets. For the most part, this provides a single source of truth. This helps for better management, security, compliance, and transparency. Cost advantages result, as there is less likelihood of purchasing duplicate technology.

One of the issues with CMDBs is that they can be time-consuming to create. Tools that can help automate the process include SolarWinds Service Desk, Freshservice, and ServiceNow CMDB.

Issues with DevOps

DevOps is not easy. This is the case anytime cultural change needs to occur in an organization.

The 2021 research report "Driving DevOps Success with Intelligent Automation and Analytics" from BMC and Hanover Research points this out. Here are some of the findings, which were based on responses from 400 technology decision-makers and influencers working at companies with at least $500 million in annual revenues:

- 41% cited a lack of familiarity with change management procedures.

- 39% indicated insufficient infrastructure for endpoint monitoring.

- 38% said they had incomplete information to make sound IT service management (ITSM) decisions.

Such problems can ripple across a company and can be magnified in large organizations that have legacy systems like mainframes. Fixing the issues will not be cheap or quick.

"It's not as simple as building it and running it, when you have to build it while dozens of heterogenous teams are managing and running their own deployments at different paces and using different processes," said Margaret Lee, senior vice president and general manager of Digital Service Operations Management at BMC. "It's also difficult to embrace DevOps when your current workforce isn't familiar with the right tools and pace. In fact, it's one of the hardest tech positions to fill today."

If anything, it's important to understand the issues with DevOps. This will help provide more realism in the process and should lead to better results.

So what are some of the other problems with DevOps to consider? Let's take a look:

Buzzwords
An organization may use the lingo of DevOps but have no true practice of its approaches and strategies. Interestingly enough, this is common. This is why it is critical to set up milestones to hit and to hold teams accountable.

Diminishing returns
As seen in this chapter, there are a myriad of ways to pursue DevOps. But the problem is that an organization may take on too many of them. This can easily lead to substantial increases in complexity, which will slow the progress of development.

Product and engineering

If either product or engineering is overemphasized, productivity could suffer. For example, the organization may focus more on product features but not enough on testing.

Training

This is a must-have priority, especially in the early stages of implementing DevOps. Developers need to learn about testing, observability, and incident response. Operations people need to have a good understanding of the process of software design and programming.

Metrics

To get a sense of whether DevOps is working, you can put together a set of key performance indicators (KPIs) that measure speed, efficiency, costs, and quality. Quite a few of them exist. So let's take a look at the main ones:

Mean time to recovery (MTTR)

The time it takes to recover from a failure of a system. For modern DevOps, the goal is to keep the time frame to minutes or hours.

Mean time to detection (MTTD)

The average time it takes to identify a problem. Often this involves having sophisticated monitoring systems.

Deployment frequency

The time it takes to get a change to staging and production. This is a key metric for evaluating Agile.

Change failure rate

The percentage of changes from services that fail, which provides a gauge for the efficiency of a DevOps environment. An organization with a top change failure rate may be 0% to 15%.

Lead time for changes

The time it takes to get committed code into production. DevOps strives to do this within a day. But unfortunately, it's not uncommon for this to be more than a month.

Mainframe DevOps Tooling

BMC and Forrester Consulting conducted a survey in 2021 of 408 software developers regarding their perceptions about DevOps tools. On the positive side, 76% of the respondents believed that mainframes were of the utmost importance to their organizations. On the other hand, 79% indicated that their mainframe development tools required major improvements. In fact, 58% said that developing for the mainframe was worse than for mobile-based systems, 48% said it was worse than cloud-native development, and 52% said it was worse than working on on-premises workloads.

Even doing easy tasks, like identifying source code changes, can be difficult. Performance and automation testing are often lacking. With the problems with tooling, there are certainly risks:

- Software is usually lower quality.
- Release times are much slower.
- Higher security risks exist.
- There is higher likelihood of issues with uptime, reliability, and stability.
- It can be more difficult to attract and retain top technical talent.

Now more organizations are trying to modernize their approaches. But as this research report shows, the pace is really not fast enough, especially when compared to the benefits and the needs for being competitive.

The study concludes (*https://oreil.ly/N8IHc*): "Our study showed that organizations who have implemented modern mainframe development tools have effectively improved the developer experience on mainframe vs. other systems by 25%. This has created a positive relationship with the mainframe platform, making it more likely for their organizations to factor a mainframe into their future plans. We also discovered that teams with modern tools are further along in their efforts to create modern mainframe applications and have fewer issues with skills gaps and top-talent acquisition."

Automation

Software tools for automation are a major part of DevOps. The technology can streamline manual processes, and this means developers will have more time to focus on coding.

A rich set of tools spans all the stages of the development cycle. In fact, it can get overwhelming.

But for mainframe environments, one of the areas to start automating is the IDE. While ISPF and TSO are efficient, they do lack lots of modern features. This can certainly lead to less productivity. It can also make it tougher to hire developers. After all, they will likely be accustomed to using modern IDEs.

One of the principles of tooling for DevOps is to not force options on developers. This is usually counterproductive. If the developers are productive with older tools, then keeping the status quo usually makes sense.

However, when it comes to IDEs, this strategy may prove to be off the mark. ISPF and TSO really are far less useful than modern IDEs. They were designed in an era when concepts like Agile were not the mainstream.

Because of this, it's a good idea to encourage programmers to make a change. This can be done with more training or enabling these employees who spend some time with developers who use modern tools.

In the next few sections, we'll look at some of the main categories of DevOps automation tools. We'll also see how the Zowe platform is making it possible to integrate modern software offerings to the mainframe.

 The Netflix platform has over 209 million subscribers across the globe. To operate this platform, hundreds of microservices and thousands of daily production changes are needed. Yet a key to scaling the operation has been automation; only about 70 operations engineers are on the DevOps team (*https://oreil.ly/XmP6x*).

CI/CD

Software is increasingly becoming interconnected. A modern application is usually made up of many APIs. In addition, various types of platforms and architectures exist—the cloud, microservices, hybrid cloud, multicloud, containers, and so on. The complexity can be mind-boggling. It's sometimes referred to as *integration hell*.

To help with this, continuous integration and continuous delivery or deployment (CI/CD) has emerged. For organizations that adopt this, they usually start with CI and then eventually implement CD.

What do these involve? CI is the automation for the building and testing of an app. The code is shared in a central repository.

But caution is needed. If developers are not collaborating, merging the branching source code can be subject to conflicts. This can easily bog down the process. Unfortunately, this is common with mainframe development.

The focus on CI, though, is to merge the code changes to a shared branch or trunk quicker. This could be on a daily basis. After this, automated testing can be done to see that the app is stable. For CI, the idea is to have testing early, and this should involve all the branches. This is often referred to as *shift left*.

In terms of mainframe development, a traditional approach to testing is still common. This involves the use of a quality assurance phase of the process. But for the most part, this has resulted in slower release cycles.

What are some of the tests available? There are many, actually. But it's common to start with *unit testing*, which tends to be quicker and cheaper. This is generally focused on small parts of the code base—say, a function or procedure.

Here are some other approaches:

Acceptance testing
Evaluates the software against business requirements. It involves closed testing, in which the tester does not know the item being tested. This is a manual approach.

Integration testing
Tests various modules of the software.

UI testing
Assesses the software's usability. This type of testing can be time-consuming and manual. However, it can be extremely useful as users want a streamlined experience.

Regression testing
Ensures that new code will not negatively impact existing features. It's about focusing on the "after effects" of code development.

 Writing solid tests is no easy feat. But one way to help is to start with the process in the early stages of the project, such as with the creation of the user stories.

A key part of DevOps tools is automation testing. This generally involves entering test data into the system under test (SUT) and then comparing the expected and actual results. From this, the software will generate reports.

Here are other steps in the process:

Software build
This includes the creation of the artifacts, which are the files for distribution packages, log reports, and so on.

CD
The software build is deployed to a testing or production environment.

Keep in mind that the CI/CD workflow is an ongoing process. This is why you will often hear talk of the *CI/CD pipeline*. The goal is to find ways to automate the process, but strong systems for monitoring should be in place.

Many useful CI/CD tools are available. Here's a look at some of them:

Jenkins (https://www.jenkins.io)
> This is the leader in the category. Jenkins, an open source project with roots that go back to 2011, has a thriving community of developers. Jenkins has two components: a server that orchestrates the CI/CD pipeline, and agents that carry out the steps. The software is available for Windows, Linux, and macOS. Jenkins includes the capability to build plug-ins, which has provided for a rich ecosystem. And since Jenkins is on premises, this may provide more security for regulated industries.

CircleCI (https://circleci.com)
> This user-friendly CI/CD system supports JavaScript and YAML. But it also offers sophisticated features, such as for graphics processing units (GPUs). A system even allows for migrating from Jenkins implementations.

GitLab (https://about.gitlab.com)
> This not only helps with CI/CD pipelines but also provides for code repositories. GitLab also has support for a myriad of languages like C, Ruby, and Java. You can also integrate Docker support. Furthermore, it certainly helps that the software is based on the open source model and has over three thousand avid contributors. As for the mainframe, GitLab does have support for Linux on the IBM Z, which is for working with LPARs and virtualized hosts.

 The DevOps concept has spun off other variations. For example, GitOps is about using Git and GitHub to track and deliver software. SlackOps uses the Slack app for DevOps functions and allows for improved collaboration.

What about mainframe-specific CI/CD tools? The IBM Z Open Development IDE has Dependency Based Build (DBB) capabilities as well as the use of Groovy, which is a Java-like scripting language. This has made it possible to integrate Jenkins, GitHub, UrbanCode (for code deployment on cloud and on-premises environments), SonarQube, and other popular CI/CD systems. For example, it is possible to run automated testing off-mainframe, which is more cost-effective.

IBM also has IBM Developer for z/OS (IDz) for its IDE. This software is for unit testing for enterprise COBOL and PL/I and uses the closed-testing approach.

BMC has a CI/CD tool called ISPW. It has its own systems for source code management and deployments. It also integrates with enterprise Git, VS Code, and ISPF.

A case study of ISPW is with Folksam, one of the largest insurance companies in Sweden. The company was having challenges with its software development. Its system, which was developed in the 1990s, required considerable manual effort and was complex. It was also difficult to find the reasons for the issues with the code.

To deal with these problems, Folksam implemented ISPW (*https://oreil.ly/wjFiL*) for its 150 core mainframe applications (the company's team had about 50 COBOL coders). The results were significant. Because of the sophisticated acceptance testing and deployment capabilities of the software, Folksam realized savings of 1.5 million krona per year. A significant increase also occurred in the acceleration of app development, with major quarterly release cycles and smaller weekly sprints.

Another widely used CI/CD system is Endevor (Environment for Developers and Operations), which is developed by Broadcom. It can run sophisticated source code and release management that is native to z/OS. The interface for Endevor is modern as it is based on the Eclipse platform. Endevor also integrates with other DevOps tools like GitHub and Atlassian Bitbucket Server.

Finally, Red Hat OpenShift Pipelines is a cloud-based CI/CD platform that operates on Tekton, which is open source software. Red Hat OpenShift Pipelines runs the pipelines in isolated containers. It also is supported for the IBM Z mainframe.

Zowe

Chapter 3 provided a demo of the Zowe Explorer. But this really just scratched the surface of the capabilities of this software platform. Consider that Zowe is becoming important in modernizing mainframe development and is a major driver for DevOps.

In this section, we'll take a look at the other parts of Zowe, which include the Zowe API Mediation Layer, the Zowe Application Framework, and the Zowe CLI.

Zowe API Mediation Layer

For mainframe environments, APIs have generally focused on local networks and virtual private networks. Some of the reasons include security and the need for managing workloads.

Yet the constraints on APIs have weighed on modernization efforts. What to do? Enter the Zowe API Mediation Layer. It is a single point of access through REST APIs to the mainframe. There is also security built in and management for the load balancing.

In terms of functions, the Zowe API Mediation Layer initiates instructions for TSO, Unix files, JES, and z/OS. New feature launches are ongoing. To help manage this, the Zowe API Mediation Layer has a graphic catalog.

For developers, you can have a local deployment of the API Layer. For example, you can do this by using a Docker container.

Zowe Application Framework

Zowe Application Framework is a system that is accessible through a browser. This software has the Zowe Desktop, a GUI that enables you to create plug-ins that access mainframe services.

The Zowe Desktop allows for the use of various languages and frameworks, such as JavaScript, TypeScript, Angular, and React. Or you can wrap a web application or content as a web page by using iframe.

Zowe CLI

Available for Windows, Linux, and macOS, Zowe CLI (*https://oreil.ly/prPpj*) is similar to how you would work on a platform like AWS, Google Cloud, or Microsoft Azure. You input your commands in a terminal on your computer.

This is certainly powerful. You can create bash or shell scripts that integrate with cloud services or open source software (for this, you can use a language like Python). The result is that it is possible to greatly expand the capabilities of a mainframe system.

For example, the following shows how you can loop through certain datasets on a mainframe and then delete the files:

```
set -e
dslist=$(zowe files ls ds "my.project.ds*")  ❶
IFS=$'\n'
for ds in $dslist
do
    echo "Deleting: $ds"
    zowe files delete ds "$ds" -f  ❷
done
```

❶ Accesses the project datasets

❷ The Zowe command to delete the files

The following are some of the plug-ins available for Zowe:

IBM Db2 DevOps Experience for z/OS
This provides DevOps approaches for database applications.

Broadcom Endevor
This is for integration with a mainframe-specific DevOps platform.

Broadcom IDMS
This allows you to interact with the company's integrated database management (IDMS) system, which provides for real-time metrics, viewing of logic, and issue management.

Zowe CLI CICS Deploy
This IBM plug-in allows for handling the CICS Transaction Server for z/OS.

ChangeMan ZMF Plug-in for Zowe CLI
This plug-in, developed by Micro Focus, provides for interacting with ZMF packages and components.

WLX Audit for Db2 z/OS
This is a sophisticated monitoring tool for databases.

If you want to create a plug-in for third parties, you will need to go through a certification process called the Zowe Conformance Program, which involves rigorous testing. According to the Zowe organization (*https://oreil.ly/r05WZ*), the program "aims to give users the confidence that when they use a product, app, or distribution that leverages Zowe, they can expect a high level of common functionality, interoperability, and user experience."

 There continues to be ongoing development from Zowe. Current projects under development include Zowe Client SDKs (these are a set of programmatic APIs for building client applications and scripts for z/OS), Zowe Mobile (smartphone access to mainframes), and ZEBRA (reusable JSON-formatted RMF/SMF data records).

In the last two sections of this chapter, we'll take a look at two demos of DevOps software. However, unless you have access to a mainframe, you will not be able to replicate them. The focus of these demos is to show the general workflow.

BMC Jenkins Plug-ins

Jenkins is generally the choice for enterprise environments. The software has a strong track record across many large companies. It also helps that Jenkins has a rich ecosystem of integrations and partners.

It's typical to install Docker (*https://oreil.ly/8kFB1*) to create a Jenkins pipeline for continuous integration. This involves four main steps to turn an application into a container that can be run on any environment:

1. Clone a repository of your app by using Git.
2. Build a Docker image. This has all the files and code for the container. The Dockerfile manages this workflow, including packaging the dependencies, creating a directory, and so on.

3. Push the container image to a registry. This means you can store and share the container on different environments.

4. Run the container image.

By using this process, the developer does not have to worry about the machine or the configuration. A container is also lighter to distribute than a typical virtual machine. There is also no need to run package managers. All in all, this can save time and allow for more reliability for the developer.

What's more, with Docker you can make Jenkins a Docker image that you can run anywhere. This is certainly key when working with DevOps. You will launch Jenkins and then create a pipeline, which is done using a Jenkinsfile. This has three stages:

1. Build the app.

2. Run tests on the app.

3. Deploy the app.

For the most part, Jenkins automates these processes. However, in terms of doing this on the mainframe, various plug-ins are used. One is from BMC and is called the Topaz for Total Test Jenkins plug-in (*https://oreil.ly/AM0fB*). It is accessed through the BMC Topaz IDE and works with COBOL batch files, CICS, and IMS programs. In addition, the TestRunner Component runs the programs on the mainframe.

Here are the other applications you will need on your system (the installation will need to be done on Jenkins as an Admin):

- Jenkins Credentials plug-in
- Compuware configuration plug-in
- Topaz Workbench CLI, which is installed on the Jenkins server
- Host Communications Interface (HCI) Connection, which runs the tests on the LPAR
- Enterprise Common Components (ECC), which includes the Topaz for Total Test TestRunner Mainframe component

Once everything is set up, you can create a Freestyle Project in Jenkins. Select New Item and enter the project name. Click OK to access the project configuration panel, where you will put in the description of the project.

Go to the Build section and enter the properties, as shown in Figure 9-1.

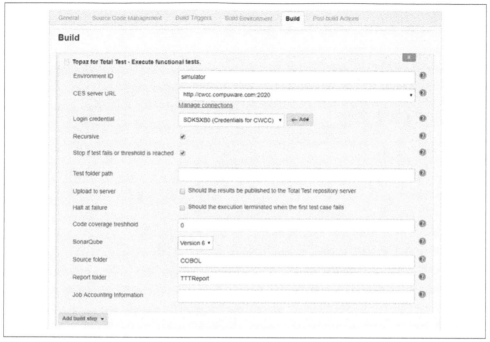

Figure 9-1. The panel to configure Jenkins with the mainframe

Here are the items to configure:

Environment ID
    The environment or LPAR where you'll run the tests.

CES Server URL
    The URL provided through the BMC configuration setup.

Login credential
    Your TSO credentials to access the mainframe.

Recursive
    The test cases will be found recursively in a subfolder to the test folder path.

Stop if test fails or threshold is reached
    The test will stop immediately if a case fails.

Code coverage threshold
    A code coverage percentage less than this value will stop the build. This is only for IBM Debug.

SonarQube
    The version used for the reports.

Source folder
> The location of the source where the SonarQube reports are linked.

Report folder
> The name of the folder for the JUnit output (this is a unit-testing framework for Java) and SonarQube reports. The default path is TTTReport.

Job accounting information
> This is optional. It is essentially an accounting information parameter for the installation.

After setting these options, click Save. Now we are ready to perform functional testing on the code. For example, you can select New Item, enter the project name, and select Pipeline. You can then enter this Pipeline script, which is written in Groovy, an object-oriented language for the Java platform:

```
stage("Run Topaz for Total Test - functional test")  ❶
{
  node{
    junit 'TTTReport/*.xml'  ❷
  }
}
```

❶ A pipeline has different stages. This one indicates that we will use the Topaz for Total Test plug-in to run a unit test.

❷ The node shows what will be performed. In this case, this translates the results of the tests into a JUnit format.

After you click Save, select Configure and Pipeline Syntax. Next, select Generate Pipeline Script. Copy the output and use it to add a line to the Groovy script:

```
stage("Run Topaz for Total Test")
{
  totaltest credentialsId: 'SDKSXB0 CWCC', environmentId: 'simulator', ↵
folderPath: '', serverUrl: 'http://cwcc.compuware.com:2020', sonarVersion: '6'  ❶
  node{
    junit 'TTTReport/*.xml'
  }
}
```

❶ This is the new line, which executes the test.

Go back to Configure and click Add in "Post-build Actions." Select the JUnit test result report and click Save. Select Build Now to see if the files were copied correctly. You can click Build # to review the test results.

Various other tests are available. And yes, the pipelines can get quite sophisticated. But for the most part, by using Jenkins, you can significantly automate the manual processes.

Zigi

While modern systems like Zowe have made progress, most mainframe shops extensively use ISPF for development. Part of this is due to how the developers were trained initially to work on mainframes. But ISPF also is highly efficient and quick.

Because of this, Henri Kuiper and Lionel Dyck developed zigi (*https://zigi.rocks*). This open source project allows for the native use of Git within the ISPF environment.

"Zigi allows developers to work on the same applications, whether on the mainframe or other systems," said Dyck. "Everyone can work with the same set of Git source code repositories. Basically, for those developers who are very productive using ISPF Edit and related tools, they can now use Git while remaining productive. They no longer must take valuable time away from development to learn new workstation tools."

Zigi, which is written in REXX, is not just a panel and a CLIST macro that pushes changes and updates to GitHub. It is a full-featured application that fits seamlessly within a mainframe developer's workflows. Through ISPF, you can use Git commands to manage z/OS datasets and OMVS files, which include binaries. You can work with other remote repositories like GitHub, Bitbucket, and GitLab. However, you cannot access VSAM, BDAM, ISAM, or RECFM=U files. Yet zigi does support load libraries that are RECFM=U as long as they are handled as binary elements.

For the installation, you download software from the Rocket Software site (*https://oreil.ly/F18sS*). You also need other software on your mainframe, like bash, Perl, and Miniconda. Then with Miniconda, install Git and all the necessary prerequisite and corequisite software.

Next, set up Git for your z/OS OMVS environment (this involves the Unix shell for scripting) and clone it using zigi (*https://oreil.ly/z3xak*). Then when in OMVS, change the Git repository to zigi and execute `./zginstall.rex`. This installs the z/OS ISPF libraries.

To use zigi, go to ISPF and enter **tso zigi** at the command prompt. If you enter Help or press the F1 key, you will get a tutorial panel (Figure 9-2).

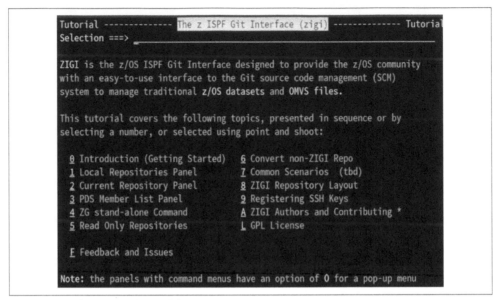

Figure 9-2. The tutorial panel for zigi

Otherwise, you will see a panel that provides a list of available zigi-managed Git repositories, illustrated in Figure 9-3. From here, you can select to work with an individual repository, create a new repository, or clone an existing repository.

If you want to check the status of one of the repositories, enter **s** on the left side of the dataset and press Enter. Just as with other Git interfaces, you should always develop in a unique branch and never in the master branch. Zigi supports creating, or changing, to other branches, as well as merging branches.

After you make a selection, you will get the panel shown in Figure 9-4. It displays the local directory and remote path for the Git repository. The repository shows a listing of the z/OS datasets and OMVS files. While zigi can manage OMVS files, including files within subdirectories, the primary benefit is managing z/OS datasets.

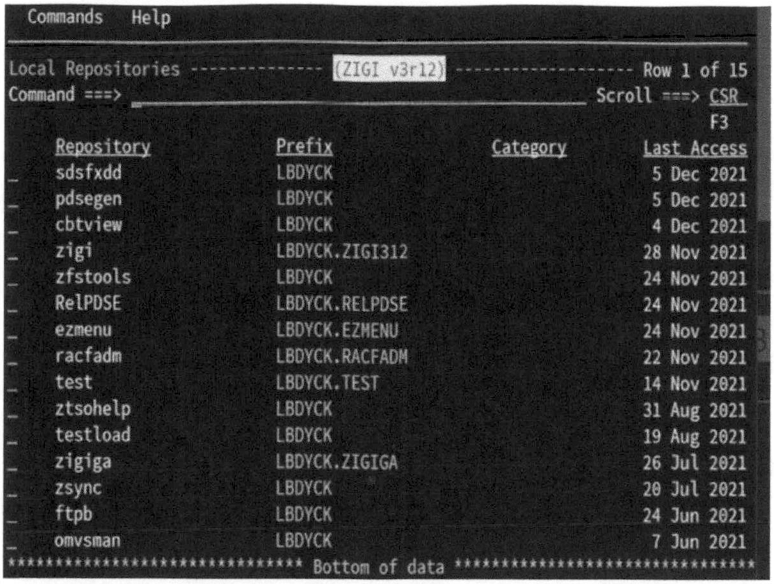

Figure 9-3. *The panel in zigi for the list of Git repositories*

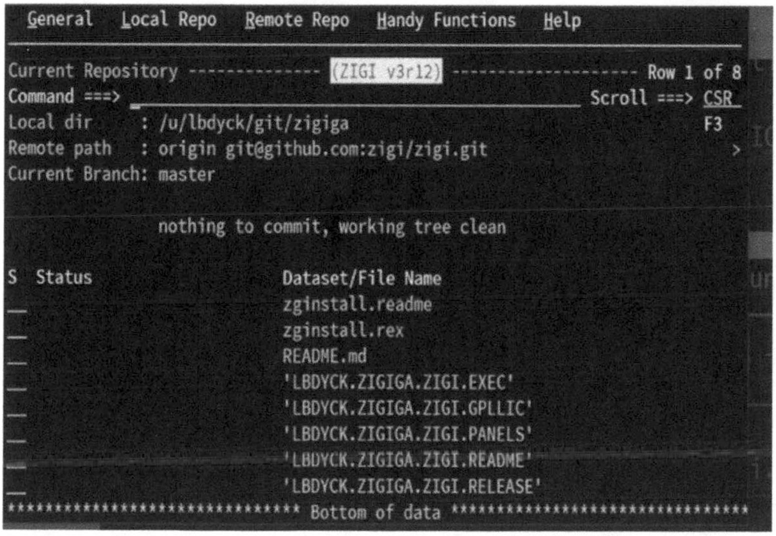

Figure 9-4. *The local and remote path for the Git repository*

Zigi is built to allow ISPF to handle the common Git commands. But if something unique is required, the software has a Git command interface (Figure 9-5).

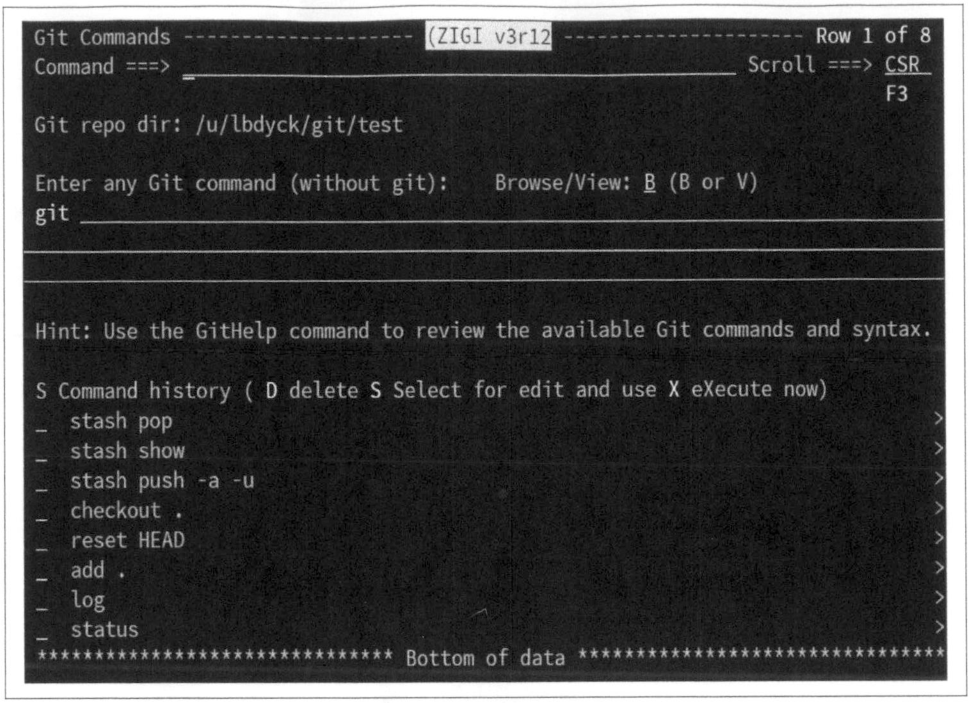

```
Git Commands -------------------- (ZIGI v3r12) --------------------  Row 1 of 8
Command ===> _____  Scroll ===> CSR
                                                                       F3
Git repo dir: /u/lbdyck/git/test

Enter any Git command (without git):    Browse/View: B (B or V)
git _____


_____

Hint: Use the GitHelp command to review the available Git commands and syntax.

S Command history ( D delete S Select for edit and use X eXecute now)
_   stash pop                                                              >
_   stash show                                                             >
_   stash push -a -u                                                       >
_   checkout .                                                             >
_   reset HEAD                                                             >
_   add .                                                                  >
_   log                                                                    >
_   status                                                                 >
****************************** Bottom of data ******************************
```

Figure 9-5. The Git command interface for zigi

Conclusion

The adoption of DevOps has been relatively slow in the mainframe world. But during the past few years, interest and urgency have increased as companies realize that they need to better integrate their mainframe departments so as to be more competitive.

In this chapter, we explored the core concepts of DevOps. We reviewed the various methodologies like Agile, Scrum, Kanban, and Lean. They generally emphasize speed and more feedback from users. We also took a look at some of the best practices for DevOps. These include using the chaos monkey, being clear with responsibilities, and providing for blameless postmortems. We then reviewed management approaches for the infrastructure side of IT, such as with deployment, upgrades, and orchestration.

Next, we took a look at the automation systems and tools for DevOps. Many options are available on the market. But we focused on the most widely used ones, like Jenkins. We also reviewed some of those that are specific to mainframes. Finally, we looked at the Zowe platform. While still in the nascent stages, it has already had a positive impact on allowing modern DevOps for mainframe environments.

In the next chapter, we will take a look at AI.

CHAPTER 10

Artificial Intelligence

Tom Siebel has an impeccable track record of understanding the megatrends in technology. He started his career at Oracle in the 1980s because he saw the promise of relational databases. By the early 1990s, he had created his own company, Siebel Systems, which pioneered the customer relationship management (CRM) industry.

What came next for Siebel was a big play on AI, with his launch of C3 AI in 2009. The platform has helped companies like Royal Dutch Shell leverage AI technology to help reduce costs and automate tedious activities.

Here is how Siebel describes that AI opportunity (*https://oreil.ly/kEis4*): "This is a significant opportunity by any standard and the largest software market opportunity that I have seen in my professional career. Digital transformation enabled by enterprise AI remains at the top of the agenda of virtually every CEO and board globally. We see increasingly robust interest and demand for enterprise AI solutions, and our pipeline continues to grow substantially across all industries and all regions."

How big is this market? According to research from International Data Corporation (IDC) (*https://oreil.ly/sHY6H*), the spending is on track to exceed a whopping $500 billion by 2024, and the growth rate is forecasted at 16.4% per year.

AI will certainly be critical for the mainframe market as well. Some of the biggest players in the market include companies like IBM, Accenture, and Infosys, which provide high-end consulting services for large enterprises.

In this chapter, we'll take a look at AI and how it impacts the mainframe category. However, it is important to keep in mind that this is meant as a broad overview. The topic of AI is extensive and constantly changing. Plenty of additional resources are available to learn more about AI.

What Is AI?

Because of the hype of the tech industry—and even the effect of movies and television shows—the definition of AI is somewhat vague and fuzzy. It is further confused with plenty of other terms such as *machine learning* and *deep learning*.

Keep in mind that AI is not new. Its roots go back to 1956, when Professor John McCarthy put together a conference at Dartmouth University called "A Proposal for the Dartmouth Summer Research Project on Artificial Intelligence." Attendees included some of the top computer science academics—Marvin Minsky, Claude Shannon, Allen Newell, and Nathaniel Rochester. In fact, the conference featured the first demo of an AI program: the Logic Theorist solved various complex math theorems.

McCarthy defined AI as follows (*https://oreil.ly/aoULg*): "How to make machines use language, form abstractions and concepts, solve kinds of problems now reserved for humans, and improve themselves." Interestingly enough, many of the attendees did not like the term *artificial intelligence*, but no one could come up with anything better.

McCarthy's conception has held up fairly well. For the most part, AI is a broad topic that comprises how computers can learn, usually by processing large amounts of data. But AI has other subtopics like ML and deep learning (see Figure 10-1).

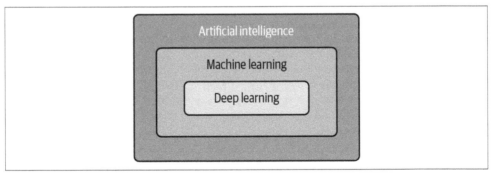

Figure 10-1. The levels of AI

The 1968 film *2001: A Space Odyssey* is considered one of the first modern depictions of AI. The story is about an onboard computer, HAL-9000, that ultimately takes control of the space vehicle and deems the crew to be useless. Interestingly, HAL is often considered to be a clever reference to IBM and its mainframes, because you can spell out IBM by looking at the letters that follow *H*, *A*, and *L* (that is, *I*, *B*, and *M*). But director Stanley Kubrick has called this a coincidence. HAL was a reference to "heuristic and algorithmic."

Why Use AI?

According to Deloitte's State of AI in the Enterprise survey (*https://oreil.ly/umogY*), which was based on interviews with over 2,700 IT and line-of-business executives across the world, there remains considerable enthusiasm for AI investments. About 57% of the respondents indicated that this technology will transform their organization during the next three years.

AI certainly offers the typical advantages for companies, such as improved automation and lower costs. But it offers many other benefits. If anything, AI is unique when it comes to enterprise software, which is often about collecting information (for sales, inventory, payroll, and so on), providing alerts, and helping with monitoring. At its core, this technology detects patterns that people may not see or have enough time to analyze. As a result, a company can use AI to anticipate changes in the markets, for example, so as to serve customers better, avoid certain risks, or find opportunities.

To get a sense of the impact of AI on a large enterprise, consider the case of a customer of C3 AI and Baker Hughes (a consortium called BakerHughesC3.ai) (*https://oreil.ly/IEdrL*). The customer, a leading oil and gas producer with hundreds of billions in revenues, wanted to find ways to reduce the costs of equipment failures. The equipment included oil well basins, offshore platforms, pipelines, retail operations, and refineries.

The company also had extensive legacy technology assets, including mainframe installations. These systems partially managed the millions of pieces of equipment across the globe. So the company needed a way to leverage its data but also use an AI platform that could scale on a global basis.

Yet success would not be about just technology. A strong leadership team was needed for the implementation. To this end, BakerHughesC3.ai established a global center of excellence (COE) that had two development teams spread across four countries. This allowed for better management, governance, and access to best practices. During the first year, BakerHughesC3.ai was able to create 2 major applications, and the goal is ultimately to have more than 15 (over the next 4 years).

One of the applications helps instrument engineers use predictive maintenance for all control valves. This has allowed the engineers to anticipate when the equipment may fail. This has not only significantly lowered costs but also improved the overall safety of field operations.

Another app, C3 AI Reliability for Compressors, allowed for predictive maintenance on all compressors for the equipment. This used a nonlinear ML module that was custom built. For the end users, the application was accessible via a web app that was built using the React framework.

Another example of the power of AI for the enterprise comes from Palantir Technologies. The company is one of the pioneers of providing AI services. For example, Palantir was critical in helping the US government after the terrorist attack of 9/11. According to many media reports, the company's technology was even used to help track down Osama bin Laden, though Palantir has declined to comment on this.

Over the years, Palantir has leveraged its technology foundation into commercial applications. Its Foundry platform is a comprehensive solution that handles backend data integration and the creation of models.

One of its customers is an automaker that was having quality and ratings problems with its manufacturing facilities. The company used Foundry to process data from warranty claims, diagnostics, dealer actions, vehicle sensors, and metadata. The resulting insights were made available to the company's plants, which could then react much quicker to emerging issues. Palantir created a sophisticated system to prioritize the actions to take. By doing this, the company was able to resolve issues 80% faster (*https://oreil.ly/cN9Kb*).

Downsides of AI

In August 2019, Apple and Goldman Sachs set out to upend the credit card market. The companies launched the Apple Card, which focused on privacy, simplicity, and low costs (there were no fees). They also leveraged sophisticated AI to help with determining the credit risks.

But unfortunately, the launch turned out to be a disaster. Twitter started lighting up with tweets from some of the legends of technology, including Apple cofounder Steve Wozniak. He noted that his wife got a smaller credit limit than him—even though she had higher income.

This gender bias was not a one-off. It appeared to be widespread. Even worse, when customers called Apple support, the response was (*https://oreil.ly/bIkEv*), "It's just the algorithm."

What's interesting is that the algorithm did not include gender. But this did not matter since other types of data can be proxies for gender and reflect certain biases. Apple and Goldman Sachs were able to resolve the problems, and the Apple Card has since become a big success. But this episode does point out the risks and complexities of AI. Even some of the most successful companies can get things very wrong.

What are some of the other ways that AI can go awry? Let's take a look:

Data

Many problems with AI are due to a lack of quality data. Lots of work usually needs to be done with the datasets to make them usable. Then ongoing monitoring must be performed. The process can be manual and time-consuming.

Fear

Feelings of misgiving about AI are common among employees. They may think the technology will ultimately take their jobs. This can result in poor adoption and failed AI projects. Therefore, extensive training and clear-cut messaging are essential. After all, AI is often not about replacing jobs but about providing more time for employees to focus on value-added tasks.

Opacity

AI models can be extremely complex and nearly impossible for people to understand. This can lead to distrust. How do we know if this algorithm is really valid? Could it just be right because of coincidence? In regulated industries, there really needs to be an understanding of the models. A new, emerging category called *explainability* allows for understanding of complex AI models.

Diversity

Diversity is generally lacking in the AI field. According to a study from New York University (*https://oreil.ly/cq3MC*), about 80% of AI professors are male. Only 15% of AI researchers at Facebook are women. This poses greater risks of bias, as we've seen with the Apple Card case. As much as possible, it is critical to have a more diverse team when it comes to AI.

Costs

Though costs are trending down, creating AI projects remains relatively expensive. The salaries for data scientists are high, as are the costs for the hardware and infrastructure. Companies looking to implement AI often need to hire IT consultants as well. Maintaining the AI models also carries costs.

According to a 2020 Burtch Works survey (*https://oreil.ly/LnMgP*), the average salary for an entry-level data scientist is about $95,000. For someone who is experienced and at a manager level, the compensation is at $250,000.

Machine Learning

In the early 1980s, philosopher John Searle sketched out his view of AI (*https://oreil.ly/XNnR4*). He saw it had two major forms:

Strong AI
> The machine is truly intelligent and can converse with humans effortlessly—to the point where it is impossible to detect that the AI is a machine. Some companies are working on strong AI, such as Google's DeepMind and OpenAI, but the field is still in the nascent stages.

Weak AI
> The computer is focused on a narrow task or domain. This would be an AI system that detects cancer or a sophisticated algorithm that can determine when a machine will break down.

Currently, we are at the stage of weak AI. But this is not to imply that the technology is lackluster. On the contrary, AI is making a significant impact across many industries.

A common approach in weak AI is ML. IBM developer Arthur Samuel came up with ML during the 1950s. He described it (*https://oreil.ly/hI3gE*) as a "field of study that gives computers the ability to learn without being explicitly programmed." At the time, he used this technology to allow a mainframe computer to play checkers. Robert Nealey, a top player of the game, lost to the computer (an IBM 7094 mainframe).

All in all, ML turned out to be a revolutionary concept, because the computer's actions could be based on data, not IF/THEN/ELSE commands or other predefined logic.

Keep in mind that there are a myriad of ML approaches, which depend on the algorithms used. But general workflows do exist. First, the ML system processes a dataset or training data, which can be labeled or unlabeled. The system then makes a prediction or classification based on the underlying patterns of the data.

Machine learning uses four types of classifications:

- Binary classification
- Multiclass classification
- Multilabel classification
- Imbalanced classification

We'll next take a look at these.

Binary Classification

Think of *binary classification* as Boolean logic—that is, true or false. But in an ML algorithm, the label is either 0 or 1. Because of discrete outcomes, you often use a Bernoulli probability distribution because it has only the results of "success" or "failure."

No doubt, binary classification is an easy approach, but it can still produce useful results. For example, a binary classification system can predict the following:

- Whether email is spam
- Whether a customer will buy
- Whether a customer will leave
- Whether a tumor is cancerous

A myriad of algorithms are used for binary classification. Popular ones include the following:

k-nearest neighbors
> This looks for clusters of similar data. It is based on the intuitive concept that values near each other will likely be good predictors. It's like the saying "Birds of a feather flock together."

Decision tree
> This is a flowchart for how a system operates. At each decision point, a probability is calculated. A decision tree is generally easy to understand and put together. It can also handle large amounts of data. However, it has the potential for error propagation. If even one of the decision points is wrong, the whole model could be useless.

Naive Bayes
> This algorithm is based on conditional probability. For example, it looks at what is likely to happen based on a prior outcome. The *naive* part means there is an assumption that the variables are independent of each other. This makes it very helpful for ML because there is usually a higher accuracy rate.

Support vector machine (SVM)
> This plots the data and determines the optimal hyperplane, which equally separates the different types of data. An SVM is usually good with handling complex relationships and outliers. However, this algorithm can consume lots of compute power and can be difficult to visualize.

Logistic regression
> This statistical method shows the correlation between variables (it is similar to regression analysis). But again, only two outcomes can result.

Multiclass Classification

A *multiclass classification* system has more than two class labels in the data. Some of its common use cases include character recognition and facial recognition. In fact, a multiclass classification system can have thousands of different labels.

A widely used statistical approach for this is the Multinoulli probability distribution. This allows for predicting where a value will belong to a certain class label. The algorithms include common ones like k-nearest neighbors, decision trees, and Naive Bayes, which we covered in the prior section. Also used are random forest, a simple algorithm comprising a set of various independent decision trees, and gradient boosting, in which a model is trained in a gradual manner.

Multilabel Classification

We have seen that binary and multiclass classification work with one label for each of the data items. But what if there are more than one? This is common for ML and is known as *multilabel classification*. An example of this is a movie that crosses genres. For example, a movie could be both a romance and a comedy.

To process multiple labels, you can use a Bernoulli probability distribution. Or you can use a transformation process that results in one label for the prediction. This means you can have traditional ML algorithms like decision trees, random forests, and gradient boosting.

Imbalanced Classification

Imbalanced classification usually involves binary data. However, one label dominates. This is common for fraud detection, in which a large number of data items are harmless, and a handful are pernicious. This is also the case with medical diagnosis, especially with rare forms of disease.

How do we handle imbalanced classification? A common approach is to use resampling techniques. This involves increasing the frequency of the class that has the minority of data items or decreasing the class with the majority. To do this, data is selected randomly.

Types of Machine Learning

An AI model can learn in three main ways. In this section, we'll take a look at each of them: supervised learning, unsupervised learning, and reinforcement learning.

Supervised Learning

Supervised learning is the most common approach (at least for business applications). Datasets are labeled, and the types of problems that are solved include classification and regression, which involve the relationship between independent and dependent variables (this analysis is often used for sales forecasts).

Let's explore a simple example. Suppose we are measuring customer churn. We analyze the level of engagement with the application, or the number of times the user visits the application. This is the input value. The supervisory signal, meanwhile, is a label that indicates whether the service has been terminated. In other words, this is a binary classification.

We then use an algorithm—such as support vector machine, naive Bayes, k-nearest neighbor, or neural networks—and run many iterations of that training data, and the weights will be adjusted. The model then detects the patterns and comes up with the predictions.

A key advantage of supervised learning is that it provides a point of comparison for the accuracy of the model. This is often based on a loss function, which finds the error rate.

But there are also downsides. First of all, you often need large amounts of data. What's more, the labeling can be challenging and subject to error. Next, you cannot use supervised learning in real time since there is no time for effective labeling. Finally, a model can consume significant compute power.

Unsupervised Learning

Unsupervised learning uses training data that is not labeled (see Figure 10-2 for a comparison with supervised learning). However, the approaches can be complex and use large amounts of compute power. Essentially, the AI attempts to find the inherent patterns in the training data. It is also difficult to determine the accuracy of unsupervised learning.

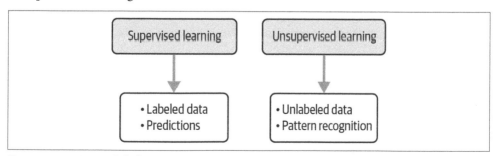

Figure 10-2. Several differences between supervised and unsupervised learning

Some of the methods for unsupervised learning include the following:

Anomaly detection
> This is about finding odd or unusual patterns in the data. This is particularly useful in fraud detection (say, for credit card transactions), as well as in making medical diagnoses.

Clustering
> In this most common approach to unsupervised learning, the AI detects groups of similar data. This is not the same as classification, as classification requires labeling but clustering does not.

Autoencoders
> A neural network translates data into a summarized version and then re-creates it. It's a complex process but has proven effective for applications like cleaning up images or topic modeling.

Association
> Data is nonnumeric; it comprises a set of relationships, like IF/THEN/ELSE statements. Association is effective with use cases like recommendation engines.

Another form of learning, *semisupervised learning*, blends supervised and unsupervised approaches. It still usually uses a lot of unlabeled data, but by using advanced AI systems, a model can create new data for the gaps. A major challenge with this approach is determining the accuracy.

 Amazon CEO and founder Jeff Bezos is a fan of semisupervised learning. Here's what he wrote about it in his 2017 shareholder letter (*https://oreil.ly/uhyEb*): "In the US, UK, and Germany, we've improved Alexa's spoken language understanding by more than 25% over the last 12 months through enhancements in Alexa's ML components and the use of semi-supervised learning techniques. (These semi-supervised learning techniques reduced the amount of labeled data needed to achieve the same accuracy improvement by 40 times!)"

Reinforcement Learning

Reinforcement learning is based on a reward-punishment system. It's similar to the way children learn. For example, when they touch the stove, they quickly realize what "hot" means and are more careful.

The technical process for reinforcement usually requires conducting many simulations. Actually, many of the applications have been with gaming. And one of the most notable examples is AlphaGo. Google's DeepMind created this model to play the board game Go, and in 2017, it beat Ke Jie, who was the world champion.

Yet reinforcement learning has more practical applications. Some use cases include robotics and investment analysis.

Deep Learning

Deep learning uses unstructured data, such as text and images, to find features and patterns. For example, a model can ingest many photos of dogs and cats. The deep learning will then find the features—like eyes, ears, and so on—that show the differences between the animals. True, a traditional ML model can also be used for recognition. Yet it will need to have labeled data.

Keep in mind that deep learning is not new. Its origins go back to the early 1960s with the efforts of computer researcher Frank Rosenblatt. He wrote a book, *Principles of Neurodynamics* (Spartan Books), that highlighted the main concepts of deep learning (though this is not what it was called at the time).

But it was not until the past 15 years or so that deep learning has become an essential part of AI. Consider that it has been the source of many of the innovations in AI. This is largely thanks to the tireless efforts of researchers like Yoshua Bengio, Geoffrey Hinton, and Yann LeCun during the 1980s and 1990s.

Several important trends have further accelerated the growth of deep learning:

Cloud computing
> This technology has made it easier to implement deep learning models, such as with the configuration and the access to data. The cloud also provides the ability to store huge amounts of data.

Data explosion
> With the ubiquity of computers, smartphones, and Internet of Things (IoT) devices, the amount of available data has grown significantly. This has made it possible to create much richer AI models.

Open source software
> Many of the top AI tools and platforms are freely available, such as TensorFlow, Keras, scikit-learn, and PyTorch. This has made it easy for anyone to create their own models.

GPUs
> These semiconductors allow for parallel processing. The pioneer of this technology, NVIDIA, used this originally for gaming. But GPUs have proven quite effective for processing AI models.

As should be no surprise, deep learning is complex. But let's get a general overview of how it works. At the heart of deep learning is a *neural network*, which is a function that processes data values and weights for each. In addition, a *bias* is a constant that helps with the calculations. All the processing is done in a hidden layer, which produces an output. This is iterated so as to get better predictions.

The *deep* part of deep learning refers to the hidden layers—usually there are many of them. But making adjustments to the weights in the model still can be problematic because traditional algorithms typically do not work well. One approach, however, has turned out to be quite useful: backpropagation. This works backward through the hidden layers to make the adjustments. By doing this, the results are usually more accurate.

Deep learning comes in various flavors. Here are some of the most common:

Convolutional neural networks (CNNs)
> These are usually for images and videos. A CNN will look at lines and then try to determine the shapes. This is done by making many iterations, which are called *convolutions*.

Recurrent neural networks (RNNs)
> These find patterns in a series of data items. RNNs have been useful for understanding language, making captions, and even predicting stock prices.

Generative adversarial networks (GANs)
> Ian Goodfellow developed GANs in 2014 after celebrating at a pub for his friend's graduation from a PhD program. He wanted to see if a deep learning model could create content. And the GAN model proved this out. It uses two deep learning models that compete against each other. GANs have been used to design clothing, mimic speech, and even create rap songs. But on the negative side, the technology has also been leveraged for deepfakes.

Data

According to John McKenny, senior vice president and general manager of Intelligent Z Optimization and Transformation at BMC, "With 30 billion business transactions traversing the mainframe daily, it is a wealth of institutional data and knowledge to be used for growth. In an environment of immense change and heightened customer expectations, mainframe data may be the key to remaining competitive. Historical mainframe data—when harnessed effectively—provides an important repository for actionable insights that could help deliver improved services, accelerate new product innovations, and determine opportunities for differentiated services."

Keep in mind that data is essentially the fuel for AI. It allows for the insights and accurate predictions that can help drive better business decisions. In other words, mainframes will be critical for AI and are likely to be a major advantage for large enterprises, such as those in the Fortune 500, in competition against startups.

Yet data can be extremely difficult to work with. This part of the AI process is often the most time-consuming and expensive. Mainframe systems have additional issues of integration with other databases and cloud platforms.

Despite this, the benefits of AI often outweigh the costs. The key is having an understanding of data and the best practices for using it. In the next few sections, we'll cover this in more detail.

Big Data

According to research by IDC (*https://oreil.ly/xFT9S*), the growth in data created from 2020 to 2023 will be more than over the past 30 years. The COVID-19 pandemic has accelerated this trend, as millions more people have had to work from home. But AI has certainly been another driver.

The use of data in an AI project is often called *big data*. This is generally defined as having three elements:

Volume
> This is the scale of the data. While there is no clear-cut definition, it is usually in the tens of terabytes. Note that volume is an area in which many tools—such as those based in the cloud—have made management much easier.

Variety
> This is about the various types of data, such as structured, semistructured, and unstructured. Sources of data also are varied and include social media and IoT.

Velocity
> This is the speed that data is created. For mainframes, an example is CICS, which generates large amounts of real-time transactional information. Among the three Vs for big data, velocity is usually the most difficult.

Over the years, other Vs have emerged. These include visualization (for graphs and charts for analytics), veracity (the accuracy of the data), and value (the usefulness of the data).

Finally, it's important to have an understanding of the different types of data:

Structured data
> This data has a defined format. For a mainframe, this is data in databases like Db2 and IMS. But it also includes VSAM and sequential files. Since this data is usually labeled, it is easier to use for AI models. However, we usually do not have enough structured data to train models. In a typical dataset, about 20% to 25% of the data is structured.

Unstructured data
> Typical examples include videos, emails, images, text files, and social media posts. Unstructured data can be extremely useful in AI models. But labeling or the use of deep learning algorithms is required to extract the features.

Semistructured data
> This is a blend of structured and unstructured data. However, the dataset often has more unstructured data. Some examples of semistructured data include XML and JSON files.

Time-series data
> This is data over time and can be structured or unstructured. A common use case is for creating AI models with IoT sensor data.

Synthetic data
> This data is created by simulations or AI algorithms like GANs. A major benefit of synthetic data is that it can be much cheaper than labeling existing data. According to research from Gartner (*https://oreil.ly/ac1Dr*), most of the data for AI will by synthetic.

Data Management

Because of the difficulties with data, it is important to start with a data strategy, which should have buy-in from the senior levels of the organization. Data is often scattered across different silos, and there may be resistance to using it in other departments (this is particularly the case with mainframe environments). But without a holistic view of data, AI efforts are likely to falter.

Another advantage of having a data strategy is that it can improve the success for IT purchases. Data solutions can be expensive, and many are point solutions. But a solid data strategy can enable a more strategic approach to purchases.

What should be in a data strategy? Here's a look at some of the key elements:

Inventory of data

What are all the sources of the data? Interestingly enough, it is common for a department to purchase a dataset even though it is owned by another department. As a result, there should be a central place that clearly identifies the data sources. There should also be use requirements. For example, how long can the database be used? It can be disastrous if there is a heavy investment in an AI project and then the data can no longer be used.

Standardization

Use consistent naming conventions for the data. Detailed notes should describe the nature of the data, including its origin, its storage location, the legal terms, and whether it is structured or unstructured.

Storage

This part of the strategy should not just be about having enough space for the data. Consideration for making it easily accessible should also be included.

Business objectives

What are the main initiatives for your organization, and how can data help? What needs to be done with the collection to get stronger results? Often this is about saving labor hours and cutting costs. But data can be essential in providing better insights. So how can the data be better used for this?

Data processing

The data plan should cover areas like data collection, preparation, and maintenance. What are the processes? Who has the roles to manage them?

Governance

Data is fraught with issues like privacy and bias. Violations can lead to fines and damaging media exposure. A process should be in place to ensure that the use of the data is appropriate. The rules should be easy to understand.

A common part of a data strategy is to use a *data lake*, a centralized repository for all structured and unstructured data. This is particularly attractive since AI is usually run on cloud platforms.

How does a data lake differ from a data warehouse? A *data warehouse* is focused on relational databases. But a data lake usually contains data in raw form. It is common for large organizations to have both types of data systems.

Not having enough data to create a model is common. A tragic example is the New Zealand mass shooting that killed 50 people in March 2019. The shooter was able to livestream this on Facebook since the AI systems could not adequately identify the incident. According to a blog post (*https://oreil.ly/8w6d7*) from Facebook's VP of Product Management Guy Rosen, "AI systems are based on 'training data,' which means you need many thousands of examples of content in order to train a system that can detect certain types of text, imagery, or video… [To detect these kinds of videos], we will need to provide our systems with large volumes of data of this specific kind of content, something which is difficult as these events are thankfully rare."

Log Data

One of the main sources of data for AI is *log data* (also referred to as *machine data*). This data can be derived from network devices, applications, and servers.

An AI model can analyze errors and outliers to detect or anticipate problems. In some cases, a system can fix the problems without any human intervention.

You can create your own models for this. But it is more common to use a log analysis tool, such as SolarWinds Loggly, Splunk, or Sumo Logic. Here are just some of the benefits:

Scale
> A log analysis tool can process enormous amounts of data. For example, Sumo Logic's platform manages more than 200 petabytes of data and over 20 million queries per day.

Integration
> A good log analysis tool has connectors to the main cloud platforms like Azure, Google Cloud, and AWS. This makes it much easier to perform AI on the data.

Dashboards and visualizations
> There are templates that can easily create these, allowing for more effective monitoring of IT environments.

Cloud
> A cloud log analysis tool will allow for the centralization of that data. Storage costs should also be lower since there is no need to make hardware purchases.

While all these are important advantages, there are still challenges with mainframe environments. Note that the built-in logging system is somewhat unique. That is, it is based on the System Management Facility (SMF), a set of system and user-written routines for the collecting, formatting, and storing of jobs and records. The logs are then written to a primary SMF dataset. And when this is full, a secondary dataset is used.

So what is the problem? The main issue is that the SMF system does not collect some of the information that can allow for better log analysis, such as data types for user identification, the job type, and so on. Rather, a systems engineer needs to create a data forwarding system, and this means that the system must work in real time. Next, filters are needed for the data to avoid overload. And finally, it is important to make sure the data is in the right format for a data analysis tool.

The bottom line: when it comes to working with mainframes and data, we should not assume that the systems work similarly to those in the cloud or on PCs. Reworking is often required. If not, the AI models are likely to provide subpar results or will just fail.

Data Wrangling

Data wrangling is the cleaning, structuring, and enriching of raw data into a form that can be usable for AI models (data wrangling is also called *data remediation* and *data munging*). Various tools can help automate the process. But human intervention—from data scientists, for example—is still needed.

As should be no surprise, many techniques can be used for data wrangling—and some can be quite complex. But let's take an overview of some of the main ones:

Outliers
This is data that is outside much of the dataset. This could be an indication that the data is incorrect. But in some cases, it could be a valuable sign—for example, in detecting fraud or malicious computer viruses.

Deduplication
It's common for data to have repetitive items. Yet this could result in inaccurate outcomes for AI. Thus, it is important to run scans for deduplication.

Merging
Various columns in a dataset may be similar, which can lead to distorted results in the AI models. You might want to consider eliminating some of the columns or merging them.

Consistency
Business data can have ambiguous definitions. For example, "revenue," "profits," and "cash flows" may have different meanings. So it is important to understand the nuances and be consistent with the data.

Validation rules

These can help improve the accuracy of the data. For example, a negative quantity in inventory is clearly wrong. The validation rules can be easy to set up with IF/THEN/ELSE statements.

Implied data

You can take several data groups and come up with new data. An example is birth dates. You can subtract these from the current date and get the ages.

Missing data

Gaps in datasets are common. Yet this does not mean that the information is bad. One approach is to smooth out the data (for example, by using averages). However, if a significant percentage of certain data is missing, it is probably best to not use it.

Binning

Sometimes we don't need data to be highly specific. Is it really important that a person is 42 or 43? Usually not. A better approach may be to group the data by ages of 20 to 30, 31 to 40, and so on.

Conversion tables

Similar to a validation table, a conversation table helps create more standardization. One example is translating the decimal system to the metric system. Or it could be for converting exchange rates for currencies.

One-hot encoding

This is a technique for working with categorical data that has nonnumeric values. For example, a column of data may list different versions of the iPhone, such as iPhone 12 Pro, iPhone 12, and iPhone 12 mini. However, to process this, we still need to assign a number to each item. We can set the iPhone 12 Pro to 1, iPhone 12 to 2, and so on. But a problem arises: the algorithm may consider iPhone 12 mini to be more important because the number is higher. To deal with this, one-hot encoding creates different labels, like "is_iPhone12Pro", "is_iPhone12", and "is_iPhone12mini". Then, for each, you have either 1 if it exists or 0 if it does not.

According to an Accenture research survey (*https://oreil.ly/L8dR3*) of more than 1,100 executives across the globe, about 48% said that they had data quality problems.

The AI Process

Any type of enterprise software deployment can be challenging, time-consuming, and expensive. But when it comes to AI, the problems are magnified. According to Gartner, about 80% of projects are never deployed (*https://oreil.ly/2nagG*).

This is why it is usually a good idea to buy off-the-shelf AI solutions. Many are available (largely because of the surge in venture capital during the past decade). AI solutions also have the benefit of being used in diverse environments and should provide access to better datasets.

Interestingly enough, many existing traditional software systems, like CRMs and enterprise resource planning (ERP) applications, already have a rich set of AI capabilities. So before initiating a major project or buying off-the-shelf software, you should learn about the capabilities of the technologies you already own. This is a good way to get some experience with AI.

Yet existing solutions may not be enough, and the best option may be to put together an AI project. If so, the process should be well planned and detailed. Here are some of the key steps:

Retain consultants
> This can be an effective way to start. You will get a team that has experience with various projects. They will understand the practical capabilities of AI, know what to focus on, help with vendor evaluation, provide training, and help navigate the risks. Consultants can also assist in building a strong foundation and even assemble an in-house team.

Focus on solving a clear business problem
> This is not as easy as it sounds. A common reason for a failed AI project is that the goals are too ambitious. A better approach is to start with a small project. For example, it could be to help automate the password-reset process. This could use natural language processing and integrations with the existing authentication system. Such a project would also be easy to measure. The idea is to get quick wins, which will help build momentum for further investments in AI.

Assess IT
> Once you have identified the goals of the project, you want to make sure your organization has the necessary technologies and datasets. As should be no surprise, there are usually some gaps. But by understanding these at the start of a project, you will save time and money.

Obtain educational resources

This step is often ignored, and that can be a big mistake. Many technical people do not have a background in data science and AI. So it is a good idea to have some workshops or online courses.

Start with a small team

One mistake is to go on a hiring spree for data scientists. This can be expensive and bog down the process. Rather, start with one data scientist and a data engineer. Then you can bring in several people from the organization who understand the business domain and the existing IT infrastructure. Such a team should be more than sufficient, especially when you have a clearly defined project.

AI projects generally follow one of two approaches. The most common one is the *analytical model*, which focuses on generating insights and forecasts. Such applications do not need real-time data. They are also easier for integration with mainframes.

Next, the *operational model* builds AI into a product—say, with a smartphone app like Uber. This is extremely complicated technology, as the models are constantly being updated and process data in real time. Then again, an operational model can be transformative for a business.

Regardless of whether you use operational or analytical AI, several important steps occur in the AI modeling process. We have already looked at one of these in this chapter: data management and wrangling. After this, other steps to consider include the following:

Model selection

A data scientist plays a key role here, because they have the experience to know which algorithms to try out, as well as what the data requirements will be. It is also common to use several algorithms (this is known as an *ensemble model*). Finally, no model will be perfect—which is known as the *no free lunch theorem*.

Model training

As you process data in the algorithms, they will learn new insights. This process includes several phases. First, the data needs to be randomized so false patterns aren't detected. Then, in a test phase, which includes 70% to 80% of the data, the data scientist tunes the model (to come up with the right parameters, for example). Next, the validation phase involves 10% to 20% of the data and provides a sense of the model's accuracy. And finally, to have a final assessment of the performance, 5% to 10% of the dataset is processed.

Deployment

This *operationalizing* of AI can be a tricky process. A new category of tools and methodologies called *machine learning operations* (MLOps) has emerged to help with this. A big part of the process is monitoring the AI system to make sure the results are accurate. But areas like compliance and data integrity may also be points of focus.

The design of the UI for an AI application is often neglected. This can be a major oversight. Since AI may be complicated to understand and use, an easy-to-use interface is often needed.

Accuracy

Since AI is based on probabilities, it is important to measure the accuracy of the model. But this can be a challenging process. For example, suppose you are using an AI model that diagnoses for multiple sclerosis and has an accuracy rate of 99%.

Sounds good, right? Not necessarily. The main reason is that multiple sclerosis is a rare disease, affecting about 90 patients per 100,000. So if a model always indicates that a person does not have the disease, it will be correct more than 99% of the time.

In such a case, the accuracy of the model can be measured in other ways. This could be looking at the chances of getting a false negative (indicating that a person does not have the disease when they really do) or a false positive.

Accuracy may be distorted by the type of datasets as well. In *overfitting*, the AI memorizes certain patterns. A very high accuracy rate, say over 90%, may indicate overfitting. A good approach for addressing this problem is to collect more-diverse data. Or you can also use a less sophisticated algorithm or set of algorithms.

Another issue is *underfitting*, in which there is a general lack of accuracy between the input and output variables. For the most part, the model is too simple and the datasets don't reflect the real world.

Some AI models are enormous in scale. This is especially the case for those focused on language understanding, such as Google Brain. It has a staggering 1.6 trillion parameters in the model (*https://oreil.ly/je8m3*).

An AI Demo

Developing AI models is fairly easy. Many of the tools are open source and powerful. So let's follow a simple demo of creating a model. We'll use a linear regression formula that predicts revenues based on the amount spent on advertising.

A good choice for this is to use the scikit-learn platform, which allows for many types of algorithms including SVM and random forests. You do not have to write these from scratch. Rather, you can just use a few commands.

To download scikit-learn, a good option is to use Anaconda (*https://oreil.ly/27Vv5*). This comes with various tools like NumPy, pandas, and Jupyter Notebook. With Jupyter, you can create a notebook for your model via your web browser, and the language is Python, the most widely used for AI and ML. Jupyter is based on a listing of cells in which you place your commands, and then you press Shift + Enter to execute each of them. But first you click New and then Python 3 to create a new notebook.

Now let's enter the code. We'll start by importing the modules:

```
import pandas as pd ❶
import numpy as np ❷
import matplotlib.pyplot as plt ❸
%matplotlib inline
from sklearn import linear_model ❹
```

❶ Allows for working with tables of data. We also use pd to set this as a variable, which we can refer to in our code.

❷ Includes functions for working with arrays.

❸ These two lines make it possible to use graphs and visualizations.

❹ The function for the linear regression model.

Then we enter code for bringing in the data and creating a table and chart:

```
df = pd.read_csv(r"advertising.csv") ❶
df ❷
plt.scatter(df.advertising, df.revenues) ❸
```

❶ Imports the data, which is in the form of a comma-separated values (CSV) file. You also probably need to specify a path for the file.

❷ Shows a table of the data.

❸ Shows a scatter plot chart of the data.

Figure 10-3 shows what a screen will look like.

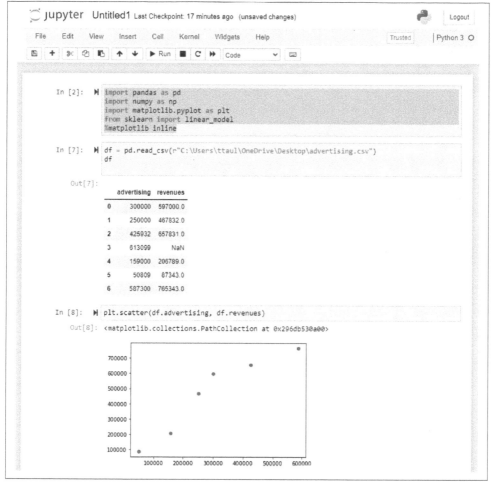

Figure 10-3. A Jupyter notebook

But the dataset has a problem. In the table, there are no revenues for item 3. This is indicated with NaN (not a number). But when using models with scikit learn, you need to have numbers in all the columns.

What to do? We can impute a value or delete it. In our case, we'll do a deletion:

```
df = df.dropna(how = "any")
```

But there is another problem: the data is not in the correct format. The data for the advertising spending must be in the form of a feature matrix, which has two dimensions. What's more, we need to make an adjustment to the revenues—we need to make them into a target vector, which is one column of data:

```
advertising = df.iloc[:, 0].values.reshape(-1,1) ❶
revenues = df.iloc[:, 1].values.reshape(-1,1) ❷
```

❶ Turns the advertising data into a feature matrix

❷ Makes the revenue data into a target vector

We then create the linear regression model:

```
regmodel = linear_model.LinearRegression()
regmodel.fit(advertising, revenues)
revenues_forecast = regmodel.predict(advertising)
```

This finds the best-fit line between advertising and revenue. This is done by creating an equation in the following form: $y = mx + b$. The m is a coefficient that estimates the slope of the line, and x is the value for the advertising spending. The b is the *intercept*, or the starting value, on the y-axis of the chart. With this, you can get a prediction for y, which represents the revenue.

We can use this code to chart the best-fit line:

```
plt.scatter (advertising, revenues) ❶
plt.plot (advertising, revenues_forecast, color='red') ❷
plt.show() ❸
```

❶ Creates a scatter graph for the advertising and revenue

❷ Creates a line graph for the best-fit line

❸ Displays the chart, which includes the scatter and line graphs

Figure 10-4 shows what the chart looks like.

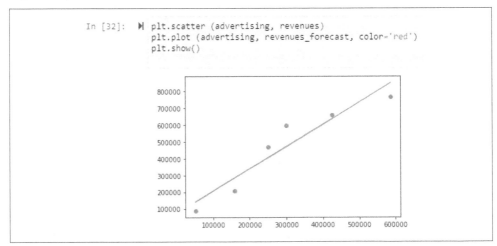

Figure 10-4. A best-fit line for a linear regression

Finally, you can measure the accuracy of this model:

```
print (regmodel.score (advertising, revenues))
```

This is the R-squared measure, and it is 0.897. This means that 89.7% of the predictions for the revenues can be explained by the model.

Again, this model is simple. But it is a good idea to start with easier ones. They are often good enough.

AI on Z

IBM has a long history of investing in AI. One of the company's innovations was Deep Blue, which was started in the mid-1980s. Its focus was on using sophisticated analytics and AI capabilities for chess playing.

Over time, the system got better and better. In 1996, Deep Blue took on world chess champion Garry Kasparov and beat him in a six-game match.

The learnings of Deep Blue would be pivotal for the next step in the evolution of AI for IBM: Watson. The first test of this system came in 2011, when it became a contestant on the TV quiz show *Jeopardy!* and prevailed against two of the show's biggest winners. After this, IBM would use the Watson platform to help companies in a variety of industries including energy, transportation, and healthcare.

So what about the company's mainframes and using AI? IBM has been retooling them with a myriad of AI tools and systems. Open source data science packages include TensorFlow, Open Neural Network Exchange (ONNX), PyTorch, scikit-learn, IBM Snap Machine Learning (Snap ML), and Apache Spark. IBM has also optimized its compilers to integrate these tools. Connections are also available with IBM proprietary platforms like Db2 AI for z/OS, IBM Z Operations Analytics, Watson, and Cloud Pak for Data.

"IBM Z is a top-grade AI infrastructure that offers the combination of low-latency, high performance, reduced complexity, and resiliency within a security-rich environment that enterprises demand," said Elpida Tzortzatos, who is an IBM Fellow and CTO of z/OS. "Therefore, our goal is to provide a comprehensive and consumable AI experience for operationalizing AI on Z, as well as build a world-class AI inferencing platform."

The strategy at IBM is to allow customers to build and train models on their platforms of choice. The company has then leveraged ONNX to easily transfer the models to Z for deployment. This means it is possible to use AI for transactional processes so as to allow for real-time analytics. There is also minimal movement of sensitive enterprise data, which improves security and governance.

"When it comes to operationalizing AI, there is a need for organizations to address the requirements related to infusing AI models into applications efficiently without impacting transactional performance and causing complexity," said Tzortzatos.

An example of this is an IBM bank client that wanted to detect fraud earlier, such as with credit card transaction authorizations. Initially, the firm deployed its AI system on a unified inference platform. But this caused a myriad of issues, such as time-outs that slowed transactions and lessened the impact of the fraud detection. But moving the model to Z resulted in a consistent response time of 1 to 2 milliseconds, which met the bank's rigorous service-level agreements (SLAs). The bank also improved its transactions per second tenfold. "By using AI on Z, the bank was able to detect fraud in real time during the credit card transaction authorization process and reduce losses due to early fraud identification," said Tzortzatos.

This is just one example. IBM has used AI on the Z mainframe for the clearing and settlement of trades, anti–money laundering, risk analysis, loan approvals, and healthcare.

AIOps

Artificial intelligence for IT operations (AIOps) is becoming a more important factor in mainframe environments. This is a new category, as Gartner coined the term in 2017. But the innovation has been fast and the results encouraging.

AIOps involves ingesting large amounts of information and applying AI and ML algorithms to it in real time. By doing this, IT managers are able to do the following:

Anomaly identification
> This could be issues with the performance of the systems or even potential cybersecurity breaches. Often the detection can be done fast, and some of the fixes may even be automated.

Improvement
> So long as the data is high-quality and the AI models are effective, the AIOps platform will learn over time. This means improvement in the operations will be ongoing.

Root-cause analysis
> A sophisticated AIOps system should be able to find the reasons for breakdowns and provide insights on how to prevent future issues.

Predictive monitoring
> This is one of the most powerful features of AIOps. The AI can provide alerts before something in the IT environment is about to break down.

As with any AI system, strong data practices need to be in place. Though this is no easy feat with mainframe environments, the benefits should be worth the effort.

Given the complexities of IT environments, relying on manual approaches is getting tougher. Moreover, traditional IT systems often generate large volumes of alerts, which puts even more pressure on staff. In mainframe environments, AIOps can provide more transparency with the systems and data. This not only improves overall performance but also helps reduce the costs of running these machines.

For example, one of the leading AIOps tools is from Dynatrace. Its software can gain insights from complex CICS Transaction Server systems, IMS web services, LPARs, and tracing for IBM MQ. There is also a root-cause analysis module that does not require configuration.

Yet this is not to imply that humans will ultimately be replaced. Rather, the automation capabilities of AIOps will mean that IT professionals will have much more time focusing on areas that need attention. In fact, Broadcom's AIOps system is focused on how to leverage the technology to increase the productivity of IT professionals. The company refers to this as *augmented intelligence*.

Successful AIOps requires a disciplined approach. "Start with a focused use case, such as detection, and inputting historical data can help demystify the process by showing how known issues are detected and help prove the value of moving to an AIOps-based approach," said BMC's John McKenny (the company has its own AIOps platform). "Gradual adoption not only ensures that your organization is employing AIOps tools to their full potential—it allows employees to learn the tools and adapt processes without the upheaval of a sudden, major change."

Conclusion

AI is likely to be one of the most important drivers for growth and innovation with mainframes. The key advantage is that these machines have access to enormous amounts of data.

In this chapter, we walked through the core concepts of AI, starting with an overview of ML and deep learning. These techniques can help automate tedious processes and provide for predictions and insights. But the AI process is difficult. This is especially the case with data management. In this chapter, we looked at how to put together a strategy and identified some best practices for data wrangling.

We also saw some unique challenges with mainframes and AI. For example, there are major differences in how mainframes use log data. In addition, this chapter explored the AI modeling process through a simple demo using open source tools.

In the next chapter, we'll discuss robotic process automation (RPA) and low-code and no-code systems.

CHAPTER 11

Robotic Process Automation, and Low-Code and No-Code Systems

Robotic process automation (RPA) allows for automating tedious and repetitive processes. This category is also one of the fastest growing in enterprise software. Based on research from IDC (*https://oreil.ly/WJoNw*), the spending is expected to go from $17 billion in 2020 to $30 billion by 2024.

One of the biggest reasons for the success of RPA is UiPath, the dominant developer of software in the industry. For 2021, the company's revenues were growing by over 60% and annual recurring revenue (ARR) was $653 million across UiPath's 8,500 customers.

In April of that year, the company launched its initial public offering (IPO) and raised $1.3 billion. The market value of the shares was about $32 billion.

Yet the early days for UiPath were rocky. By 2015, the company was on the verge of going bust. But cofounder and CEO Daniel Dines did not give up. He set out to reimagine RPA by using technologies like computer vision to read screens for better automation and low-code systems to allow for developing automaton bots without having to be a coder. As a result, he was able to help enterprise customers better implement automation of their IT systems.

Keep in mind that—in the RPA category—many of the early customers had mainframe environments. The technology would prove effective in improving performance and lowering costs.

But this type of automation is still in the early phases. Other technologies like low code and no code will likely have a big impact. So in this chapter, we'll take a look at all of these to see how they can provide for modernization of the mainframe.

What Is RPA?

The RPA industry has been around since 2003, when Blue Prism launched its first software platform. The technology relied primarily on screen scraping to automate user interfaces—for example, for CRM and ERP systems. The main focus was usually for back-office operations.

The RPA industry, though, was actually considered a low-growth category. The perception was that the technology was rudimentary and the growth opportunities were not particularly promising. But Blue Prism, as well as other companies like Automation Anywhere, were building strong businesses in the RPA market.

In 2012, the chief evangelist at Blue Prism, Pat Geary, coined the term *RPA*. Before this, the software category was ill-defined and was described in different ways.

The term *RPA* is somewhat muddled, though. The word *robotic* does not refer to a physical robot. Instead, it is software, often referred to as a *bot*. This program performs a set of automations, such as cutting and pasting, logging into an application, accessing a database, selecting certain buttons on a screen, extracting content from PDFs, and so on.

The *process* part of the term is also not quite accurate. This implies a comprehensive approach, not the handling of specific tasks.

Regardless of the ambiguities of the term, RPA technology has nonetheless proven to be effective in implementing automation in enterprise environments. In fact, RPA has been shown to generate a strong return on investment (ROI) within a relatively short period of time. Consider a 2019 survey from Computer Economics Technology Trends (*https://oreil.ly/QmIRo*), which included 250 companies. Of those that implemented RPA, about half reported a positive ROI within 18 months. The other respondents reported a break-even performance.

According to a survey from LinkedIn (*https://oreil.ly/nUTOR*), the job category with the second-highest growth rate is robotics engineer. The increase was 40% in 2020. Also, in a study from UiPath called "State of the RPA Developer Report," about 84% of respondents indicated that having RPA skills would be a benefit for their careers.

RPA has a multitude of benefits:

Digital transformation
  This describes the general process of a traditional company that looks to transform its business with new technologies. This can be a big challenge: retooling or eliminating legacy systems can be difficult as they often are used for mission-critical operations. RPA provides a way to mitigate these issues. Bots are relatively easy to create and deploy. RPA can also be a way to build a foundation for more sophisticated automation systems, such as business process management or AI.

AI
  More RPA systems are leveraging AI technology. This allows for more agility and flexibility with the automations. If anything, AI allows bots to take on tasks as a human would.

24/7
  Except for occasional downtime for maintenance and updates, bots work on a continuous basis. This is one of the reasons ROI is so high for RPA.

Process analysis
  Some RPA tools do process analysis. One popular approach is to use process mining (we will look at this later in this chapter). Often this means using sophisticated ML and AI to map out the existing processes and determine more optimal ones. No doubt, this can greatly increase the effectiveness of the automations.

Employee impact
  Implementing RPA means that employees will spend less time with tedious and repetitive tasks. As a result, they will likely be more productive and satisfied with their roles. RPA can also be instrumental in providing insights and better approaches to handling certain issues.

Compliance
  A bot will always carry out the same task. A high level of accuracy results, which will improve compliance.

Power of small changes
  Saving a few minutes on a task may not seem significant. But for a global enterprise, the impact can certainly be great.

Customer experiences
  More streamlined operations for the back office can mean improved customer satisfaction. For example, a bot can automate various tasks for the processing of a mortgage loan, which can mean getting approval in minutes, not days. But RPA can also be useful for front-office applications, such as a chatbot for automated customer service applications.

Scalability

> If a surge in activity or customer demand occurs, bots can easily handle the volume. This was critical for many companies to handle the impact of the COVID-19 pandemic.

Integration

> RPA is built to automate many types of applications. This greatly enhances automation opportunities. Moreover, there is little need for configuration with the applications.

The Disadvantages of RPA

RPA definitely has some downsides and risk factors. One of the notable ones is the cost. Multiyear subscriptions and licenses might be added on top of that. In the meantime, costs for training and consultants need to be considered. But of course, there are other issues, such as the following:

Assessment

> If the RPA developers lack a good understanding of existing company processes, RPA could be far from optimal. In a sense, bad practices could be automated, leading to bad performance.

Breakage

> If a bot is too rigid, it may not work. This is usually the case when a task is subject to period changes. This breakage issue can also make RPA difficult to scale across a large organization. Interestingly enough, the system may require considerable monitoring and ongoing maintenance, which can easily become a large and unexpected cost.

Security

> An RPA system may handle sensitive information, such as for employees, vendors, and so on. Thus, if appropriate cybersecurity policies are not in place, a breach could happen.

Macros, Scripts, and APIs

Software applications certainly provide for extensive automation. Databases are prime examples. They have brought major efficiencies to businesses and have been a key for growth for mainframe computers, as seen with Db2 and IMS.

But applications cannot do everything. This is why other forms of supporting automations have emerged, such as macros and scripts. Even though these are technically simple, they have still been quite effective.

Yet these approaches have their own problems. They can be tough to manage and may be rigid. So to deal with these problems, application programming interfaces (APIs) are often used. This software connects two or more applications to perform a task. Actually, APIs have become a massive business. Just look at Stripe, which is a fast-growing startup. The company's APIs make it much easier—say, with just a few lines of code—to connect to existing financial systems to help speed up the development of fintech apps. Even though the company was founded in 2009, the valuation of this startup is over $100 billion.

Mainframes use a myriad of APIs. We already looked at Zowe and how it can connect to many of the key services like CICS, z/OS, and Db2.

But APIs have their downsides as well. First of all, they do require some technical background to use. Next, the testing needs to be stringent and ongoing (although services can help with this). And finally, no good APIs may be available for certain systems.

So how is RPA different? What makes it more than just a macro or API? RPA is essentially a development tool, allowing for the creation of variables, loops, IF/THEN/ELSE statements, and so on. Such capabilities are seamlessly integrated with the UI of many applications. Because of this, you do not have to rip out existing systems.

An RPA platform also has orchestration, which allows management of the automations—for example, for monitoring and governance. But it can also help with implementing APIs.

Keep in mind that the development tools for RPA are often downloadable Windows software. This increases speed and improves integrations. The orchestration is usually a cloud-based system that hooks into the Windows software.

Types of RPA

RPA is not monolithic. It comes in different flavors, even though some platform systems may use all of them. Here's a look at the main types of RPA:

Attended RPA

> This may also be referred to as *robotic desktop automation (RDA)*. Regardless of the name, this technology is used to help people perform their jobs better. A typical use case is in a call center. When a call comes in, the attended RPA can provide relevant information, and the employee can use automation to move this data to another application.

Unattended RPA

> This automates tasks without the intervention of people. For example, an RPA bot will be triggered when an invoice is received, and the system will process it. Much of the attended RPA is handled in the back office.

Cognitive automation
> This uses AI and ML for automating tasks. One popular approach is natural language processing (NLP), which "understands" written or spoken language. This can be used to create a chatbot to manage certain customer interactions.

Process Methodologies

Before any RPA system is implemented, existing processes should be evaluated. This often involves bringing in consultants who understand the various process methodologies. They may also use tools like process mining.

Here is a look at the main process methodologies:

Lean
> Toyota developed this in the 1950s for the production of high-quality cars at scale (we learned about this in Chapter 9). This methodology is one of the key reasons the company was so successful in gaining market share in the US. For the most part, this approach is focused on continuous improvement. Some elements of Lean include value (what the customer considers important and worth paying for), value stream (the mapping of processes across development, production, and distribution so as to optimize workflows and reduce waste), and flow (the breaking down of processes to identify bottlenecks).

Six Sigma
> This uses advanced statistical metrics to measure and track process improvement in an organization. Six Sigma originated in the mid-1980s with Motorola, and then it was adopted by the legendary CEO of General Electric, Jack Welch. Six Sigma measurements are based on the bell curve. Its focus is on having defects less than six standard deviations from the mean. Six Sigma also has different levels of proficiencies for the people involved. For example, a White Belt is a novice, whereas as Master Black Belt has the highest designation and is in charge of the project.

Lean Six Sigma
> This is a blend of Lean and Six Sigma. Essentially, it involves statistical concepts along with continuous improvement.

Which one is best? There is no bright-line answer to this question. It is common to start with Lean and then perhaps move over to Six Sigma. Some organizations have their own variation of the different approaches.

What is important is that structure and discipline are involved in understanding and optimizing existing processes. If not, the RPA software is likely to show poor results or even fail.

Optical character recognition (OCR) technology has been around for many years. It includes a document scanner, which could be a smartphone, that uses software to recognize text. OCR is a critical part of most RPA systems because they work with paper documents. With the innovations in AI and fuzzy logic, OCR has become much more accurate, though problems still exist. So when it comes to evaluating RPA software, it's a good idea to look at the OCR capabilities. For example, some use cases need to be able to recognize handwriting.

RPA Roles

While RPA can provide significant improvements in automation, a support staff is still needed. This is especially the case for enterprise implementations.

One key role is the RPA sponsor. This person is usually an executive and has the overall responsibility for the RPA platform. But let's take a look at the other roles:

RPA champion
>   This is the evangelist for the RPA system. They help with the messaging—say, with videos and blog posts—and the training. This person may also be the RPA change manager. This person's role involves coming up with approaches to get buy-in and adoption of the technology.

Business analyst or subject-matter expert (SME)
>   This person has experience with a certain department or function within the organization. An effective business analyst helps identify the areas that could be improved with automation. They should also have some proficiency with technology (for example, to evaluate vendors). What's more, a business analyst comes up with the process design document, which is a guide for the types of automations to develop. This person also helps with the management of the project.

RPA developer
>   This person codes the bots. Usually, they have certifications for platforms like UiPath or Automation Anywhere. They also have backgrounds in computer languages like #C, Java, or .NET, as well as experience with databases and enterprise applications.

RPA infrastructure engineer
>   This person helps with the server installation and configuration of the RPA system. They can also help come up with the right IT architecture. As a result, an RPA infrastructure engineer should have a background in network/administration, cloud systems, virtualization, and databases.

RPA solution architect

This is similar to an RPA developer. However, an RPA solution architect usually provides help in the early stages with mapping out the technology strategy. This usually means selecting the right tools and understanding the integrations. The goal should be to build the right foundation for scaling the RPA implementation and allowing for the adoption of next-generation technologies like AI.

RPA supervisor

This is the manager who handles the day-to-day activities. This person typically has a blend of business and technical expertise. They should also have a track record of putting budgets together and delivering projects on time.

RPA service support

This role is often overlooked. But RPA systems do need to have ongoing support for technical questions from users.

Something else that can be helpful for the success of an RPA implementation is the center of excellence (CoE). This team, which doesn't have to be a large group, helps with the overall strategy for development, deployment, and monitoring of the platform.

Two approaches can be used to organize a CoE. In a *centralized CoE*, one team manages the strategy for all departments. In a *federated CoE*, each business unit has a separate team.

Of course, you can also blend the two. This is what UiPath does with its own CoE: a core group is at the headquarters, and then RPA champions are in every department.

Evaluating RPA Software

Well over 80 types of RPA systems are on the market. And this should be no surprise. Since RPA is a hot market, venture capitalists and angel investors have shown lots of interest.

However, this has also made it much more difficult to evaluate an RPA solution. The reality is that it is impossible to look at all of them.

Then what to do? Let's take a look at some strategies:

Research

An effective way to winnow down the list of RPA vendors is to check out analysis from firms like Gartner. They have teams of analysts that try out the software and talk to many customers. Various websites also provide user-generated ratings and commentary. Top ones include G2.com and TrustRadius (*https://www.trust radius.com*).

Standard features

Some RPA solutions do not have the kinds of functions that a platform should have. You should ensure that standard features are included, like a system to create bots, integrations with many enterprise applications, and a good system to track the bots.

Backing

You want an RPA vendor that has been able to attract substantial venture capital funding, is publicly traded, or is part of a larger company. This indicates enough resources for support and ongoing innovation of the platform.

Ecosystem

A key to the power of RPA is integration with your IT assets. But even the largest software vendors cannot do everything. That's why it is important for there to be an application store system to allow for third-party developers. No doubt, this has been critical for growth for the larger RPA companies like UiPath, Automation Anywhere, and Blue Prism.

Costs

As mentioned earlier in this chapter, some RPA systems can have substantial fees. If you are evaluating two systems with comparable features, take the one with the lower costs. What's more, you can usually negotiate for discounts, as the competitive environment in the industry is quite intense.

Try before you buy

Once you have a short list of RPA vendors, you can try out the software. There is often a free trial or community edition (this is always free but has limits on the number of users). For the evaluation, make sure the software has a full set of RPA features. Next, how easy is it to create bots and monitor them? Also, are security features built in? And finally, look at the training resources. Will they be sufficient to make for a seamless implementation?

It's true that the evaluation process for an RPA system can be time-consuming, but being thorough is essential. After all, it can be difficult to move to another one. So before making a purchase, make sure the RPA vendor has a platform that meets your needs and the resources to ensure strong innovation.

Process Mining

As we've seen earlier in this chapter, it's recommended to map and analyze current processes before implementing an RPA system. If not, inefficient processes could be automated.

But analyzing an organization's processes is time-consuming and subject to interpretation. It can also be difficult for massive enterprises.

This is where *process mining* comes in. It's software that detects processes and finds the bottlenecks.

The origins of process mining go back to the 1990s. Wil van der Aalst, a professor of computer science at the Eindhoven University of Technology in the Netherlands, was frustrated about current approaches to process automation. He thought they essentially were disconnected from the reality of modern organizations.

So he set out to come up with a better approach, which he called *process mining*. His thesis was to analyze event data, such as the logs created by systems and applications. This would be a more objective approach to understanding the interrelationships.

Yet getting adoption was excruciatingly slow. There were problems in getting access to datasets as well as difficulties in getting the attention of data scientists.

But van der Aalst was persistent. He wrote a myriad of papers on process mining and encouraged other universities to teach his approach. He also was critical in providing assistance for the creation of open source software projects. Then he wrote a book entitled *Process Mining: Discovery, Conformance and Enhancement of Business Processes* (Springer). Because of these efforts, the process-mining industry started to pick up speed—and has seen nice growth during the past decade.

After all, a variety of startups in the space have raised large amounts of venture capital. Large RPA players, like UiPath, have made acquisitions to bolster their process-mining capabilities.

How does process mining work? The technology is quite complex. But let's take a high-level look at it. Again, there will be the analysis of event logs. Yet the scale is enormous in order to allow for much better pattern recognition. It's similar to how AI works.

In terms of the analysis, one of the approaches is discovery. This evaluates a process on an as-is basis, which involves mapping the workflows and creating visualizations. With the discovery of information, it is possible to create baselines for more sophisticated analysis.

Next is a conformance stage. A set of advanced algorithms detects outliers and deviations in the event logs. By doing this, the process-mining system can find bottlenecks and more optimal workflows.

Finally, the analytics component evaluates the "to be" processes. This looks at the root causes of the processes—say, the time spent on unnecessary tasks, the effectiveness of certain workflows, and so on.

While process mining is often used for RPA, other use cases exist. One is DevOps. Process mining can be an effective way to provide insights into IT environments. Or you can use this technology for internal audits—say, to help find problems with duplicate payments.

In terms of using process mining with mainframes, this has been done by automating ERP software like SAP. But IBM has been moving into the category as well—for example, through a strategic partnership with Celonis, one of the largest process-mining vendors. According to Mark Foster (*https://oreil.ly/ARXZ0*), chairman of IBM Consulting, "I do think that moving the [Celonis] software into the Red Hat Open-Shift environment is hugely powerful because it does allow in what's already a very powerful open solution to now operate across this hybrid cloud world, leveraging the power of OpenShift which can straddle the worlds of mainframe, private cloud, and public cloud."

IBM has also been investing heavily in the RPA market. To this end, the company acquired WDG Automation in July 2020.

How to Create a Bot

In the remainder of this chapter, we'll take a more hands-on approach. We are going to create a bot for the UiPath platform, and then create a bot for a mainframe.

Why use UiPath? It is the most widely used in the RPA industry, and it has a comprehensive set of capabilities. The company also has a strong offering of documentation, videos, and forums.

Creating a UiPath Bot

You do not have to be a programmer to create bots in UiPath. The system has low-code approaches—such as with drag-and-drop—to allow the creation of bots. However, if you want to develop sophisticated ones, you need to learn UiPath's language. It looks like Python or JavaScript, including elements such as these:

Variables
> There are a variety of types, including Booleans, integers, strings, objects (these are custom data types), Browse for Types (for opening up menus in an application), arrays, and System.Data.DataTable (for large datasets). UiPath variables also have local and global scope.

Conditionals and loops
> You can evaluate conditions using the IF/THEN/ELSE structure. UiPath also has several types of loops, like For Each, Do While, and Switch.

UiPath has two systems. The *Enterprise edition* requires paying a license (based on the number of users and bots created). You can evaluate this for up to 60 days. The *Community edition* is a free version with access to the support forum. But of course, you cannot deploy this software in enterprise environments. For our purposes, we'll look at the Community edition. Consider that both editions are for the Windows operating system. There is no version for Linux or Mac. However, the Orchestrator is a cloud application that will track the bots. You also have to create an account to access the download. This software is called StudioX.

Let's see how to install the Community edition. Go to the UiPath site (*https://www.uipath.com*) and click Try UiPath Free. You can create an account with your email or a login with Google, Microsoft, or LinkedIn. You then fill in some information about yourself and your organization. After this, a dashboard will appear.

Click Download UiPath Studio to download the Windows executable. The first screen asks you to use the *https://cloud.uipath.com* URL by clicking the Sign In button. The next screen provides you with three profiles. Select UiPath StudioX, which is for citizen developers and business users who want to create simple automations. After this, a screen will pop up for introduction videos, tutorials, and free training for the UiPath Academy. These are definitely worth checking out.

You will then see a screen to create a project. For this, you can use a template or load an existing project. But for our demo, select Blank Task. Then enter the name of the process, choose a path where the project will be stored, and write a description. The StudioX Design View opens, as seen in Figure 11-1.

Figure 11-1. The UiPath bot editor

This screen has a ribbon at the top with numerous icons:

Export as Template
  This allows you to easily turn a project into a template that you can reuse.

Project
  There are two options. One allows for changing the Project settings. The other is to load another Project.

Notebook
  This is an Excel file that stores information for the process automations. Thus, to update something, you could just change the file.

Manage Packages
  This allows you to make updates for any packages that are used and project dependencies.

App/Web Recorder
  This is a key part of RPA. Instead of coding the different steps in an automation, the App/Web Record will log these instead. Our demo will show you how to do this.

Table Extraction
  You can use this to get information for files, like spreadsheets or databases.

Analyze
  This shows whether your automations meet best practices for RPA (for example, based on your corporate standards). There is also a feature to validate for any errors.

Publish
  This deploys the bot to the Orchestrator or to a folder.

Run
  This executes the bot.

The Activities panel is on the left side of the screen. Here you have access to over one hundred components that you can drag and drop into your bot. These can automate such tasks as files for Excel, PowerPoint, SAP, Word, and so on. There are also extensive integrations for internet interfaces.

You will see the Data Manager panel on the right side of the screen. This is where you manage the resources in your project, such as the notebooks and the variables.

Now let's create a simple bot by using the screen in the middle. Here's the scenario: suppose you spend part of your morning copying the number of new employees— from an Excel spreadsheet—to your HR web-based application.

To create this bot, click the Excel icon on the Activities panel and select Use Excel File. Then drag the file to the Drop Activity Here section and choose the new employee file. Figure 11-2 shows the result.

Figure 11-2. Extracting information from an Excel file

For this demo, we will not use an actual HR application. Instead, we'll have a simple online notepad (*https://oreil.ly/fHTRh*) that does not require a login. For our bot, go to App/Web and select Use Application/Browser. Drag and drop the Use Application/Browser icon below the Excel component. Next, click the button that reads "Indicate application to automate (1)," and you will then get a message to install a plug-in for your browser. After you do this, navigate to the online notepad and select it with a click of your mouse. As you can see in Figure 11-3, we are essentially building a visual workflow.

You need to specify how to put the information into this app. Go to the Activities panel and enter **Type Into** in the search box. Drag and drop the Type Into icon under the online notebook component. Then go to "Indicate target on screen (1)" and navigate to the online notebook. Click the area where there are lines for text and choose Confirm.

Figure 11-3. Using your RPA system to connect to a web app

How do you get the information from the Excel spreadsheet to the online notebook? You go to the online notebook component and click the plus sign. Then choose Excel → Indicate in Excel. You will get a message to load in the Excel package. After this, you will be taken to the Excel spreadsheet. Select the cell for the information to copy and then click Confirm.

And that's it—you have your first bot. To see how it works, click Run.

Creating a Bot for the Mainframe

What about creating a bot for a mainframe? For this, you need to use the Terminal package. Go to Manage Packages and enter `UiPath.Terminal.Activities` in the search box. Then click Install and Save. Then search for `Terminal` in the Activities panel and drag and drop Terminal Session to the middle of the screen. Figure 11-4 shows what this looks like.

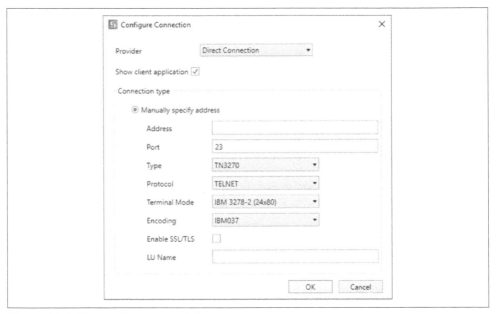

Figure 11-4. Connecting to a mainframe

The first option, Provider, shows the various 3270 emulation software systems to connect to the mainframe. These include Rocket BlueZone, IBM Personal Communications, Reflection for Unix, and IBM EHLLAPI. Or you can use a direct connection.

Depending on which one you select, you will get a different "Connection type." This is where you can configure the access. For example, if you select Rocket BlueZone, you can do either of the following:

Use an existing profile
     This is one you have already created.

Manually specify address
     Here you indicate the server address for the mainframe, the port number, and the type of the connection, which is usually TN3270.

When you log in, you will get the UiPath Terminal Wizard. At the top of the screen, a menu helps with the creation of the bot. The Stop/Start button, for example, records interactions with the application. As this is done, the wizard generates a list of the Recorded Actions on the right side of the screen.

Next, you can use buttons for the text on the mainframe screen, which is in the middle. You can use Set Text to input the label. For the field currently highlighted on the mainframe screen, you can view Field Properties on the right side of the screen, including the start of the row on the screen and the column. This is known as *coordinate identification*.

You can also use *visual identification*. This is done by using LabeledBy (the label before the selected field), FollowedBy (the label after the selected field), and Index (this is 1 or greater and is for fields with the same labels). With this approach, you will be able to continue to track the fields if a change occurs in the position on the screen, which can lessen the risk that the bot will break.

Regardless of which approach you use, you can then record the actions for the mainframe, and they will be embedded into the bot. One common use case is for the login to ISPF or other mainframe services. Other use cases for mainframe bots include automations for creating reports or querying data.

Such bots often save considerable time, but the added benefit of fewer errors is key. After all, when it comes to manual input—especially with tedious activities—it is easy for employees to make mistakes. However, a bot will do the same thing every time.

To get a sense of the real-life applications of RPA on mainframes, let's take a look at Genpact. The company, originally part of General Electric, is a global professional services business that focuses on helping companies transform their processes. The company has over 90,000 employees.

"Mainframe RPA automation has been growing rapidly in line with overall growth in mainframe processing and the need for bidirectional integration with next-generation SaaS systems," said Ben Chance, the vice president of Intelligent Automation at Genpact. "We have engaged with multiple clients that are using RPA to exchange mainframe data with SFDC and other products."

One example of a Genpact engagement was with a large insurer. The company had challenges with its receivables reconciliation process, in which the policies resided on the mainframe and the customer data was on a separate system with no interface. Genpact was able to use terminal emulator bots to access data across nine separate mainframe processes and load the data into a customer database. Doing this reduced cycle time by 66% and significantly increased accuracy.

RPA Issues with Mainframes

Since maintenance is a major part of working with mainframes, RPA can be a big help. Automating even simple processes can provide more time for working on more important projects. Besides, there simply may not be integrations or APIs to work with certain functions on the mainframe. Thus, RPA can be a good alternative. However, using this technology with mainframes has various downsides:

Screen scraping

This is the typical use case for mainframes. As we've seen in this section, you can identify fields and then create an automation with them. But this process may have issues. It can be difficult for complex automations—say, when working with different screens, screen dependencies, or even color highlighting. Note that no available RPA platform is specific for mainframe environments.

Coding

Some RPA systems may require using lots of code to create an automation. But this could make things more difficult to manage. A better approach is for an RPA platform that has low-code/no-code capabilities (we'll look at this in the next section of this chapter).

Templates

These are common for RPA platforms and can speed up the bot development process. However, usually not many templates are available for mainframe environments. Additional custom development may be needed.

Transactions

RPA automations can be slow. This is because they have to move from the network server to the mainframe and then back to the server. The result is that there can be a substantial increase in latency, which slows interactions. This can be particularly problematic for CICS environments, which may handle millions of transactions per day.

Orchestration

Using a terminal RPA system to interact with the mainframe often involves extensive tracking, which can weigh on performance and increase transaction costs.

Short-term approach

RPA is a good alternative when you need to build an automation quickly—say, in a couple of weeks. But this is not necessarily a long-term strategy for modernization (we'll look at this in the next chapter).

Now third-party solutions can address some of the problems. Just look at HostBridge Technology. Founded in 2000, HostBridge is a leader in providing services and solutions for CICS environments.

"The IT group sees steadily increasing CPU consumption coming from automations, but they don't know how to optimize them," said Russ Teubner, the company's CEO and cofounder. "So they call us and we are able to do analysis to find out which automations are the biggest generators of transaction volume, and which ones are consuming the most CPU cycles. We can then go in and create RESTful services that run these transactions, which UiPath automations can invoke via a simple HTTP request."

HostBridge has a platform called JavaScript Engine (HB.js), which allows for the creation of APIs to work with data without using screen scraping. Moreover, a big learning curve is not required since the underlying code is JavaScript.

The software is resident inside the CICS platform, which results in much less latency. In one test by HostBridge, an automation that had a sequence of 16 screens took 53 seconds on an RPA system but only 1 second for JavaScript Engine.

"Lately, our customers are using HB.js to write RESTful services that their UiPath bots/automations can call," said Teubner. "Integrating bots to the mainframe in this way provides a scalable, high-performance integration path that lets you avoid the perils of screen-scraping. It takes very little time to write services and APIs using HB.js."

Low-Code and No-Code Systems

A *low-code system* allows nonprogrammers to create enterprise applications. Often this involves using drag-and-drop, templates, and simple commands. *No-code systems* are similar but usually use no commands.

Regardless of the variation, the market has been growing briskly. According to analysis from Forrester Research (*https://oreil.ly/3O57x*), the total spending on low-code and no-code systems is forecasted to reach $21.2 billion by 2022, with the compound annual growth rate at roughly 40%.

Various catalysts are driving this strong growth. One is that enterprises have needed to find ways to create web and mobile apps that seamlessly connect to legacy IT systems. This generally takes extensive coding and integration. But with a low-code/no-code system, the development time can be shrunk considerably. Think of this technology as being a blend of off-the-shelf and custom software.

Another driver is to find efficiencies with corporate processes. In other words, a low-code/no-code system can be similar to an RPA platform.

A low-code/no-code system also has the benefit of rich user interfaces. This certainly saves a lot of development time. What's more, it means that the user experience will be much better—and this should lead to improved adoption of the applications.

 A traditional business typically spends much of its IT budget on maintenance, not just innovation. According to the journal *Applied Computing and Informatics*, about 75% of the budgets for banks and insurance companies (*https://oreil.ly/JSNen*) are for this purpose. But with the emergence of RPA and low-code/no-code systems, more opportunities exist to reduce these costs.

Some low-code/no-code offerings are general-purpose, but this may not be enough to fulfill customer needs. Because of this, some of the more useful platforms are focused on a certain industry, which allows for more relevant workflows and templates to be created or deployed. It's also possible to build in compliance features, such as for industry regulations.

As for low-code/no-code for mainframes, the technology has shown promise. But to make this work, integration is usually needed to make the connection to the machine. An example is webMethods CloudStreams from Software AG. The system provides for sophisticated management of the flows of data between on-premises applications, such as on mainframes, and software as a service (SaaS) applications. Numerous connectors are predefined and easily configurable with wizards.

The system can handle the sync of the data—allowing for bidirectional access—as well as network outages. Functions manage the governance—for example, with SLAs, auditing, monitoring, traffic analysis, and so on.

Yet the use of low-code/no-code has its drawbacks:

Data translation
> You usually need to find tools for data conversion. Even something like translating IBM's EBCDIC to ASCII can be a challenge.

Orchestration
> Even though integration tools can help with this, there still needs to be lots of planning with the processes and ongoing monitoring of the low-code/no-code applications. This is to ensure that the updates across the different systems are consistent and do not violate any governance rules.

Data ingestion
> Mainframe files may have billions of records, and this could be a problem with low-code/no-code systems. The migration process can take months. In fact, when evaluating a system, make sure to ask about the data management capabilities and limits.

Training
> Low-code/no-code systems usually have a learning curve. It can easily take a few months to train new employees to use this technology effectively.

Conclusion

In this chapter, we took a look at how RPA and low-code/no-code can be helpful in modernizing mainframe environments. These technologies have shown to have quick ROI. If anything, they can be a good way to transition to more sophisticated approaches, such as AI.

This chapter has shown that RPA and low-code/no-code are about much more than installing software. To have a successful implementation, a company's current processes need to be mapped. This often involves the use of process methodologies like Six Sigma and Lean. Emerging technologies, like process mining, can help with this, such as by showing the bottlenecks.

In light of the growth of the RPA and low-code/no-code industries, the evaluation of the software is not easy. Many solutions are available, and it can be challenging to find those that are the right fit. In this chapter, we took a look at some of the best practices for this process.

We also got a demo of how to create a bot by using the UiPath platform. For the most part, it is fairly easy but powerful. We then showed how to use the UiPath system's Terminal Wizard to interact with a mainframe.

We also reviewed some of the issues with RPA and no-code/low-code. For example, CICS environments may not be ideal for these types of automations. In addition, issues may occur with training and managing bots.

In the next chapter, we will explore the various strategies for mainframe modernization, including migration and hybrid approaches.

CHAPTER 12

Mainframe Modernization Strategies

Large enterprises are very interested in modernizing their systems and are willing to make the necessary investments. But some difficult problems exist. In a 2021 survey (*https://oreil.ly/3nu6E*), 64% of respondents reported using mainframe applications that are between 10 and 20 years old, and 28% use ones that are 20 to 30 years old. In fact, the average mainframe application has a whopping 8.86 million lines of code.

Advanced, a global organization that helps companies with application modernization services, conducts the annual survey, which examines the current mainframe market and the challenges facing enterprises. The respondents are companies that have over $1 billion in revenues.

Results from the survey are published in Advance's *Mainframe Modernization Business Barometer Report*. As the report notes, "Mainframe applications tend to pass through many hands over many decades, often without proper documentation of features or functional relationships. For many organizations, mainframes are like 'black boxes'—vast entanglements of code written by developers who may have retired or left the business long ago."

As a result, applications continue to fail or are difficult to upgrade. Finding talent with the right technical expertise to help with those efforts can also be difficult. Now, this is not to imply that the situation is hopeless. Many organizations have been successful with modernization. And in this chapter, we'll take a look at the strategies as well as the tools and systems.

Why Modernize?

The question of whether to modernize may seem strange. Shouldn't all companies be interested in improving their IT systems?

This is true. But there can be considerable risks, as many mainframe applications handle mission-critical processes. Problems, if they arise, could severely damage the business. This is why it is important to set the right priorities and goals.

Chapter 1 covered some of the reasons in favor of modernization. These included the urgency for digital transformation and the impact of COVID-19. Yet one of the biggest reasons many businesses opt to modernize is fear of being disrupted by a startup or a mega tech operator like Amazon or Apple.

But another factor is the cost of operating mainframes, which is often expressed in terms of MIPS. This cost comprises software licensing, hardware, maintenance, and operational expenses. These can certainly add up. According to research from Advanced, the average is $4,266 per MIPs annually.

However, the focus on costs can be too narrow. One reason is that it does not look at the ROI, which can be quite attractive for mainframes. This is especially the case for handling intensive transactional processes.

Besides, the alternative to a mainframe—which is often a distributed environment of lower-cost x86 PCs and workstations—may not have much of a cost advantage, especially when you include expenditures for software licenses, staff to manage the distributed environment, and consulting. Take a look at a study from IDC and Rocket Software, which surveyed over 440 businesses. One of the respondents said (*https:// oreil.ly/L0xvg*), "For every $1 we spent on IBM, it would have been at least $2 to go with a different solution." There were even greater discrepancies for those companies that have more frequent system updates.

Now, when it comes to modernization, one of the most important considerations is the cloud. Gartner predicts that the spending on this technology (*https://oreil.ly/ mQolc*) will go from $270 billion in 2020 to $397.5 billion by 2022.

Then again, cloud technology has clear advantages, such as the following:

Costs
> There is no need to manage data centers. The systems are instead handled with a third party, such as Amazon, Microsoft, or Google. These companies have the technical talent, scale, and resources to manage seemingly unlimited workloads. What's more, costs for the customer are generally based on usage. Another benefit is that an enterprise can focus its IT talent on more value-added activities, not on such things as setting up servers or spinning up storage systems.

Mobile
> The cloud allows for access to corporate data via mobile devices. This is critical as these devices have been a ubiquitous way for customers to interact with companies. Mobile applications are also a more convenient way for employees to connect to corporate data—for example, to help make better decisions.

The cloud makes it possible to centralize data, and this makes it easier to use applications like ML and artificial intelligence. Such capabilities can be major competitive advantages for companies.

Track record

In the early days of cloud computing, enterprises were very skeptical about the scale, security, and performance of this technology. But cloud computing has shown to be quite durable. For the most part, many of the fears have proven to be unfounded.

Using a Hybrid Cloud

Cloud computing is far from perfect. For example, some industries have strict data privacy requirements and have little choice but to maintain some of their data on their own data centers. This is certainly common for large organizations that have mainframes.

Because of this, a common strategy is the *hybrid cloud*. As the name indicates, this is about creating an environment that blends the public, private, and on-premises solutions. This also means that companies will likely not get rid of their mainframes. If anything, these systems will likely be an essential part of a successful digital transformation strategy. This is why IDC, in a research report (*https://oreil.ly/aakUu*), has called this the "transformative mainframe."

Some of the benefits of this hybrid cloud approach include agility, security, and much higher performance, which have led to improved revenue streams and improved efficiencies. The IDC report shows that using a hybrid approach increases value sixfold.

It certainly helps that more organizations are pushing innovation. One strategy has been to leverage a microservices architecture, which means creating small independent services that are connected with APIs. Some of the benefits include the following:

Improved productivity

It's easier to build and maintain applications. It is also possible to use different computer languages, technology stacks, and software stacks.

Scale

A DevOps team can choose the best microservices for a particular task and add them without downtime. Deploying microservices on various servers is also fairly easy.

Resiliency

Because microservices are more compact and easier to understand, they can allow for better identification of issues. This can make a big difference in lessening the impact of a failure.

Customization

Since a microservice is self-contained, it can be built for more specialization for a particular function.

Besides microservices, more companies are looking to capitalize on their data assets with ML and AI. With a more holistic approach to enterprise IT assets, use of these capabilities improves.

Finally, with systems like Zowe, developers can use more modern platforms and tools. It's possible to use a VS Code editor, a Jenkins CI/DC system, Kubernetes, or Docker.

Of course, this means getting the benefit of top-notch technologies, which can go a long way to improve productivity. But another benefit is that many people already know how to use these tools.

 An Enterprise Management Associates (EMA) Research Report (*https://oreil.ly/n8mME*), which was based on a survey of 207 individuals from a broad cross-section of enterprises, showed that 88% of respondents believed that mainframes would remain important for at least the next decade. According to the 2021 report, "Companies are evaluating and adopting the latest technologies, but the mainframe still serves as the critical core of their technology vision."

Setting Goals

For mainframe environments, it's common for the development to be somewhat ad hoc. And this should not be a surprise. After all, many development projects include maintenance of existing applications within the mainframe.

However, if an organization wants to achieve transformation, a strategic approach toward these development efforts must be taken. Otherwise, the business could face a threat of disruption.

When it comes to setting goals, what are some factors to consider? A good first step is to evaluate your mainframe environment. Interestingly enough, this is often avoided since it can be time-consuming. But to boost the success of a transformation effort, it's critical to have a good understanding of the main components, such as the applications, the interconnections, and usage of systems like Db2, CICS, and IMS.

Transformation efforts are far from easy and are fraught with risk. In Advanced's 2021 mainframe survey, about 36% of respondents reported considering their own efforts to be failures. Moreover, 77% indicated that they had at least one failure.

Through this evaluation process, you will get a sense of which parts of the mainframe system are most critical for the business. You'll likely also get a better understanding of what areas to start with in terms of the modernization.

Consultants can certainly be helpful in assessing the mainframe environment. For example, they can provide assistance on how to approach the project but also recommend certain data and code-scanning tools to speed up the process. They also benefit from having specialized teams that have worked on a variety of projects.

But the assessment of a mainframe environment should not be completely outsourced. It is important to have some of the organization's own mainframe experts to help provide details on the layouts and systems.

Once the assessment is finished, analysis is needed on the first steps of the modernization project, with a clear-cut timetable, deliverables, and goals. The temptation often is to be overly ambitious and to try to take on too much. In the early stages of a project, many ideas and strategies will be discussed.

For a project to be successful, a better approach is to have narrow objectives, as mainframe systems are complex and have many interconnections. It's also important to keep in mind that many organizations have multiple transformation efforts already in progress.

Areas of focus are generally divided into two categories. The first is functions related to day-to-day business operations, such as processing data for payroll or customer interactions. There can definitely be opportunities to find efficiencies or improve agility. However, internal operations for mainframes—especially handling of intensive transactions—are usually highly optimized already. Thus, you need to be careful with these types of projects since there may not be an opportunity to get meaningful ROI.

The second category is areas in which innovation is the goal. An example is adding a new mobile app for customers or building an application to help enter a new market.

Then what to do? There is no hard-and-fast rule, but it is probably best to focus on one of these two approaches. In fact, the first project can also be fairly simple. For example, it could be about taking non-mission-critical data and migrating it to the public cloud. Such a project would be straightforward and clearly defined, and it should provide measurable results.

There are also many variations in modernization approaches. Gartner has identified several, including encapsulating, rehosting/replatforming, refactoring/rearchitecting, and replacing/rebuilding. In the following sections, we'll look at these.

Encapsulating

Encapsulating involves accessing mainframe resources by using APIs. A common use case is connecting a mobile app for customers or employees.

All in all, the encapsulate strategy has proven quite popular since costs are lower than that of other modernization efforts. However, it has downsides as well. Creating APIs for mainframes can be difficult since it's common for the applications to be highly complex. In other words, there is the risk that the APIs could break and no longer work. The reason is that the original developer of the mainframe application—who is perhaps not even still with the company—may not have intended for the application to work under certain conditions.

Rehosting or Replatforming

Rehosting, or *replatforming*, is the process of transferring applications and data from a mainframe to another platform. This could be to the public cloud or a distributed x86 environment. This approach is also known as *lift and shift*.

The other platform will use rehosting software, which compiles the applications. A big benefit is that there is little need for changes in the code or the underlying business logic. This helps lessen the risk of malfunctions or errors in the software. Here are some other advantages:

Speed
> A rehosting project can take less than a year. The need for training is reduced since the applications will operate the same as before.

Costs
> Major reductions can occur in infrastructure and operating costs. According to Micro Focus (*https://oreil.ly/vSt6t*), which has used its rehosting software for over 1,000 projects, the estimated savings are up to 90%.

Performance
> Since the applications will be on a more modern platform, software productivity can significantly improve. Micro Focus estimates that application performance gains can be up to 75%, and development productivity improvements can be up to 30%.

Hiring
> There is little need to recruit more staff for mainframe languages and tools because most existing code will not undergo rewriting.

In light of the benefits, rehosting has become one of the most popular approaches for mainframe modernization. The following are two real-world examples (*https:// oreil.ly/OcteU*) that used software from TmaxSoft. TmaxSoft has more than 2,000 customers, and many of them are on the Fortune 500.

Major US retailer
This company had 10 core business systems hosted on 6 IBM mainframes. Costs were rising each year as workloads increased, and the company wanted to find ways to generate savings. The retailer used TmaxSoft software to rehost applications for the IMS database. The result was a 50% reduction in costs.

Property and casualty insurer
One of the company's applications, which was housed on an IBM mainframe, had 19,000 batch-processing functions. The company realized that this would be a good candidate for rehosting. As a result of the rehosting, transactions per second improved fourfold, and the response time was only 200 milliseconds. In fact, during a five-year period after the implementation, cost savings reached $17.5 million.

However, it is important to note that rehosting is really for a limited number of scenarios. Here is a look at some of the factors to consider:

Standards
The mainframe environment should use standard tools and languages like PL/I, COBOL, JCL, CICS, IMS, and Db2. If this is not the case, the rehosting software may not be as effective.

Workloads
Based on research from Tata Consulting Services (TCS) (*https://oreil.ly/eSvYk*), a major IT consulting firm, the MIPS should be below 5,000.

Source code
Source code should be available, and having adequate documentation is helpful.

In cases where some of these factors could hinder full rehosting, partial rehosting may be a viable option.

Refactoring or Rearchitecting

Refactoring, or *rearchitecting*, is about finding ways to improve and optimize the existing applications on a mainframe. Legacy code, like COBOL or PL/I, is converted into Java or another more modern language. This often involves the use of sophisticated automation tools for conversion.

However, the functions of the software will change little. This helps lessen the risks that the programs will have errors. However, extensive testing of the code base should still occur. After some time—when the program is stable in a production environment—further modernization can be undertaken.

One example of a refactoring is a major project with the US Air Force (*https://oreil.ly/1GuN6*) that involved a variety of companies like Array, NTT DATA, TSRI, and Datum Company. This team set out to modernize a large COBOL application for an ACAT III Major Defense Acquisition Program that had over 18,000 users across 260 locations across the globe. It was built more than 50 years ago. This system was for day-to-day supply-chain and equipment support for military missions and processed more than $30 billion in inventory.

Here are some other metrics on the application:

- The application had 1.3 million lines of COBOL.
- The annual operating costs were $30 million.
- The system processed about 500,000 transactions per day, based on a data management system with 1.2 million lines of COBOL.

The US Air Force wanted to transition this application to an x86 Red Hat Enterprise Linux (RHEL) platform, which would be hosted on AWS. The goals for this project were to lower costs, increase agility, and improve security.

Back in the 1990s, the Air Force had attempted a program to modernize the system, but it was a failure. So this time around a different approach was taken, relying more on a refactoring strategy. And while this attempt to modernize the system ultimately turned out to be a success, it still took nearly three years to complete.

Here are the three main phases of the project:

Phase 1 (18 months)
> This turned out to be the most complicated part of the project. It involved using an automated system for the COBOL-to-Java conversion. Because of the complexities of the code structures, there was a need for an intermediate object for the code base as well as the use of a translation language. The original COBOL identifiers were maintained so as to help with the testing of the Java code.

Phase 2 (12 months)
> This was about handling the COBOL remnants, which involved more testing and design improvements. Just some of the work included eliminating GOTO statements, using more modern workflow structures, and getting rid of redundant code sections. For this, TSRI JANUS Studio was used. However, the process still involved much manual work from developers, data engineers, and SMEs.

Phase 3 (3 months)
> The whole system was migrated to AWS. By doing this, the Air Force was able to use systems like modern DevOps and CI/CD tools. Estimated annual cost savings reached $25 million.

While there are various methods to migration, the Air Force's three-phase approach is definitely a good one. It focuses on clear-cut goals, and the phases built on each other. It certainly helped that not much was added along the process, which could have easily increased the complexity and extended the timelines.

Replacing or Rebuilding

Replacing or *rebuilding* existing applications is the most extensive strategy for mainframe modernization. Often this results in completely eliminating the mainframe footprint.

This approach, which is sometimes referred to as a *big bang rewrite*, requires a development team with backgrounds in legacy languages and modern ones (usually Java). But the end result is a new code base and documentation, which means that Agile development will become much easier.

Yet the risks are daunting. The timetable is usually in years, and the costs are substantial. The reality is that feature creep often bogs down the project. In the meantime, there will be turnover, which makes the situation even worse.

Another issue is that the mainframe system needs continued maintenance. So then, as you have a rewrite, what will the updates be for the existing applications? Should they be synchronized? This is probably a good idea. But it will add to the time and costs of the project.

Keep in mind that some of the biggest failures in mainframe modernization have been with rewrites. Here's a look:

California Department of Motor Vehicles
> The state government initiated a $208 million project (*https://oreil.ly/MBg6B*) for modernization of this mainframe system. However, within a few years, it had to be canceled. The reason: little progress had been made in the project.

Michigan mainframe systems
> In 2005, the state started a 10-year project for modernization (*https://oreil.ly/0C5fo*). The existing system was originally built in the 1960s and was used by 131 offices of the secretary of state. But within eight years of starting the project, the lead vendor was fired. Michigan also launched a $49 million lawsuit against the firm. Simply put, the vendor did not deliver even one of the functions.

Unemployment insurance

After the 2008 financial crisis, the US federal government wanted to modernize the state unemployment systems and provided funding for this. But there was a key stipulation: states would have to work together. In theory, this made sense, as standardizing the systems would result in efficiencies. But unfortunately, the stipulation would ultimately lead to failure, as Vermont, Idaho, and North Dakota terminated their partnership (*https://oreil.ly/BZsqA*). For the most part, it was difficult to coordinate resources and reconcile the differences in state unemployment programs. The cancellation of the partnership came in 2020, when the pandemic hit and the systems came under tremendous pressure.

Texas Child Support Division

In 2007, the Texas government agreed to revamp this system. Originally, the project was budgeted at $60 million, but costs ballooned to $340 million. By 2019, the project had failed to live up to its requirements and was terminated. Yet the mainframe system continued to process the child support payments, which came to $4.4 billion per year. According to Texas Congressman Giovanni Capriglione (*https://oreil.ly/r5Kay*), "If there's any good that can come of this, it is that we are now learning all of the things we should never do when we write contracts."

However, this is not to imply that replacement projects are doomed to failure. Success stories certainly exist. The company Amadeus is one example. Launched in 1987, Amadeus operates the largest transportation reservation system in Europe.

In 2018, the company retired its last mainframe computer; its IT system had been transitioned to a platform that relied exclusively on open systems (primarily on Linux machines). According to a blog post from Denis Lacroix (*https://oreil.ly/7pEKa*), senior vice president of Core Shared Services at Amadeus, "The switch was like changing an aircraft engine mid-flight, demanding precision engineering and mission critical skills."

The migration had its roots in the early 2000s, as the company started to focus on open source software. Over time, the project would ultimately involve 400 engineers across the world working full time. The total hours came to 2,000 effort years.

Working with the Hyperscalers

The *hyperscalers* include the mega cloud operators like Amazon, Microsoft, and Google. These companies operate the largest cloud platforms and are growing their enterprise businesses at a rapid clip. The hyperscalers also view the mainframe market as critically important for long-term growth. After all, there are huge footprints of data and applications.

While the hyperscalers would like to completely convert all this to the cloud, this is not a part of the road map—at least in the near term. Keep in mind that the focus is generally on a hybrid strategy. Customers usually do not have the appetite to rip out their older systems from data centers and migrate the workloads to the cloud.

The hyperscalers certainly have considerable advantages. Many companies already use their cloud services as well as business applications like Microsoft Office or the G Suite. Of course, the hyperscalers have huge systems to handle any type of workload and a long history of strong uptime for services. In fact, the hyperscalers have the ability to run LPARs across different virtual networks throughout the world.

For the next few sections, we'll take a look at the programs of Amazon, Microsoft, and Google.

Amazon Web Services

Amazon is the pioneer of the enterprise cloud industry. The company started this venture in the early 2000s primarily to manage ecommerce sites for third parties. But this also came at a time when Amazon was restructuring its IT infrastructure into APIs and microservices to allow for a more modular approach to development.

At first, Amazon Web Services (AWS) was focused on helping startups. But as the platform grew and became more mature, it attracted larger customers. One of the first major ones was Netflix, which completely hosted its entertainment service on AWS.

Fast-forward to today: AWS is the largest cloud service in the world. During the second quarter of 2021, its revenues jumped by 37% to $14.8 billion (*https://oreil.ly/EKtlG*). Consider that AWS is the largest driver of operating profits for Amazon.

In terms of the mainframe market, this is a high priority for AWS and a long-term source for growth. To this end, Amazon has two parts to its program: Migration Solution and the AWS Mainframe Migration Competency Program.

AWS Mainframe Migration Solution

To see how the AWS Mainframe Migration Solution works, let's look at an example. Venerable is a privately held financial services company that manages variable annuities. It has about $240 billion in assets under management.

In the 1980s, the company developed a mainframe-based system for handling agent commissions. But over the years, the application became more complex, with about 3.8 million lines of COBOL and assembler code. The system had 650 online screens, performed 250 batch jobs that used over 2,000 programs and a CICS transaction system, had 110 VSAM files (with variable and multirecord formats), and contained 25 Db2 tables that had 15 GB of data.

For the modernization project, Amazon partnered with Heirloom Computing, which provided the software solutions for the conversion, and Cognizant, which offered its professional services. Cognizant had a team that ranged from 6 to 12 employees, and Heirloom dedicated 3 senior solution architects to the project. Venerable contributed a full-time SME.

Using the Heirloom Probe software, the team was able to do the following:

- It created a detailed analysis of the application with a baseline and map of the assets, metadata, and dependencies.
- The software refactored the CICS BMS screens into HTML5 and JavaScript web pages. The look and feel was similar to the BMS screens so as to not hamper the user experience.
- A VSAM-to-data conversion allowed the use of the Microsoft SQL server on Amazon Relational Database Service (RDS) without having to make code changes.

Cognizant also had its own proprietary tools, which it used to convert Easytrieve programs to intermediate COBOL programs. Then Python scripts were developed to translate VSAM file data into a relational format.

All in all, the project took roughly 16 months to complete (the original estimate was 24 months). The Venerable application became fully cloud-native in Java, and the cost savings came to $1 million per month, with an 80% reduction in operating expenses.

AWS Mainframe Migration Competency Program

The AWS Mainframe Migration Competency Program includes a set of partners like Advanced, Blu Age, Deloitte, Micro Focus, TSRI, Accenture, and Wipro. The goal is to provide customers with top service providers and software developers to streamline the process of migrating to AWS. Furthermore, Amazon has set a high bar for those who want to be a part of the program.

Microsoft

When Bill Gates was in high school, he learned to program computers by working on a General Electric mainframe. He would access this machine by using a Teletype Model 33 ASR terminal. He was so proficient that he was hired as a contract programmer for Information Sciences, to write a payroll program in COBOL.

A few years later, he cofounded Microsoft with schoolmate Paul Allen. While they would go on to usher in the PC revolution, they still developed software for the mainframe. One of the tools, which came out in 1981, was the TN 3270 emulator. Microsoft even developed a version of COBOL.

As the company grew at a furious rate, its software became heavily embedded across millions of businesses across the world. Therefore, Microsoft gained much experience working with integrations with mainframe environments.

Today, Microsoft's priority is Azure, its cloud platform. The business is ranked second in the industry in terms of revenue.

What about the mainframe, then? The Azure platform emulates many of the traditional components (*https://oreil.ly/oixtM*). Here's a look:

Online transaction processing (OLTP)
Azure works with CICS, IMS, and the Terminal Interface Processor (TIP). It is possible to move applications to the platform to run as an infrastructure as a service (IaaS) using VMs. This is done "as is" since there are no code changes, which reduces the risks of the migration. The screens are then managed using web servers, and the database connections use such tools as Microsoft ActiveX Data Objects (ADO), Open Database Connectivity (ODBC), and Java Database Connectivity (JDBC).

Batch processing
Azure has easy-to-use command-line utilities like AzCopy that can copy data and move it to cloud storage. Azure Data Factory can handle data from disparate sources.

Databases
Microsoft usually rehosts the data tier. This is done by moving the workloads to the SQL Server as well as open source databases and other relational databases. There are also tools to integrate with mainframe databases like Db2 and IMS.

LPARs
With Azure, VMs are used to emulate these systems. There are VMs for the application tier, other VMs for the data, and another for the development environment. This allows for more-optimized processing.

Let's look at an example of an Azure implementation. This involved one of the largest auto insurers, GEICO. The company manages over 17 million policies in North America.

GEICO wanted to transition its mainframe system for its sales application, which included 16 subsystems. It handles such processes as the issuance, rejections, and quotes for the policies.

The migration project was definitely risky. Since it impacted sales, there was the potential for disruption if the systems failed. Maintaining onerous regulatory compliance was also necessary.

GEICO believed that a cloud platform like Azure could provide more agility, though. The company also selected Microsoft because it already relied on many of its software systems and shared a long history of working as partners.

For the most part, the migration project was fairly smooth and involved the help of Microsoft partner Applied Information Sciences. The sales application was cloud-native on Azure and allowed for the use of APIs, SQL Server databases, and VMs.

As a result, GEICO was able to have release cycles for major upgrades to its system every three weeks. Before the migration, release cycles generally occurred every six weeks.

Google Cloud

Among the hyperscalers, Google was late to the game. But the company has been aggressively making up for lost ground. In the second quarter of 2021, revenues from its Google Cloud division jumped by 54% (*https://oreil.ly/0QHw1*) and are on track to reach $18.5 billion annually. This places the company as number three in the cloud industry.

Google has some clear advantages. It has deep experience in managing some of the most trafficked web properties, like YouTube, Google Search, and Gmail. The company was also the innovator in using commodity servers and systems to build sophisticated IT infrastructures.

And Google has other advantages:

Analytics
> Google has been an innovator with AI in its development of tools such as TensorFlow.

Data
> The BigQuery system is a powerful cloud-based data warehouse. It not only handles huge amounts of data but also provides for intensive real-time transaction processing.

Cybersecurity
> Since the early days of Google, the company has been at the forefront of cybersecurity. This has allowed the company to snag numerous major clients in heavily regulated industries like financial services and healthcare.

Even though such advantages are key for mainframe customers, Google still did not have much experience with this industry. But in February 2020, the company acquired Cornerstone Technology (*https://oreil.ly/geLs1*). Founded more than 30 years ago in the Netherlands, it built a mainframe migration product called G4, which is used by customers like Capgemini and Deutsche Bank AG's Postbank segment. It also has assembled its own team of consultants and advisors.

The G4 platform is now at the heart of Google's mainframe business. The technology can translate complex COBOL, PL/I, and assembler programs into Java applications and microservices. This allows companies to get the benefits of containerized environments. G4 also comes with a set of programs that transfer databases and mainframe files. Its dashboard provides metrics to help with testing and fine-tuning applications.

 Automated writing of new applications in object-oriented languages, like Java, provides the best value over time, according to a 2021 ISG Research study (*https://oreil.ly/mx6jG*). This study of 70 mainframe modernization projects from 30 service providers and software vendors showed cost savings ranging from 40% to 80%.

An example of a customer that used G4 successfully (*https://oreil.ly/aVMrq*) was a large credit bureau. Because of a change in government regulations, the company needed to manage an expected fivefold increase in credit queries. But the existing mainframe system would not be able to handle this cost effectively. It had both IBM AS/400 and Z mainframes that included various COBOL applications connected to CICS, Db2, and Easytrieve.

With G4, the conversion was for both the batch and online systems. The technology dealt with the business rules conversion. As for the Google cloud tools, a development team used Cloud Composer for batch processing and Compute Engine for transaction processing. The database was then converted from Db2 to Postgres.

Automation Tools

Automation tools can convert mainframe languages to modern ones, such as Java or C#. These systems are quite fast, converting over 20 million lines per hour. This also includes handling complex workflows and data structures.

However, the automation is far from perfect. When code is converted, it still may look similar to the structure of COBOL. This is known as *JOBOL*. This is not necessarily bad. Mainframe coders may want this similarity. However, some automation tools will make the conversion look more like native Java or C#.

Automated tools can find dead code. This should not be a surprise since mainframe programs have often been built over decades. You can certainly delete the dead code. But this is often not done. Because mainframe apps are generally for mission-critical applications, companies are often conservative with any changes.

Extensive testing and quality assurance are needed, which means manual changes to the code base will be ongoing (it's common to use a Jenkins pipeline for management of this). This is why mainframe development experts are needed, such as those with expertise in COBOL, CICS, Db2, or IMS.

As a result, general estimates can be made for conversion costs, and companies often use a professional services firm for this. A 2021 report from ISG (*https://oreil.ly/G8MZP*) offered these figures:

Modernization and code refactoring
    25 cents to $2.30 per line of code, with a project duration of 2 to 36 months

Transformation and code conversion
    50 cents to $8 per line of code, with a project duration of 6 to 60 months

Given the complexities of a project, no tool can do everything. Using several is common for a modernization project. In the following sections, let's take a look at some of the automation tools.

Heirloom Computing

Among the operators in the mainframe automation category, Heirloom Computing is one of the younger ones. The company got its start in 2010 with a goal to transform mainframe workloads to the cloud. It's the only migration solution that was built from the cloud, from the ground up.

The company's Probe software acts as an orchestrator to automate the whole process, including inventory analysis and collection, code refactoring, data migration, packaging, and deployment. Here are some of the benefits:

Speed of delivery
    The software uses a compiler core technology to migrate code to Java and datasets to relational databases. The company has been able to get projects done in as little as 90 days.

Cloud-native end state
    The Heirloom applications are 100% cloud-native Java and can be deployed to any cloud platform. "Because they are just plain old Java applications, they 'plug & play' with the target cloud platform," said Gary Crook, CEO at Heirloom Computing. "It's then the target cloud platform that takes care of scalability, high availability, and the management and monitoring of the deployed applications."

Agile
    Heirloom software exposes all the business rules as REST services, which allows for faster UI modernization and helps break monolithic functions.

Bimodal development

Heirloom does not dictate a target language. For example, after a migration, you can still use COBOL, PL/I, Java, or any mix. This is a nice feature since people may prefer to program in legacy languages.

Databases

Heirloom has an easy-to-use system to read and manage databases, such as IMS and Db2, that includes integration with security systems like RACF. Figure 12-1 shows this system.

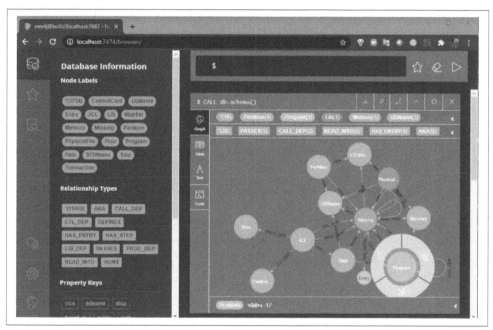

Figure 12-1. The Heirloom database tool

EvolveWare

Founded in 2001, EvolveWare focuses on automating IT processes, and a key part of this has been through using ML and AI. The company has been awarded five US patents for its unique metadata technology, which has helped with its modernization capabilities. EvolveWare's customers include Fortune 2000 companies and government agencies.

The company started with two main products: Legacy Modernizer and Legacy Maintainer. It consolidated these into a cloud-based platform in 2015. Called Intellisys, the platform can automate more than 20 languages and has end-to-end capabilities that include discovery, analysis, rules extraction, code optimization, and migration. It can even automate documentation. Code translation is done without using proprietary

APIs or libraries, which allows for more flexibility for the customer. Over the years, the platform has processed over 100 million lines of legacy code.

Advanced's Automated COBOL Refactoring

Advanced has its own software platform, called Automated COBOL Refactoring. The system, which was part of the acquisition of Modern Systems, has processed billions of lines of COBOL into Java.

One advantage Advanced has is its extensive professional services organization. After all, modernization efforts require considerable planning and customization. Note that the company has been a part of over 500 projects.

A key to the software platform is the Native Java Framework. This set of libraries supports common functions for I/O, logging, various utilities, and application life-cycle management. There is even emulation for JCL, sequential files, CICS, and VSAM files. These functions are then translated to be used seamlessly with the standard versions of Java.

Astadia

For more than three decades, Astadia has helped large organizations migrate mainframe deployments. The company has an end-to-end platform that works with Azure, AWS, and Google Cloud. The migrations include automations for databases, code conversion, and automated testing and validation. "By the time we're ready to flip the switch, we know exactly how the migrated system will behave, and how well it will perform," said Scott Silk, Astadia's chairman and CEO.

Data Migration

A common way for companies to use sophisticated analytics with mainframe data is by utilizing extract, transform, load (ETL) techniques. This transfers data to data warehouses, where BI tools can run the operations. But this can result in using considerable MIPS and can also take significant time. The problems can then be exacerbated by data that is stored on tapes or a virtual tape library (VTL).

However, some companies are looking to address this by using the modern ETL approach. This moves mainframe-formatted data directly to any object storage target before using the target platform to transform it for use in analytics or AI applications.

One company that is innovating this category is Model9. Its Cloud Data Manager for Mainframe allows for seamless migration of data without needing to change mainframe applications. "This is a low-risk/no-risk proposition that can provide immediate payback," said Gil Peleg, CEO and founder of Model9. "Then, with that certainty, we can help our customers build and accelerate modernization or migration, as well as support hybrid multicloud strategies."

An example of the use of the system (*https://oreil.ly/dUUq6*) is a leading transportation business. The company wanted to lower its mainframe costs as well as move away from its legacy systems. This was done by using the Model9 platform with Amazon S3 storage. Snowflake—which replaced Db2—was used for analytics.

Another example of a company that is innovating with the use of data and mainframes is GigaSpaces. Founded 20 years ago, it is the pioneer of in-memory computing technology that allows enterprises to load data into memory, and power applications with extreme performance when accessing their data. For example, its Smart DIH product helps decouple digital applications and mainframe systems of record. Transactions can be offloaded by Smart DIH and not consume resources on the mainframe. Key benefits include lower MIPS costs, protection from the core mainframe systems from overload and bottlenecks, and high availability (if a mainframe is down or inaccessible, the data is still available).

Conclusion

This chapter provided an overview of the ways that organizations are modernizing their mainframe environments. We first looked at setting goals and targeting the best areas for restructuring.

Then we covered the numerous strategies for modernization. They include encapsulating, rehosting/replatforming, refactoring/rearchitecting, and replacing/rebuilding. While they do have some overlap, they represent gradual levels of change within mainframe applications. They also show the different levels of risk and rewards. As we saw, the replacing/rebuilding strategy can have significant benefits, including agility. But this approach can be time-consuming and very costly.

Then we looked at the impact of the hyperscalers. They see the mainframe market as a major opportunity for growth in their cloud businesses. Thus, if a developer is looking for opportunities in the mainframe industry, one option is to work for Amazon, Microsoft, or Google.

Next, we took a look at automation tools for modernization. Some of the companies covered included Heirloom Computing and EvolveWare. In light of the move toward digital transformation, the automation tools space is likely to see more growth in the years ahead.

Finally, we reviewed some of the players in the data migration market. These companies have created interesting technologies that have made it easier to transition data to the cloud so as to better use such things as AI and ML.

In the next and final chapter, we will look at some of the trends for mainframe development.

CHAPTER 13

The Future

The mainframe market is definitely large and diverse. As we've seen in this book, it includes maintaining applications, developing new programs, innovating around DevOps and AI, and performing migrations.

However, this is not to imply that the mainframe industry is seeing growth everywhere. As with any category, certain pockets stand out in terms of the long-term growth prospects. In this chapter, we'll take a look at these, as they may be worth considering for those seeking a career in mainframe development.

Innovation of the Mainframe

Mainframes are truly amazing machines. They can process massive workloads, such as 19 billion encrypted transactions a day at about 220,000 per second. This is absolutely critical as digital interactions continue to grow at a rapid pace. Moreover, their performance will continue to get better and better. This has been the case for decades.

"We are seeing large organizations that are not looking to replace their mainframes," said John McKenny, senior vice president and general manager of Intelligent Z Optimization and Transformation at BMC. "Rather, they are looking to add these machines. There may even come a time when startups—say, in the fintech sector—will consider mainframes because of their durability, performance, and security."

The 16th Annual BMC Mainframe Survey (*https://oreil.ly/Ck5n8*) points to these positive trends:

- 92% see the mainframe as a source of long-term growth.
- 72% of the respondents have half their data on mainframes.

All this should not be a surprise, either. IBM has continued to invest heavily in innovating mainframe platforms. IBM's long involvement with Linux technology has been a big part of this and has been bolstered by the Red Hat acquisition. But IBM also has leveraged its extensive capabilities in AI, blockchain, and cloud computing for its mainframe systems. For example, the company has developed a cloud-native platform, called Wazi Developer, that allows developers to use the IBM Z for multi-cloud environments and uses modern DevOps approaches.

Perhaps the most important initiative is with AI. "For tasks like fraud prevention, IBM Z is not only bringing AI insights directly to where your mission-critical data lives, but we're coupling that with unmatched security," said Ross Mauri, general manager of IBM Z. "Since last year, we have been working to enable our clients to embed AI into their mission-critical enterprise workloads and core business processes with minimal application changes—giving them the ability to score every transaction while meeting even the most stringent SLAs."

In terms of the hardware side of the IBM Z, impressive innovations continue. Consider the introduction of Telum, the next generation of the mainframe processor. "This is so important because to date there have been chips that are dedicated to AI, and there are server processors that run enterprise workloads like databases and transactions—but not one that can do both," said Mauri. "The Telum chip brings those capabilities together to enable our clients to embed AI directly into their transaction workloads."

Security is another key selling point for the IBM Z, especially as the number of cyber breaches continues to increase and new threats emerge, such as those created with AI. In the meantime, more regulatory requirements are protecting data.

Here are just some of the security benefits of the mainframe:

Walled system
> The difficulties in accessing a mainframe are definitely an advantage. This means that the typical way to hack a system—through phishing or visiting a site that has viruses—is rare. Even if malware is installed on a mainframe, it likely would not be able to operate on the z/OS system.

Resource Access Control Facility
> RACF is a security system for the mainframe. For the most part, it requires permissions to get to certain areas of the system, including third-party software.

Logging
> This is built into a mainframe. In other words, a machine will track any security intrusions.

Finally, IBM is taking sustainability seriously with its mainframes. For example, Linux on IBM Z servers will use 7,673 kWh of energy and 103,000 square feet of floor space. By comparison, distributed servers will consume 38,400 kWh and take up 687,000 square feet.

"More than ever, we're also seeing pressure from leadership, particularly in the banking sector, to focus on improving sustainability," said Mauri. "Amid growing data centers and rising costs, floor space and efficiency have also become a sustainability concern." When it comes to the mainframe, IBM is certainly not the only source of innovation either. Third-party software vendors like BMC, Broadcom, and Rocket Software are modernizing their stacks and adopting open source solutions. Startups are also being launched in the mainframe market, such as Model9 and OpenLegacy.

 According to a recent Forrester report about financial services (*https://oreil.ly/Yvjph*), about 56% of respondents indicated that a hybrid strategy was a critical priority. Moreover, they said that usage on the mainframe increased by 4% to 8% in the past year, and the expectation is that this will increase to 6% to 8%.

Enterprise Integration

IT integration, also known as *systems integration*, has been around for decades. This involves connecting data, applications, machines, and APIs. However, integration should not be confused with continuous integration. This instead is about managing code bases for faster and higher-quality development.

IT integration has various approaches, including these:

Point-to-point integration
> This is the most basic. It connects two applications, and data flows in one direction. Point-to-point integration is usually a good place to start. But as an IT environment gets more complex, exploring more sophisticated approaches becomes necessary.

Hub-and-spoke model
> This is for more complicated environments and involves the use of a central hub or message broker. This is essentially middleware that communicates across the systems. The hub-and-spoke model allows for much more scalability and is easier to upgrade. Yet one of the drawbacks is that the centralization can cause bottlenecks.

Enterprise service bus (ESB) model
> This is a set of different middleware systems that connect the parts. Unlike the hub-and-spoke approach, each system has its own integration engine. This is really for highly complex environments or those with quite different technologies, such as between the cloud and the mainframe.

Tools, called *connectors*, are used to make the connections. The main ones are as follows:

APIs
> This is the most widely used and involves connections by using web services.

Middleware
> This is a software layer that melds distributed systems, devices, and applications. The services are broad, such as with the data management, authentication, messaging, and even API management.

Electronic Data Interchange (EDI)
> This is a data format for exchanging information. This can be done on a private network or via the web.

Webhooks
> This involves the use of making calls in real time using HTTP. These are generally used for notifications.

Now with the increase in digital services, IT integration has turned into a growth business. But there are other benefits as well, like lower costs, leveraging existing IT resources, and getting more scale.

In fact, IT integration tools companies are looking at the mainframe market as a major opportunity. Just look at Boomi. Founded in 2000, the company is a leader in providing software solutions for IT integrations and has over 17,000 customers.

Boomi has an integration platform as a service (iPaaS) platform that provides extensive critical managing of business processes and slotting. An example of a customer for this technology is Kenco Logistics, a provider of third-party logistics and supply-chain management. Onboarding a new customer on its system—which operates on IBM AS/400 mainframes—took 40 to 60 hours of manual work with the EDI system. But with Boomi, this shrunk considerably. Other benefits included powerful analytics and forecasts of usage and customer trends.

"With companies wanting more insight into data than ever before, being a good citizen of digital connectivity provides future-proofing for mainframe technologies, and for businesses that still depend on them," said Rajesh Raheja, senior vice president of R&D and Engineering at Boomi. "While mainframes aren't built for that level of analysis or flexibility, by integrating mainframes with other applications, people, partners, and so on, data takes on a new life and can provide new insights to the business. In addition, low-code platforms from Boomi and our partner Flynet, which specializes in legacy application connectivity, make it easier than ever to leverage data from a mainframe across the business for impactful, actionable insights."

Among the integration approaches, though, the use of APIs is definitely seeing lots of traction. "API enablement is crucial for companies leveraging legacy tech alongside other applications to drive development," said Dr. Alex Heublein, president of Adaptigent. "Organizations, industries, and the federal governments are introducing or upgrading API offerings, making API enablement that much more important."

Yet API development remains challenging for the mainframe. The costs can also be significant. "Consultants can often charge upwards of $125,000 per API—costs that many companies are not willing or able to spare, as totals can add up quickly," said Heublein.

But the good news is that emerging low-code and no-code solutions can help with the API development process. Microservices are also becoming an important part of the toolbox for mainframe modernization. This type of technology is a software function for a single business process and can be deployed when needed.

One company that has been innovating in this category is OpenLegacy, which raised $70 million in venture capital. The company's general focus is helping enterprises transition to cloud-native platforms. OpenLegacy's platform makes it easier to create the microservices without having to make changes to the code base.

A customer of OpenLegacy is Union Bank, one of the 20 largest financial institutions in the US, with close to 400 branches. Over the years, the company has been focused on digital transformation of its mainframe systems (*https://oreil.ly/S7sNn*).

A big issue was that the company had a complex web of middleware that made it difficult to make changes. To deal with this, Union Bank implemented Apache Kafka for real-time data as well as the OpenLegacy mainframe integration system. Note that OpenLegacy was connected directly to CICS, which bypassed the middleware and allowed for the use of microservices and APIs. It took only two weeks to deploy five use cases, and ultimately the time-to-market for new applications accelerated tenfold.

The Hybrid Model

Perhaps the most important trend—and opportunity for mainframe developers—is the hybrid model. As we saw in Chapter 12, this approach is becoming the standard for modernization because of the lower costs, reduced risks, and concrete benefits. Besides, there remain considerable advantages for the mainframe.

"The robust architecture of mainframes will continue to be favored for core critical transaction processing workloads," said Gil Peleg, CEO of Model9. "Furthermore, there is the growing trend—and regulatory requirements—toward mandatory data residency and personal privacy and data ownership. However, no enterprise can survive for long without the agility cloud provides as well as evolving possibilities, such as AI and ML that are available at a compelling price point. Moreover, cloud economics for some of the old 'table stakes' functions of the data center—especially archival storage—are extremely compelling."

This transition is still in the early phases, but the growth is accelerating. Experienced consulting firms will be needed to manage these complex projects—that is, there will be lots of opportunities for mainframe developers.

A new category called *CloudOps* is also emerging. In a mainframe migration, an application will often be containerized (for example, by using Kubernetes). This helps with the integration with databases or other functions that remain on the mainframe. But this also adds to the complexity of the IT environment, such as with the orchestration, compliance, security, and so on. With CloudOps, a plan is in place to help with this. According to a blog post from David Linthicum (*https://oreil.ly/HuPaq*), chief cloud strategy officer at Deloitte Consulting, "You need to understand the cost, risk, and ROI of deploying 5 different security systems, 20 different development platforms, and 30 different databases on 3 different public cloud brands."

Mainframe as a Service

There is a trend to innovate the business model for mainframes, to make them more affordable. One approach is mainframe as a service (MFaaS). With this, a company does not have to manage a data center or have a team of technical people. Rather, this is managed by an IT company that specializes in these capabilities.

For example, MFaaS can provide for the following:

- Outsourced management of complex requirements, such as for configurations, dealing with software licenses, and managing upgrades. Companies are not burdened with talent recruitment.
- The costs are generally lower. After all, the MFaaS vendor will benefit from economies of scale and specialization. More resources should be available for monitoring the systems, which will mean higher reliability.
- You may have access to a dedicated mainframe or one that is shared.

Often MFaaS is an approach for more of a short-term engagement—say, for less than three years. The reason is that this is usually about a way to migrate away from a mainframe setup.

Conclusion

We are now at the end of the book. And we have definitely covered a lot of topics. The first part of the book was primarily about providing a foundation of the traditional tools and software systems, such as COBOL, ISPF, TSO, CICS, and Db2. Granted, they may be old and seem somewhat archaic, but they are powerful and widely used. More important, if you want to be a successful mainframe developer, you need to have an understanding of this software.

Then, in the second half of the book, we delved into modern topics. The good news is that the mainframe has seen considerable innovation—and this is likely to continue. We saw the growing importance of DevOps, RPA, AI, and hybrid approaches.

The bottom line: being a mainframe developer is a great opportunity, and there will be growing demand for motivated and bright coders. Good luck on your journey!

Additional Resources

Articles by Broadcom's Jessielaine Punongbayan on Medium (*https://oreil.ly/NshHJ*)

BMC's Mainframe Blog (*https://oreil.ly/dHMZN*)

COBOL Facebook Group (*https://oreil.ly/T6hA4*)

COBOL Fridays Webcast Series (*https://oreil.ly/PyRfN*)

DancingDinosaur Blog (*https://oreil.ly/zPhc0*)

IBM Z Blog (*https://oreil.ly/d8Eoy*)

Open Mainframe Project (*https://oreil.ly/fFxou*)

Planet DB2 Blog (*https://oreil.ly/j0mvo*)

Tom Taulli's COBOL Courses on Pluralsight (*https://oreil.ly/mzL5g*)

Glossary

Agile

An approach to software development that focuses on speed, customer feedback, and collaboration.

alphabetic

In COBOL, this is a data type that can have only letters.

alphanumeric

In COBOL, this a data type that can have letters, numbers, and special characters.

artificial intelligence (AI)

Algorithms processing large datasets to come up with insights and predictions.

attended RPA

Also known as robotic desktop automation (RDA), this RPA technology is used to help employees perform their jobs better. A common use for this is in the call center.

batch processing

Processing done at certain intervals. For example, the input into a system could be during business hours, and the processing would then be done during off-hours.

bot

Software that is created by an RPA system. It is for automating a task, such as logging into an application, accessing a program, or selecting buttons on a screen.

business analyst or SME (subject matter expert)

A person who has experience with a certain department or function within the organization. They can be extremely helpful when implementing RPA.

center of excellence (CoE)

A group of people who manage an RPA implementation. They help with the strategy, development, deployment, and monitoring.

continuous integration/continuous delivery or deployment (CI/CD)

This includes best practices and automation tools for the application development process, from the initial idea to the deployment and monitoring.

Common Business-Oriented Language (COBOL)

The standard language for mainframe application development. It has the types of features that are important for business use cases, such as handling large-scale batch- and transaction-processing jobs.

cognitive automation

A type of RPA that involves automating tasks using AI and ML. This is commonly done by using natural language processing (NLP), such as with a chat bot.

columns

For a mainframe language, code is put into different columns on the screen. This arose from the use of punch cards during the early days of computers.

compiled language

A computer language that is converted into machine language and then made into an executable. This helps to increase its speed. An example of a compiled language for the mainframe is COBOL.

concurrency

Allows for more than one program to be executed at the same time. This is possible because a CPU's resources are usually idle or not heavily used.

configuration management

The use of tools to help automate hardware, the operating system, services, and network connectivity.

control interval

The minimum (4 KB) and maximum (35 KB) amount of data that is transferred when accessing files on a mainframe.

DATA DIVISION

For a COBOL program, this is where you will include the data structures. There are three areas for this: WORKING-STORAGE SECTION, FILE-SECTION, and LINKAGE-SECTION.

dataset

A file for a mainframe system. A dataset is also put into a catalog to provide easier access.

ddname

The name of the file used for a JCL script.

deep learning

A form of AI that uses unstructured data, such as text and images, to find features and patterns.

delimiter

A character that marks the end point of a certain type of data in a file. One common delimiter is the carriage return.

DevOps

A set of practices for improved software development and IT operations.

direct access storage device (DASD)

The disk drive for a mainframe.

DIVISION

There are four in the COBOL language: IDENTIFICATION DIVISION, ENVIRONMENT DIVISION, DATA DIVISION, and PROCEDURE DIVISION. They are meant to provide more structure to the code.

dynamic access

Enables a file to be read sequentially or randomly.

edited field

In COBOL, a data type that can format a field, such as for a currency or a date.

entry sequence dataset (ESDS)

A VSAM file type and similar to a sequential file organization. This is common for databases like IMS and Db2.

ENVIRONMENT DIVISION

In a COBOL program, this is where you specify the files to be accessed.

Extended Binary Coded Decimal Interchange Code (EBCDIC)

IBM's own system for the character set of the mainframe.

file status codes

Provide information about the accessing of files. They often help identify errors or issues.

filler

In COBOL, a data item that does not have a name. This is commonly used for formatting reports.

high-level qualifier (HLQ)

The first name in a dataset name. It is often based on a user name.

IDENTIFICATION DIVISION
>In COBOL, this is where you put the name of the program and other high-level information about the program.

indexed file
>A file that is used for transaction processing.

Integrated Development Environment (IDE)
>A tool that allows for software development.

Interactive System Productivity Facility (ISPF)
>A menu-driven system that allows for software development on a mainframe.

interpreted language
>A language that converts commands into machine language while in run-time. A common example is BASIC.

Job Control Language (JCL)
>A scripting language to help combine data files with a program.

Kanban
>A way to manage a software project that involves a physical or virtual board. The idea is to provide a visual way to understand the workflow.

key sequence dataset (KSDS)
>The most common type of VSAM file. With a KSDS, you can access files randomly and use variable-length records. There is also sorting on a key field.

Kernel-based Virtual Machine (KVM)
>An open source virtualization module for the Linux kernel. KVM essentially makes the kernel function as a type 1 hypervisor.

Lean
>A software development approach that focuses on reducing wasted activity.

level number
>In COBOL, this is used for the hierarchy of the data. The level numbers go from 1 to 49.

log data
>Data that is derived from network devices, applications, and servers. Such data is often used for analytics and AI.

logical partition (LPAR)
>A form of virtualization, in which a mainframe can be divided into separate mainframes (it's based on a type 1 hypervisor). The current z15 system allows for up to 40 LPARs.

low-code
>A platform that allows for the creation of an application using a small number of commands, templates, and drag-and-drop.

lowest-level qualifier (LLQ)
>This is the last name in a dataset name.

machine learning (ML)
>A subset of AI that enables computers to learn without being explicitly programmed.

margin A or area A
>In COBOL, this is where you put the main headers for the code, for divisions, sections, paragraphs, and level numbers.

margin B
>In COBOL, this is where you put the main code for the program.

master file
>A file for a large collection of information for a department in a company, such as sales, accounts payable, accounts receivable, inventory, and payroll.

no-code
>Similar to low-code, in which a system is used to create software. But there are usually no commands for this. Instead, no-code relies on drag-and-drop, templates, and so on.

online transaction processing (OLTP)
>Processing of transactions is done in real time, such as with airline reservations. IBM has sophisticated platforms for this

like Customer Information Control System (CICS).

partitioned dataset (PDS)
A file and directory system for a mainframe.

partitioned dataset extended (PDSE)
An enhanced version of a PDS, with more directories and records per member.

PIC
In COBOL, this specifies the number of digits or characters a field can have. This is short for *picture*.

PROCEDURE DIVISION
In COBOL, this is where you perform the logic of the program.

Processor Resource/Systems Manager (PR/SM)
Firmware for a mainframe that enables virtualization with the LPARs.

program function (PF) keys
Function keys on the keyboard for a mainframe. They do such things as navigate a screen, get help, and end a session.

punch card (or punched card)
A piece of stiff paper that has perforations representing information. Punch cards were used to program and operate early mainframe computers.

record
A group of related fields of information. For mainframes, a file is typically made up of various records.

REDEFINES
In COBOL, this command allows for changing the data type.

reinforcement learning
A form of AI in which the learning is based on a reward-punishment system.

robotic process automation (RPA)
Software that creates software bots that automate tedious and repetitive processes.

RPA developer
A person who codes bots using an RPA platform. They also usually have a certification.

RPA sponsor
Usually an executive who has the overall responsibility for the RPA platform.

screen scraping
A key function of an RPA. This allows for automating the user interface—say, for customer relationship (CRM) and enterprise resource management (ERP) systems.

Scrum
An approach to managing a software project, which usually involves small teams and multiple development sprints.

sequential file
A simple text file for a mainframe, in which records are stored consecutively.

spooling
Allows for the managing of the queue for certain functions like printing or file handling.

strong AI
A machine that is truly intelligent—for example, able to converse effortlessly with humans.

structured data
Data that has a defined format. For a mainframe, this is data in databases like Db2 and IMS.

supervised learning
The most common approach for ML. It involves using algorithms to process data.

System/360
The pathbreaking mainframe system that IBM developed in the 1960s. It quickly became the standard in the industry. One of the key benefits was backward compatibility, as older programs could be run on newer machines.

systems administrator

Similar to a systems programmer, but this person typically specializes in certain areas.

systems operator

Monitors the operation of the mainframe.

systems programmer

A person who provides engineering and administration for the mainframe and z/OS. Duties include installation, configuration, training, and maintenance.

terminal

A machine that nontechnical people can use to interact with a mainframe computer. Common use cases include agents who book flights or insurance agents who process claims.

time-sharing

A system that allowed for the renting of mainframe computers.

Time Sharing Option (TSO)

A command-line system that enables native access to z/OS.

TN3270 emulator

Software that allows access to a mainframe, such as via a PC.

transaction file

A file that collects information for activity for a period of time.

type-1 hypervisor (or bare-metal hypervisor)

For virtualization, a software layer installed directly on top of the physical machine or server. This generally results in higher performance and stability.

unattended RPA

Involves the automation of tasks without the intervention of people.

unstructured data

Data that is not in a certain format, like videos, email, and images.

unsupervised learning

A form of AI in which the data for the algorithms is unlabeled.

virtual storage access method (VSAM)

A dataset and access method for the IBM mainframe. The VSAM makes file processing easier. It also provides strong performance, efficiency, and security.

virtualization

Allows for getting much more resources from existing machines. This can be done by hardware or software systems.

waterfall method model

One of the earliest approaches to software development and has had a big influence on mainframes. It is highly structured, and its steps include conception, initiation, requirements, design, implementation, and testing.

weak AI

AI that is focused on a narrow task or domain.

z/OS

The main operating system for IBM mainframes.

Zowe

An open source platform that allows access to a mainframe.

z/TPF

An OS for the mainframe that is focused on transaction systems. The first use of this was called Sabre, which handled airline transactions.

z/VM

An OS that is based on virtualization, which IBM introduced in 1972. This involves the use of a type 1 hypervisor, a software layer that's installed on a physical machine or server.

z/VSE

An OS for the mainframe that is targeted for smaller businesses.

Index

C

---

memory, 143-145
message processing region (IMS), 167
message switch (IMS Transaction Manager), 167
metrics
  key performance indicators for DevOps, 208
  provided by G4 platform, 287
  tracking with table in COBOL, 119
MFaaS (mainframe as a service), 298
Micro Focus survey findings on COBOL, 9
microcode (software layer) for System/360, 16
Microsoft, 284-286
  Azure cloud platform, 285
ML (machine learning), 224, 228-233
  binary classification, 229
  classifications, types of, 228
  cognitive automation in RPA, 256
  EvolveWare's use of ML to automate IT processes, 289
  imbalanced classification, 230
  multiclass classification, 230
  types of, 230-233
    reinforcement learning, 232
    supervised learning, 231
    unsupervised learning, 231
MLOps (machine learning operations), 243
models in AI, 242
  accuracy of, 243
  creating a model, demo of, 244-247
modernization of mainframes, 21, 273-291
  automation tools, 287-291
    Advanced's Automated COBOL Refactoring, 290
    Astadia, 290
    data migration, 290
    EvolveWare, 289
    Heirloom Computing, 288
  benefits of, 273-275
  setting goals, 276-282
    analysis on first steps of process, 277
    encapsulating, 278
    evaluating mainframe environment, 276
    refactoring or rearchitecting, 279
    rehosting or replatforming, 278
    replacing or rebuilding, 281
  using a hybrid cloud, 275
  working with hyperscalers, 282-287
    Amazon Web Services, 283-284
    Google Cloud, 286

Microsoft, 284-286
MOVE command (COBOL), 70, 74
multiclass classification, 230
multilabel classification, 230
multilevel tables, 120-123
Multinoulli probability distribution, 230
MULTIPLY command, 78
multiregion operations (MROs), 186
mythical man month, 198

N

naive Bayes algorithm, 229
.NET, 56, 158
  IMS Data Provider for Microsoft .NET, 169
Netflix, automation at, 210
neural networks, 234
nibble or nybble, 144
no free lunch theorem, 242
no-code systems, 269
Node.js, 52
Nonaka, Ikujiro, 198
nonoperational SQL, 182
numerics, 65
  numeric edited fields in COBOL, 68, 73
  numeric fields in COBOL, 68
  using MOVE command with numeric fields, 75

O

object-oriented programming languages, 142
  object-oriented COBOL, 158
OCCURS command, 116
  iterations for total sales, 119
  specifying table indexes, 124
OCR (optical character recognition), 257
offsets (VSAM files), 111
OLTP (online transaction processing), 26, 285
ON SIZE ERROR clause, 76
  use with COMPUTE command, 80
one-level tables, 116
one-to-many relationships, 174
one-to-one relationships, 174
online calculator converting binary to decimal, 144
online transaction processing (OLTP), 26, 285
opacity of AI, 227
Open Mainframe Project, 51
open source software in AI, 233
OpenCobolIDE, 57

Z

About the Author

Tom Taulli has been writing code since he was in the eighth grade, when his father bought him an Atari 400 (this was during the early 1980s). After a year or so, he started publishing his applications in magazines (in those days, they actually had listings for readers to type in!). From the experience, he knew he wanted to be a part of the tech world.

When he got into college, he worked at a local bank and helped with COBOL development and updates. Taulli would next start his own company. It was in the e-learning space and involved the development of applications for exam preparation.

But as the internet emerged, he would transition to this technology and start another company, Hypermart.net. It was essentially a first-generation Shopify. Growth was strong (hey, it was the late 1990s), and he sold the company to InfoSpace.

Along the way, Tom would also write for publications including Forbes.com (he still does to this day). He also wrote books including *Artificial Intelligence Basics* and *The Robotic Process Automation Handbook* (Apress).

Besides his writings, Tom is an online instructor. He has developed courses for COBOL and Python for Udemy and Pluralsight. He also is a frequent panelist and moderator for virtual conferences and webinars.

Colophon

The animal on the cover of *Modern Mainframe Development* is an Aldabra tortoise (*Aldabrachelys gigantea*). Named for the Seychelles atoll to which it is native, the Aldabra is one of the largest species of land tortoise, reaching up to 550 pounds or more in weight and 4 feet in length.

These visually striking giant tortoises are dark gray to black in color and feature a thick, highly domed outer shell. Their long necks aid them in browsing the vegetation that comprises the bulk of their diet. However, Aldabra tortoises are opportunistic feeders and will eat fresh meat or carrion when it can be easily accessed.

Prolific sleepers, Aldabras reportedly slumber an average of 18 hours per day. They are also believed to be among the longest-lived animals and may frequently achieve lifespans in excess of 100 years. Yet, despite this notable longevity, the current conservation status of the Aldabra tortoise is "vulnerable." Like all animals featured on O'Reilly covers, the Aldabra tortoise's importance to our world cannot be overstated.

The cover illustration is by Karen Montgomery, based on an antique line engraving from Lydekker's *Royal Natural History*. The cover fonts are Gilroy Semibold and Guardian Sans. The text font is Adobe Minion Pro; the heading font is Adobe Myriad Condensed; and the code font is Dalton Maag's Ubuntu Mono.

Printed in the USA
CPSIA information can be obtained
at www.ICGtesting.com
JSHW072035040923
47807JS00017B/128